FRENCH IN ACTION

FRENCH IN ACTION

A Beginning Course in Language and Culture

The Capretz Method

STUDY GUIDE - Part II

Barry Lydgate

Wellesley College

with

Sylvie Mathé
Université de Provence,
Aix-Marseille

Norman Susskind
Oakland University

John Westlie
William Jewell College

Laurence Wylie
Harvard University

Yale University Press

New Haven and London

French in Action is a co-production of Yale University and the WGBH Educational Foundation, in association with Wellesley College.

Major funding for French in Action was provided by the Annenberg/CPB Project. Additional funding was provided by the Andrew W. Mellon Foundation, the Florence J. Gould Foundation, Inc., the Ministries of External Relations and of Culture and Communication of the French government, the Jesse B. Cox Charitable Trust, and the National Endowment for the Humanities.

The authors wish to express their thanks to Ann Noack and Susan Hafer, and to the Wellesley College Science Center, for help in preparing Part II of the French in Action Study Guide.

Published with assistance from the foundation established in memory of Calvin Chapin of the Class of 1788, Yale College.

Printed in the United States of America by Murray Printing Company.

International standard book number: 0-300-03940-9

Study Guide, Part I   ISBN 0-300-03939-5
Study Guide, Parts I and II as a set   ISBN 0-300-03787-2

10 9 8 7 6 5

Contents

INTRODUCTION
Using the Study Guide

The purpose of this guide is to show how the video, audio, and print components of *French in Action* fit together into a coherent learning system, and how individual users can get the most out of the course.

Before beginning, you should read lesson 1 in the textbook, which describes the function of the different components of the course. Each lesson is made up of:

- a video program
- an audio program
- a textbook chapter
- a workbook chapter
- a study guide chapter

The study guide will lead you through each lesson, and you should follow it step by step. Briefly, the principal steps are these:

1. Preview the study guide. Read carefully the story summary at the head of each lesson, and review the notes on culture and communication. These will prepare you for the video program.

2. View the video program. You will retain more from each video program if you can view it more than once. If you are using the course via broadcast at home and have access to a videocassette recorder, tape the lesson off-air. If the video programs are available in a language lab or media center, review them there. Remember, though, that the purpose of the video program is to expose you in a preliminary way to the material of the lesson and to help develop your feel for communication in French. You will not need to take notes, and you shouldn't worry if you don't understand everything you hear and see. Your objective is to get the gist of what is going on. You won't be expected to learn any word or structure in depth from the video program alone. More extensive practice in understanding and using French comes later, as you work with the workbook, audio program and textbook.

3. Complete the lesson. After you have watched the video program, you should start immediately with the section of the lesson called *Text work-up,* and proceed through the workbook, audio program, and textbook, with the study guide as your companion and road map.

As you begin *French in Action*, keep the following in mind:

• **The importance of regular study.** You will achieve the best results in this course if you do the lessons regularly. Learning a language is like creating a painting or writing a short story: success depends on consistent, steady effort over time. Avoid letting too much time go by between periods of study. And avoid trying to complete several lessons at one sitting; the day-to-day contact you need in order to develop your listening and speaking skills can't be compressed.

• **Determining what is basic.** At the beginning of each study guide lesson you will find a list of features of the language treated in that lesson. Check marks (√) identify the basic, minimal material of the lesson—material that you will be expected to learn and that you should cover carefully. While the balance of the lesson is not optional (you should complete the entire lesson), you may choose how much to concentrate on the remaining material, according to your interest and the time available.

• **Testing; written and oral assignments.** This course has been designed to help you get into a regular rhythm of study and practice. At the end of the study guide you will find a summary quiz for each lesson. If you are taking *French in Action* as a telecourse, your instructor will very likely assign these quizzes, and you should complete and return them following the information in your course syllabus. The summary quizzes for even-numbered lessons (beginning with lesson 4) contain an oral production section for you to record on an audiocassette and submit to your instructor. In addition, topics for additional written and oral assignments are suggested in each study guide lesson. These are optional, and may or may not be assigned by your instructor; again, check the course syllabus for directions.

• **Dealing with overload.** Most language-learners experience a certain amount of disorientation at their first contact with a new language. If you are new to language-study, or if you have studied language via more conventional approaches, you may find the early lessons of this course particularly challenging and time-consuming. If you do, it is because the course **immerses** you in French and asks you to make sense of the language on its own terms, without the aid of English.

This immersion approach is highly effective, but it is a bit unconventional, and you may find it overwhelming and even frustrating at the beginning. You will quickly get used to it, however. First of all, like any new skill, understanding and speaking French gets easier as you learn the ropes. After a few lessons you will build up a critical mass of familiarity with the course and with the language. From that point on, everything will go faster and more smoothly. Second, and even more importantly, although you may find it frustrating at first to study French without the crutch of English, you are developing survival skills that will serve you well in the long run—skills that you would not be likely to acquire in a conventional course.

   ● **Using the audio program.**   As you work with the audio program, resist the natural inclination to whisper or mumble when you repeat and answer. Your goal is to learn to speak French, and there is no reason to be modest. Get into the habit of saying everything **out loud**, as if you were talking back to a telephone answering machine, or speaking to someone halfway across the room. If it helps, try to mimic the voices you hear, as though you were making fun of them. (Most students are experts at making fun of their teachers, so here is a golden opportunity.)

   ● **Audio cues.** Most of the workbook exercises have an audio component. You will notice that the phrases you hear on the audio program for many of these exercises are printed in the study guide, just below the instructions for completing each exercise. You should be able to do most of the exercises without looking at these phrases, and you should always try to do so. The printed cues are given for reference if you need them.

   ● **The importance of participation.** Anyone can learn to communicate in French and discover the satisfaction—and the fun—of being able to say steadily more and more. The speed with which you progress, however, depends on your willingness to take the initiative in speaking. That is why your active, verbal participation—your **performance**—in this course is so important.

   As you practice speaking up and speaking out, you will get a great deal of support in the lessons that follow. There are role-playing and interactive exercises in abundance in this course, and for good reason. The ability to imagine yourself as a speaker of French is an indispensable first step toward actually becoming one. By assigning you various French-speaking parts, these role-playing exercises help you get used to lending yourself to the language and projecting yourself as a speaker of it. The faster you can cultivate this skill, the more rapid your progress will be.

   Good luck—*bonne chance!* And *bon travail!*

PHONETIC SYMBOLS
The sounds of French

In the workbook and study guide lessons, you will see the sounds of French written as symbols contained between two slashes: / /. These are symbols of the International Phonetic Association. They are used because conventional letters are not reliable guides to the sounds of a language—too many of them can be pronounced differently from language to language, and even within a single language.

Below are the symbols for the basic sounds of French, grouped into categories of related sounds. Next to each sound is a word that contains it. You will learn how to make these sounds, and see which spellings are associated with them, in the lessons that follow.

Oral vowels

/i/	il
/e/	divorcé
/ɛ/	père
/a/	grave
/o/	gros
/ɔ/	personne
/u/	toutou
/y/	tutu
/ø/	deux
/œ/	soeur
/ə/	le

Consonants

/p/, /b/	papa, banc
/t/, /d/	taxi, drame
/k/, /g/	calcul, garçon
/f/, /v/	fille, Véronique
/s/, /z/	poisson, poison
/ʃ/, /ʒ/	chat, jardin
/l/	elle
/r/	mardi
/m/, /n/	madame, Noël
/ɲ/	saignant

Nasal vowels

/ɛ̃/	hein
/ã/	roman
/ɔ̃/	allons
/œ̃/	aucun

Semivowels

/j/	voyons
/ɥ/	huit
/w/	Louis

On a beautiful spring morning, his first day in Paris, Robert Taylor sets off to explore the Latin Quarter. He follows some student demonstrators into the courtyard of the Sorbonne. Mireille Belleau, on her way to school, happens to end up in the same place. They catch each other's eye, and meet.

They see each other a number of times over the next several days, sharing interests and experiences. They discover they have an acquaintance in common. As they get to know each other, they seem unaware that a mysterious man in black has taken an interest in their banter.

Mireille and Robert get invited to dinner at the home of their common acquaintance. By this time Robert has become very interested in Mireille—an interest fueled, perhaps, by her friendly but non-committal attitude toward him. Robert would love to accompany Mireille on a trip she plans to take to Chartres. After dinner, he asks her when he can see her again. She gives him her phone number, and tells him to call her the following Monday.

LESSON 27
All manner of transportation I

The story

9:00 a.m. Monday. Mireille's phone rings. Wrong number; the caller wanted the Salvation Army. 9:03: this time it's Robert. Timidly, he asks if he can see her today. She's going to Chartres, to visit that little museum near the cathedral. Could he come along? If he insists. Rented car? Too expensive. Bus? Too slow. Airplane? Chartres is too close. On foot? It isn't that close. Bicycle, horseback, motorcycle, hydrofoil, helicopter, all rejected. What, then? The train! Of course! All Robert has to do is take the métro to the Gare Montparnasse. Lost? Ridiculous! No one gets lost in the métro!

We next see Robert lost in the métro—or nearly, in spite of Mireille's excellent directions. Finally, only ten minutes late, he finds her at Montparnasse. Robert wants to buy two first-class tickets, but Mireille already has hers, and it's second class. When everything is in order they board the train, which departs right on time.

As the train passes through Versailles, Mireille suggests they drop the formal *vous*. Even though *tu* is common among young people, this represents a step forward. And she invites him to dinner with her family on Thursday and to a movie afterward. Things are moving along!

Notes on culture and communication

● **Le train.** Trains in France are one of the best and safest means of transportation. Frequent, fast, comfortable, and punctual, they make traveling through the country easy and pleasurable. The national rail network is administered by the Société Nationale des Chemins de Fer (SNCF), a state-run company whose latest achievement is the development of the *train à grande vitesse* or TGV, the fastest train in the world.

● **Le château de Versailles** began as a hunting pavilion under Louis XIII (1601-1643). Louis XIV (1638-1715) turned it into a monumental palace and made it his capital; it remained the royal seat until the fall of the monarchy. An architectural masterpiece, its elaborate interior decoration, furniture, and works of art and its incomparable gardens make Versailles the archetype of French classical art.

• **Body language and the telephone.** Only words are transmitted in telephone conversations, yet the role of the body in communication is so automatic that expressions and gestures contribute to the message even though their share of it does not get through. Turn off the sound and watch Robert's and Mireille's facial expressions and gestures on the phone: the eyes, for example, which roll up as the speaker searches for a solution when a woman gets the wrong number and asks Mireille for the Salvation Army, when Robert asks Mireille if he may accompany her to Chartres, when he ponders the best way to get to Chartres, when Mireille ponders her replies.

Content and learning objectives of lesson 27

This lesson shows ways in which French speakers insist, express fear, and talk about making mistakes. It also shows how they talk about getting places via various modes of transportation.

The following points are highlighted in lesson 27 (you should concentrate on sections marked with a √):

- *Se tromper de*
- *Avoir peur*
- *Tenir à*
√ • *A* and *en* with means of transportation
√ • The pluperfect (27.16, 27.17)
√ • The conditional (27.18-27.21)

ASSIMILATION OF THE TEXT

27.1 Text work-up

The *mise en oeuvre* of the text will give you a working familiarity with the important words and structures of the lesson, in preparation for explanations of their function and practice in their use.

Bear in mind that you are not expected to learn word for word all the material contained in the work-up. Its purpose is to single out and help you focus on elements of the text that you will be working with in detail later on.

• You should begin the *mise en oeuvre* as soon as possible after you have viewed the video program for lesson 27. Listen to the *mise en oeuvre* on the audio recording, repeating and answering according to the musical signals (short signal = repeat; long signal = answer.) Complete 27.1 on the audio program **before** you look at the printed text in the textbook. Remember to speak up and speak out.

27.2, 27.3 Aural comprehension and oral production

This section will give you practice in associating French phrases with mental images of the situations to which they refer, without having to go through the laborious process of translation.

- In 27.2, you see a series of illustrations. In phase 1 of the exercise, study the numbered pictures as you listen to the phrases that correspond to them on the audio recording. In phase 2, these phrases are presented in a different order, labeled A through H. Find the illustration that best fits the phrase you hear and write the identifying letter beneath it.

√ Check your answers in key 27.2 at the back of the workbook.

- In 27.3, you will hear a series of dialogues. Take the part of one of the characters, as indicated, mimicking his or her speech as closely as possible. You will hear the line again for confirmation. (The characters you are to play are indicated in the workbook.)

THE "TEXT" AND THE TEXTBOOK

Turn to your textbook and study the text of lesson 27 and the accompanying illustrations. Then read the questions that follow the text and answer them out loud. (They will be familiar to you from the *mise en oeuvre* you just completed.) If you find you have any difficulty answering, return to section 27.1 and repeat it, looking at the questions in the textbook as you listen to them on the recording.

TOWARD COMMUNICATION

27.4 Activation: Pronunciation; vowel sounds

- Repeat the words and expressions you hear, paying close attention to the vowel sounds. Be especially careful

1. not to stress them too much (there should be a slight stress—no more—on the final vowel of a rhythmic group, and nowhere else);

2. not to diphthongize them (that is, not to let your voice slide from one vowel sound to another in the same syllable, as often happens in English: *how = ha-oo*);

3. not to let their sound be influenced or distorted by the sound of the following consonant.

27.5, 27.6 Observation and activation: Errors; *se tromper de*

Everyone makes mistakes, so *se tromper de*, followed by a noun, is a very valuable expression. Use the noun to express the kind of mistake that has been made: if Robert has once again gotten the wrong door, say *il s'est trompé* **de porte**; if the woman who calls the Belleaus wanted to reach the Salvation Army, say *elle s'est trompée* **de numéro**, and so forth.

• The statements you hear in exercise 27.6 draw attention to people's errors. Say they have made a mistake, and indicate what kind of mistake by using *se tromper de* and the appropriate noun. Notice in the example that the noun will not always be contained in the sentence you hear. You will need to infer it from the context.

27.7, 27.8 Observation and activation: Easy solutions; *n'avoir qu'à* + infinitives

Need to get to the Gare Montparnasse? The expression *n'avoir qu'à* used with an infinitive suggests a simple solution to your problem: "Vous **n'avez qu'à** prendre le métro!" All you have to do is what is indicated by the verb in the infinitive following *n'avoir qu'à*.

• In exercise 27.8, various people find themselves in situations that require an immediate solution. They are told what to do. Point out how simple each solution is, using *n'avoir qu'à* followed by an infinitive.

27.9, 27.10 Observation and activation: *Avoir peur*

Mireille is afraid she and Robert will never make it to Chartres if they drive a rental car. What worries her is the possibility of a breakdown, and she expresses her fear by using *avoir peur* with *de* and an infinitive, as chart 27.9 demonstrates.

• In exercise 27.10, various people don't want certain things to happen. Ask whether they're afraid of these things taking place, using *avoir peur de* followed by an infinitive.

Audio cues (for reference):
27.10 Activation orale: Avoir peur de

1. Je ne veux pas tomber en panne!
2. Elle ne veut pas tomber en panne!
3. Nous ne voulons pas tomber en panne.
4. Robert et Mireille ne veulent pas tomber en panne.

5. Robert ne veut pas prendre l'avion.

6. Robert ne veut pas se tromper de train.

7. Robert ne veut pas être en retard.

8. Robert ne veut pas rater son train.

9. Il ne voulait pas rater son train.

27.11-27.13 Observation and activation: Insistence; *tenir à*

Although he gets lost a lot, Robert is a tenacious fellow. He has his heart set on going to Chartres with Mireille, a desire that can be expressed by *tenir à* and an infinitive: "il **tient à** aller à Chartres."

Notice that what one insists on (*à* and the entire expression that follows it) may be replaced by *y:* "il tient **à aller à Chartres**" ⇒ "il y tient."

• In exercise 27.12, you will be asked whether various people very much want to do certain things. Say they do, using *tenir à.*

Audio cues (for reference):
27.12 Activation orale: Tenir à

1. Vous tenez à aller à Chartres?

2. Tu tiens à aller à Chartres?

3. Robert tient à louer une voiture?

4. Vos parents tiennent à vous accompagner?

5. Tu tiens à venir?

• In exercise 27.13, you will be asked whether you or other people want to do certain things. Say yes, you and they insist on doing them, using *tenir à.*

Audio cues (for reference):
27.13 Activation orale: Tenir à

1. Robert veut aller à Chartres?

2. Mireille veut aller à Chartres aujourd'hui?

3. Robert veut voir la cathédrale?

4. Vous voulez absolument venir?

5. Vous voulez y aller en voiture?

6. Vous ne voulez pas y aller en train?

7. Vous ne voulez pas y aller à pied?

27.14, 27.15 Observation and activation: Means of transportation; *en, à*

Some conveyances enclose travelers and others simply carry them perched on top. Discussing how to go to Chartres, Robert and Mireille use *en* when they talk about riding inside (**en** *voiture*, **en** *train*). When they discuss means of transportation that require standing or straddling, they use *à* (à *cheval*, à *ski*, à *bicyclette*).

• In exercise 27.15, determine whether each conveyance encloses the traveler or not and complete the sentences, using *en* or *à* as appropriate.

√ Check your answers in key 27.15 at the back of the workbook.

27.16, 27.17 Observation and activation: The pluperfect

The present represents the moment at which we are speaking. When we want to refer to actions that took place before the present moment, we use a past tense.

It occasionally happens that we want to refer to events that took place not only prior to the present, but prior to other events in the past. The **pluperfect** tense is used to express this kind of anterior action. It indicates that an event is not only past in relation to the present, but also in relation to some other point in the past. It shows a past in the past, a "double" past.

Suppose we are narrating the story of Robert and Mireille in the present. "C'est lundi," we say, "et Robert **téléphone** à Mireille." Then we remember we should probably mention the last time they saw each other, at the Courtois dinner the Friday before. We shift to the *passé composé:* "Ils **ont dîné** chez les Courtois vendredi." So far, so good. Then we realize we need to reach further into the past to explain how Mireille happened to be at the Courtois's. So we shift again, this time to the *plus-que-parfait:* "Mireille **avait téléphoné** jeudi." Home free.

Like the *passé composé*, the pluperfect is a compound tense. It is composed of an auxiliary (*avoir* or *être*) and a past participle, as the charts in 27.16 show. The auxiliary is in the **imperfect**. The choice of whether to use *avoir* or *être* as auxiliary is made exactly as it would be for the *passé composé:* use *avoir* for verbs that can take direct objects; use *être* for reflexive verbs and the fifteen or so verbs of movement and change of status that do not take direct objects (see lesson 22).

• Listen to the sentences you hear in exercise 27.17 and decide whether the verb they contain is in the *passé composé* or the pluperfect. (In practice, this means figuring out whether the auxiliary is in the present, in which case the verb is in the *passé composé*, or in the imperfect, in which case the verb is in the pluperfect.) Mark the appropriate box on the grid.

√ Check your answers in key 27.17 at the back of the workbook.

27.18-27.21 Observation and activation: Reality and conditional supposition

You saw in lesson 2 that in addition to having different **tenses** to refer to action at various times (present, past, future), verbs come in a variety of **moods** that correspond to different functions (indicative, infinitive, imperative).

The function of the **indicative** is to indicate, to say what's what. If Robert, stuck in a phone booth without exact change, says "La vie n'est pas facile," he is using the indicative.

Fortunately, language does not limit us to talking about what is or is not. It also allows us to speculate, to suppose, to imagine what might or might not be. The **conditional** fulfills one of these speculative functions. It is used to hypothesize about how things would be if a certain **condition** were present.

Robert knows that in life there are all sorts of problems: *La vie n'est pas facile*. That is a fact, and so *est* is in the indicative. But he feels that the problems Mireille mentions when he tries to wangle an invitation to accompany her to Chartres are not real ones. If there were no more serious problems than those, "la vie **serait** facile!" (although in fact there are, and so it isn't). Since the condition (= no problems) is definitely contrary to reality, its outcome is equally unreal, and so this outcome is expressed in the **conditional**.

Chart 27.18 contrasts the conditional and the indicative.

Charts 27.19 and 27.20 show how the conditional is formed from the stem of the future and the endings of the imperfect.

• In exercise 27.21, decide whether the sentences you hear are in the indicative or the conditional, and mark the appropriate box on the grid.

√ Check your answers in key 27.21 at the back of the workbook.

27.22 Activation: Dialogue between Mireille and Robert

This interactive exercise is designed to strengthen your role-playing and pronunciation skills, and to help you learn some short, useful French phrases.

Listen to the conversation between Mireille and Robert on the audio recording, and memorize Robert's lines. Imitate Robert's voice as carefully as possible, until you can answer Mireille yourself. Try to complete the exercise

without looking at the written text of the dialogue beforehand. Above all, avoid looking at the written text as you do the exercise.

TOWARD FREE EXPRESSION

27.23 Words at large

Words at large will give you practice retrieving and reusing words and structures you have learned in lesson 27 and in previous lessons.

The questions in 27.23 can be answered in a large variety of ways. A number of possibilities are given in the workbook; read them and add as many other examples as you can. If you work alone, say your answers out loud (you may write them down as well if you like). If you work with a partner, go back and forth orally and see how long you can keep the alternatives coming.

27.24, 27.25 Role-playing and reinvention of the story

Role-playing and reinvention exercises give you an opportunity to make creative use of what you have learned so far, and to adapt the story to your own tastes and preferences.

In 27.24, Robert and Mireille are discussing what kind of transportation to take to Chartres. Imagine their dialogue, out loud, using the alternatives given in the workbook as a point of departure. If you work with a partner, take parts and complete the exercise, then switch roles and do it again.

In 27.25, Robert is on his way to the Gare Montparnasse to keep his appointment with Mireille. Needless to say, he gets lost. Imagine his adventures, saying them out loud. You may use the suggestions in the workbook to get started, or you may invent the whole story yourself. If you work with a partner, tell parallel stories, each one giving his or her alternative to each scene.

• **Suggested written assignment.** Write out a version of Robert's adventures in 27.25. Write 50-75 words. Send this assignment to your instructor (see the course syllabus for details).

OPTIONAL EXERCISES FOR WRITING PRACTICE

These exercises will give you additional practice writing French.

Listen again to exercises 27.12 and 27.13 on the audio recording and write out the audio cues you hear.

Check what you have written against the printed text in the study guide.

SELF-TESTING EXERCISES

The test exercises in 27.26-27.29 are keyed to principal points covered in lesson 27; they allow you to measure what you have learned from the lesson, and to help you review.

• To complete exercises 27.26 and 27.27, select the appropriate phrase from those given in the title and write its correct form.

• In 27.28, complete the sentences with the appropriate pluperfect form.

• Complete 27.29 by listening to the sentences on the audio recording and marking whether each contains a verb in the indicative or in the conditional.

√ Check your answers in keys 27.26-27.29 at the back of the workbook. If you have made errors, follow the references at the end of each exercise to sections of the workbook and audio program for review.

SUMMARY QUIZ

A summary quiz for lesson 27 can be found at the back of this guide. For information about completing it and handing it in, consult the course syllabus or check with your instructor.

LESSON 28
All manner of transportation II

The story

The train arrives in Chartres right on time. Robert seems surprised, but Mireille tells him that French trains are **always** on time—well, nearly always. They have a bite to eat in a small restaurant. Mireille refuses to take a taxi to the museum and the cathedral, which are only a ten-minute walk away. After witnessing an accident, they take time to look at the cathedral (Mireille is in no big rush). We note that in spite of his tirade at the Closerie des Lilas against all but the most utilitarian studies, Robert seems sincerely impressed by the beauty of the place. There's hope for the kid yet.

Mireille leaves for the museum. They will meet here, at the West Portal, in exactly one hour, at 3:00 on the dot. After her departure, Robert does some window-shopping. He'd like to buy something for Mireille, but he doesn't dare. His stroll has brought him near the museum. Suddenly he thinks he sees her exchanging smiles and disappearing with a cute young Swedish-looking hunk. Is it Mireille, or isn't it? He can't be certain. Perturbed, Robert goes back to the West Portal. Mireille joins him at 2:59, but the triumph of her punctuality is spoiled for Robert by the loud engine of a sports car pulling away. At the wheel is . . . the Swede?

Notes on culture and communication

● **Notre-Dame de Chartres.** Begun in 1145, rebuilt at the beginning of the thirteenth century, the cathedral of Chartres is the first masterpiece of the mature Gothic style. The magic of its interior space, its sculptures, and its incomparable stained-glass windows make it a triumph of beauty and majesty and one of the most celebrated monuments in the world.

Content and learning objectives of lesson 28

In this lesson you will find expressions for being early, on time, and late, and for recalling or anticipating events. The lesson shows ways in which French speakers refer to something near or far away in time. It also presents expressions for feeling and causing pain.

The following points are highlighted in lesson 28 (you should concentrate on sections marked with a √):

10

√• Expressions of time: *en avance, à l'heure, en retard* (28.6, 28.7)
√• *Il y a une heure, tout à l'heure, dans une heure* (28.8-28.11)
  • *Faire mal, avoir mal*
√• Expressions of quantity, review (28.22, 28.23)
  • The conditional, review
  • Plural of words in -*au*, -*eau*, -*al*, and -*ail*

ASSIMILATION OF THE TEXT

28.1 Text work-up

• You should begin the *mise en oeuvre* as soon as possible after you
have viewed the video program for lesson 28. Listen to the *mise en oeuvre*
on the audio recording, repeating and answering according to the musical
signals (short signal = repeat; long signal = answer.) Complete 28.1 on the
audio program **before** you look at the printed text in the textbook. Remember to speak up and speak out.

28.2-28.4 Aural comprehension and oral production

• In 28.2, you see a series of illustrations. In phase 1 of the exercise,
study the numbered pictures as you listen to the phrases that correspond to
them on the audio recording. In phase 2, these phrases are presented in a
different order, labeled A through H. Find the illustration that best fits the
phrase you hear and write the identifying letter beneath it.

√ Check your answers in key 28.2 at the back of the workbook.

• In 28.3, you will hear a series of dialogues. Each dialogue is followed
by a question. Answer the question. You will hear the correct answer for
confirmation. (The questions you are to answer are indicated in the workbook.)

• In 28.4, you will hear a series of dialogues. Take the part of one of
the characters, as indicated, mimicking his or her speech as closely as
possible. You will hear the line again for confirmation. (The characters you
are to play are indicated in the workbook.)

THE "TEXT" AND THE TEXTBOOK

Turn to your textbook and study the text of lesson 28 and the accompanying illustrations. Then read the questions that follow the text and
answer them out loud. If you find you have any difficulty answering, return

to section 28.1 and repeat it, looking at the questions in the textbook as you listen to them on the recording.

TOWARD COMMUNICATION

28.5 Observation and activation: Pronunciation; vowels (review)

• Repeat the words and expressions you hear, paying particular attention to the sound /a/. Avoid overstressing /a/, and be careful not to slide from /a/ into some other vowel sound or into the sound of the following consonant.

28.6, 28.7 Observation and activation: As time goes by; *en avance, à l'heure, en retard* (review and extension)

Study chart 28.6 to review these ways of talking about being early, on time, and late.

• In exercise 28.7, people were expected for various times. They arrive before, after, or on the dot of the appointed time. Analyze each case and conclude that they are early, late, or on time, using *en avance*, *en retard*, or *à l'heure*.

Audio cues (for reference):
28.7 Activation orale: Le temps qui passe; en avance, à l'heure, en retard

1. Robert attendait Mireille à 3h. Elle arrive à 3h et quart.
2. Nous vous attendions à midi. Il est 1h.
3. Mireille attendait Robert à 11h. Il arrive à 11h et quart.
4. Les Courtois attendaient Robert à 8h, et il est arrivé à 7h!
5. Je t'attendais à 5h, et il est presque 6h!
6. Vous m'attendiez à 11h, et bien il est 11h pile!
7. Robert a rendez-vous avec Mireille à midi, au Luxembourg. Il est 11h et il est déjà là!

28.8-28.11 Observation and activation: As time goes by; *il y a une heure, tout à l'heure, dans une heure* (review and extension)

Chart 28.8 shows how to refer to precise moments in the past and future from the point of view of the present.

For the very recent past and the very near future, the expression is the same: *tout à l'heure*. The verb will tell you whether *tout à l'heure* refers to the past or the future: "Elle **est partie** tout à l'heure" (past), "elle **va partir** tout à l'heure" (future).

For points in time beyond the immediate past and future, *il y a* is used with expressions of time (*trois heures*, *dix jours*, and so forth) to refer to the past. *Dans* is used with similar expressions of time to indicate the future.

• Exercise 28.9 will sharpen your ability to associate these three expressions with various situations. Analyze each situation as you hear it, keeping in mind that it is now 4 p.m., and select the phrase that best expresses the situation. Mark the appropriate box on the grid in your workbook.

√ Check your answers in key 28.9 at the back of the workbook.

• In exercise 28.10, it is still 4 p.m. Various actions are described as taking place at different times between 3 and 6 p.m. Say when they happened or will happen, using *il y a . . .* , *tout à l'heure*, or *dans une heure*.

Audio cues (for reference):
28.10 Activation orale: Le temps qui passe; il y a une heure, tout à l'heure, dans une heure

1. Il est 4h. Mireille est partie à 3h.
2. Il est 4h. Elle est partie à 3h50.
3. Il est 4h. Elle va revenir à 5h.
4. Il est 4h. Elle va revenir à 6h.
5. Il est 4h. Je l'ai vue à 4h moins le quart.
6. Il est 4h. Je l'attends à 5h.
7. Il est 4h. Elle était là à 3h.
8. Il est 4h. Elle sera là dans quelques minutes.
9. Il est 4h. Nous avons rendez-vous à 5h.
10. Il est 4h. Nous avions rendez-vous à 3h!

• In 28.11, the time is no longer 4 p.m. but varies, from 6 p.m. to noon to Wednesday. Say when the actions you hear mentioned take place or will take place, using *il y a . . .* or *dans* with the appropriate expression of time.

Audio cues (for reference):
28.11 Activation orale: Le temps qui passe; il y a, dans

1. Il est 6h. Elle est partie à 4h.
2. Il est midi. Elle va revenir à 3h.
3. Il est presque midi. Elle va arriver à midi.
4. Il est midi. Robert a vu Mireille à midi moins dix.
5. C'est mercredi. Robert va voir Mireille vendredi.
6. C'est mercredi. Robert et Mireille se sont rencontrés lundi.

28.12, 28.13 Observation and activation: As time goes by

The expressions in chart 28.12 give you a variety of ways to talk about being early, on time, or late for an appointment scheduled for 3:00.

• In exercise 28.13, listen and decide whether the situations you hear described indicate that you are early, on time, or late; mark the corresponding box on the grid in your workbook.

√ Check your answers in key 28.13 at the back of the workbook.

28.14-28.16 Observation and activation: Distance measured in time

Chart 28.14 shows how the time it takes to get from one point to another may be indicated by *c'est à* followed by the amount of time needed. If the point of departure is named it is preceded by *de*.

If, in addition to giving the facts, you want to stress how nearby or how far away the destination is, you can add *au plus* or *au moins*.

• In exercise 28.15, say how long it takes to get to a given place from different points of departure (here, the station, Paris) by various means of transportation (on foot, by car, and so forth). Use *c'est à*, and indicate the amount of time needed and the means of transportation used.

Audio cues (for reference):
28.15 Activation orale: Distance mesurée en temps

1. D'ici, à pied, il faut une heure.
2. De la gare, à pied, il faut 10 minutes.
3. De Paris, en voiture, il faut une heure et demie.
4. D'ici, en métro, il faut un quart d'heure.
5. De Paris, en avion, il faut 7h.

• In 28.16, say how long it takes to get to different places. If you think the destination is far, add *au moins* to your statement. If you think it is near, add *au plus*.

Audio cues (for reference):
28.16 Activation orale: Distance mesurée en temps

1. C'est tout près. Il faut 20 minutes.
2. C'est loin. Il faut 20 minutes.
3. C'est tout près. Il faut une heure.
4. Ce n'est pas tout près. Il faut 40 minutes.

5. C'est très loin. Il faut 2h.

6. Ce n'est pas loin du tout. Il faut un quart d'heure.

28.17–28.21 Observation and activation: *Faire mal, avoir mal*

Chart 28.17 shows that *mal* is used in a number of ways to refer to discomfort or pain. *Avoir mal* is used to talk about **feeling** pain, usually in a particular part of the body. Notice that the part of the body in pain is preceded by the **definite article**.

Faire mal is used to talk about **causing** pain. One can be hurt by other people ("tu lui fais mal"), or one can hurt oneself (*faire mal*, used reflexively: "il s'est fait mal"), or some area of the body can cause pain ("la jambe lui fait mal"). The sufferer is referred to with an **indirect object** pronoun: "ça lui fait mal."

• In exercise 28.18, you are asked whether you and other people have hurt yourselves. Say no, you haven't, using *se faire mal*. In the last sentence, tell the person who thinks he has hurt himself that he really hasn't.

Audio cues (for reference):

28.18 Activation orale: Se faire mal

1. Vous vous êtes fait mal?

2. Le cycliste s'est fait mal?

3. Elles se sont fait mal?

4. Tu t'es fait mal?

5. Aïe, je me suis fait mal!

• In 28.19, you will hear someone complain of pain in various parts of the body. Show interest, and ask if those areas hurt, using *avoir mal* and the appropriate part of the body preceded by the **definite article**.

Audio cues (for reference):

28.19 Activation orale: Avoir mal

1. Ouh! Mes jambes!

2. Ouh! Mon bras!

3. Ouh! Mes dents!

4. Ouh! Mon ventre!

5. Ouh! Ma tête!

6. Ouh! Mes oreilles!

• In 28.20, someone is asking you to watch out and complaining about various parts of the body. Ask if you are hurting that person there, using *faire mal*.

Audio cues (for reference):
28.20 Activation orale: Faire mal

1. Eh là! Mon pied!   4. Eh là! Mon doigt!
2. Eh là! Ma jambe!   5. Eh là! Ma main!
3. Eh là! Ma tête!   6. Eh là! Mes oreilles!

• In 28.21, someone is drawing attention to pain in various parts of
the body. Ask if that person has hurt himself or herself there, using
se faire mal.

Audio cues (for reference):
28.21 Activation orale: Se faire mal

1. Ouille! Ma jambe!   4. Ouille! Ma main!
2. Ouille! Mon pied!   5. Ouille! Mon nez!
3. Ouille! Mon doigt!   6. Ouille! Mon genou!

28.22-28.23 Observation and activation: Expressions of quantity (review)

Chart 28.22 contrasts two ways of talking about quantities of things.
Recall from lesson 26 that *du*, *de la*, *de l'*, and *des* are used with nouns to
refer to an unspecified amount of a larger whole. When the amount is
specified, the expression that specifies it is linked to the noun by *de* alone.

• Listen to exercise 28.23 on the audio recording and describe what
Robert and Mireille have ordered for lunch. You will need to figure out the
proper word to express the quantity (*une assiette*, *une carafe*, *un pichet*).

Audio cues (for reference):
28.23 Activation orale: Expressions de quantité

1. Mireille voulait des crudités. Qu'est-ce qu'elle a demandé?
2. Elle voulait de l'eau. Qu'est-ce qu'elle a demandé?
3. Robert voulait de la charcuterie et du vin rouge. Qu'est-ce qu'il a commandé?

28.24-28.29 Observation and activation: The conditional (review and extension)

You saw in lesson 27 that the conditional allows us to speak hypothe-
tically, to refer not to the way things are but to the way they **would be** if a
given condition that is not fulfilled **were** fulfilled. The action of a verb in
the conditional has an unreal, often wishful quality precisely because it does
not correspond to actual reality.

Chart 28.24 illustrates a related function of the conditional—a kind of by-product of its role as a vehicle for expressions that are purely hypothetical.

Section 28.24 shows the conditional used for the sake of politeness. Since it is less direct than the indicative, it can be brought in to take the edge off a declaration or to soften the feeling of confrontation created by an abrupt request. The examples in the conditional in 28.24 are more diplomatic, less demanding than their equivalents in the indicative. Recall also Robert's way of asking Mireille if he can walk her home (lesson 14): not "je vais vous accompagner!" which would be much too forward, but the more polite "est-ce que vous **voudriez** bien me permettre de vous accompagner?" which is in the conditional, and which works.

Note that the conditional sentences in 28.24 presuppose a condition that is not expressed, but that is understood nonetheless. For example, when Robert says he would love to go to Chartres with Mireille, some condition such as "if you're willing" is understood, although it is not spelled out.

Chart 28.25 contrasts the indicative, which describes real situations, with the conditional, which describes situations that are unreal or unrealizable. The conditional presupposes a **condition** ("si la voiture n'était pas en panne . . .") and projects a hypothetical **outcome** (". . . nous pourrions aller à Chartres").

The part of the sentence stating the condition is introduced by *si*: "Si vous vouliez, nous pourrions louer une voiture." Notice that the verb in the **imperfect** describes the **condition** ("si vous **vouliez**"), while the verb in the **conditional** describes the **outcome** ("nous **pourrions** louer une voiture").

Before beginning exercises 28.26-28.29, look again at lesson 27.19 and 27.20 to review how to form the conditional. Then complete the exercises.

• In exercise 28.26, you will hear that when people want to do things, they can do them (where there's a will there's a way). Make each statement hypothetical, using *si*, the imperfect, and the conditional.

• In 28.27, say that if Mireille did something you would, too. You will hear the conditions, expressed by verbs in the imperfect. Complete each statement using the same verb in the conditional.

• In 28.29, certain actions are not occurring because the necessary conditions are not present. Say what would happen if these conditions **were** present. Before rewriting each sentence be sure you can tell which part lays down the condition (it is introduced by *parce que*) and which describes the outcome. Study the example carefully before you begin. As you work, bear in mind that since the conditional represents the opposite of reality, your rewritten sentences will reverse the originals (what was negative in the original will be positive in your version). Start each sentence with *si*.

√ Check your answers to 28.29 in the key at the back of the workbook.

28.30 Observation: Singular and plural (review and expansion)

The chart presents the plurals of words whose singular forms end in -*au*, -*eau*, -*al*, and -*ail*. Note that all the plural forms end in -*aux* **except** *portails*.

28.31 Activation: Dialogue between Robert and Mireille

Listen to the conversation between Robert and Mireille and memorize Mireille's lines, imitating and repeating as usual.

• **Suggested oral assignment.** Record the dialogue in 28.31, giving each character's name before you say his or her lines. Send this assignment to your instructor (see the course syllabus for details).

TOWARD FREE EXPRESSION

28.31 Words at large

Proceed as usual. (Refer to lesson 27 for directions.)

28.33, 28.34 Role-playing and reinvention of the story

In 28.33, Robert and Mireille have just arrived in the train station at Chartres. Imagine their dialogue. You may reconstruct what they say from the material of the lesson, using the suggestions in the workbook as a point of departure. Or you may make their conversation up yourself.

In 28.34, describe what might have happened between Mireille and the young Swede in Chartres.

DOCUMENT

In the textbook chapter for lesson 28 you will find a brief passage for reading practice by the essayist and poet Charles Péguy (1873-1914).

Péguy, a strongly committed nationalist and patriot, was also a fervent, almost mystical Catholic. In this excerpt from a longer poem about Chartres, he describes the annual student pilgrimage from Notre-Dame de Paris to Notre-Dame de Chartres, from one magnificent cathedral rising up over the buildings of the Ile de la Cité in Paris to the other presiding over the fertile plain of the Beauce region of France.

OPTIONAL EXERCISES FOR WRITING PRACTICE

Listen again to exercises 28.11 and 28.15 on the audio recording and write out the audio cues you hear.

Check what you have written against the printed text in the study guide.

SELF-TESTING EXERCISES

- Complete and check 28.35 and 28.36 as usual.

SUMMARY QUIZ

Consult the course syllabus or check with your instructor for information about completing and handing in summary quiz 28.

LESSON 29
All manner of transportation III

The story

The train back to Paris is packed. Robert, in a foul mood, keeps grousing, even when Mireille finds a compartment occupied by only one person (a man dressed all in black). She knows a lot about automobiles, and she waxes lyrical about the model driven by that Swedish hunk, which doesn't improve Robert's mood. It's only natural that she should know cars; her father, after all, is in the business.

Mireille doesn't mind hitchhiking on occasion. It offers all the advantages and none of the drawbacks of owning a car. She once hitched from Paris to Geneva in eight hours. That's very good time. She admits it's a little risky, but that's the fun.

Robert suggests dinner on a sightseeing boat, but that sort of thing is just for American tourists. Besides, Mireille must grab a bus to visit a friend on the Boulevard Saint-Germain. She'll see Robert at dinner on Thursday. Tomorrow is out, too. She's going to Provins. Robert can't stop thinking about the Swedish hunk. (Could our boy be jealous?) He hails a cab and searches the entire Saint-Germain area . . . in vain.

Notes on culture and communication

• **Saint-Germain-des-Prés.** The Left Bank neighborhood of St.-Germain-des-Prés is a district bordering on the Latin Quarter. Its geographical and spiritual center is the church of the same name. Its many cafés, restaurants, and nightclubs have made it the rendezvous of intellectuals since the existentialist movement of the late 1940s and 1950's. The nightlife of St.-Germain is still among the most intense and colorful in Paris.

Content and learning objectives of lesson 29

This lesson presents expressions for talking about automobiles and describing the advantages and limitations of common means of transportation. It also shows how French speakers express admiration, phrase suggestions, and react to the unexpected.

The following points are highlighted in lesson 29 (you should concentrate on the section marked with a √):

- *Mettre* and expressions of time
- The conditional, review
- *Arriver: ça arrive!*
√ • The past conditional (29.23-29.25)

ASSIMILATION OF THE TEXT

29.1-29.4 Text work-up, aural comprehension, and oral production

Proceed as usual in these sections. (Refer to lesson 28.1-28.4 for directions, if necessary.) Work with the text of lesson 29 in the textbook, as in previous lessons.

TOWARD COMMUNICATION

29.5, 29.6 Observation and activation: Pronunciation; forward quality of consonants in French

Compared to consonants in English, French consonants are produced quite far forward in the mouth.

To produce a /t/ in either language, the tongue must touch somewhere in back of the upper front teeth. The precise point where the tongue meets the area behind the teeth to produce a /t/ is called the **articulation point** of that sound. The articulation point of /t/ in the English word *taxi* is the alveolar ridge behind the teeth. The articulation point of the /t/ of the **French** word *taxi*, however, is further forward: the tip of the tongue taps against the front teeth themselves. This forward articulation is characteristic of French pronunciation in general.

- In exercise 29.6, repeat the words and expressions you hear, being careful to articulate the consonant sounds well forward in the mouth.

29.7 Observation: Perspicacity

Chart 29.7 groups together a number of useful expressions for predicting what will happen, and for announcing after it happens how right you were.

29.8 Observation and activation: Braking

The verb *freiner* and related words refer to the process of stopping a vehicle. Note the difference between the two nouns: *un frein* is the mechanical component that actually slows down the wheels; *le freinage* is the result of applying *les freins*.

29.9, 29.10 Observation and activation: Admiration

The exclamation *ça c'est . . . !* expresses enthusiastic approval. It suggests that the object of your admiration conforms to the highest standard that can be applied to it. When the object of admiration is expressed by a noun, the noun is generally used with the partitive article.

Mireille has been knowledgeable about cars since childhood, and the Renault Alpine is her idea of a real car: "Ça, c'est **de la** bagnole!"

• In exercise 29.10, give an enthusiastic response to the questions you hear, using *ça c'est . . . !*

Audio cues (for reference):
29.10 Activation orale: Admiration

1. Alors, qu'est-ce que vous en dites? Ce sont de bons freins?
2. Alors? Ce sont de bonnes reprises?
3. Alors? ça vous plaît comme bagnole?
4. Alors, ces vacances? Ça vous plaît? C'est bien?
5. Alors, c'est du bon cinéma? Ça vous plaît?

29.11-29.13 Observation and activation: *Ça arrive!*

Ça arrive is used to talk about events that are unforeseen or occur on exceptional or rare occasions (outside of a regular pattern or routine). Everybody's car breaks down at some time or another: *ça arrive!* Mireille has been known to hitchhike—*ça lui est arrivé*—although she does not make a regular practice of it. Persons to whom these things happen are indirect objects of the verb *arriver:* "ça **leur** arrive.

• In exercise 29.12, you will be asked whether you or other people ever do certain things. Say yes, you've had occasion to, using *ça arrive* and the appropriate indirect object pronoun. Notice that when the question is in the present, you will use the present of *arriver* ("Ça m'**arrive!**"); when the question is in the *passé composé*, you will use the *passé composé* of *arriver* ("Ça m'est arrivé!").

Audio cues (for reference):
29.12 Activation orale: Ça arrive!

1. Vous prenez l'avion quelquefois, vous deux?
2. Vous prenez le train quelquefois?
3. Vous êtes tombés en panne quelquefois?
4. Tu fais de l'auto-stop?
5. Tu as déjà fait de l'auto-stop?
6. Mireille a déjà fait de l'auto-stop?
7. Les parents de Mireille prennent l'avion quelquefois?
8. Est-ce qu'ils ont pris un aéroglisseur?

• In 29.13, you will again be asked whether various things ever happen to you or others. Say no, they never do (or no, they never have if the question is in the *passé composé*), using the negative expression *ça n'arrive jamais* (*ça n'est jamais arrivé* in the *passé composé*), and the appropriate indirect object pronoun.

29.14, 29.15 Observation and activation: Advantages and drawbacks

Chart 29.14 gives the benefits and the drawbacks of a number of modes of transportation.

• In exercise 29.15, decide whether the phrases you hear refer to an advantage or a drawback, and mark your responses on the grid in your workbook.

√ Check your answers in key 29.15 at the back of the workbook.

29.16, 29.17 Observation and activation: The time it takes

The verb *mettre* is used with expressions of time to state how long it takes to complete a given activity. When the activity is mentioned, it is expressed as an infinitive preceded by *pour*.

• In exercise 29.17, you will hear when certain people and a train left for various destinations, and when they arrived. Do a quick calculation and say how long it took them, using *mettre* and the appropriate expression of time.

Audio cues (for reference):
29.17 Activation orale: Le temps qu'on met

1. Mireille est partie de Paris à 10h du matin, et elle est arrivée à Genève à 6h du soir.
2. Robert est parti du Home Latin à 10h et demie et il est arrivé à la gare à 11h 10.

3. Nous sommes partis à 5h et nous sommes arrivés à 7h.

4. Vous êtes partis à 2h? Il est 3h maintenant.

5. Robert et Mireille sont partis du restaurant près de la gare à 2h moins le quart. Ils sont arrivés à la cathédrale à 2h moins cinq.

6. J'ai commencé à 1h. J'ai fini à 3h.

7. Quand Mireille va à la Fac elle part de chez elle à 11h. Elle arrive à la Sorbonne à 11h 10.

8. Il y a un train qui part de la Gare Montparnasse à 18h 06 et qui arrive à 19h 06.

29.20-29.22 Observation and activation: The conditional (review)

You have seen (lessons 27 and 28) that the conditional is speculative; it refers to a hypothetical outcome that depends on a condition that is not present. The condition, introduced by *si*, is expressed by a verb in the imperfect ("**si j'avais** assez d'argent . . ."); the outcome is expressed by a verb in the conditional (". . . j'**achèterais** une petite voiture"). Chart 29.20 extends discussion of the conditional to situations you have encountered in lesson 29.

• In exercise 29.21, you will hear that people are not doing one thing or another because certain conditions are not present. Say that if these conditions were fulfilled they would do those things, using conditional sentences. Bear in mind that the conditional sentence, since it is contrary to fact, will state what is negative in the indicative sentence as positive, and vice versa. Study the example carefully before you begin the exercise.

• In exercise 29.22, you will see pairs of sentences that present actual situations. The second sentence of each pair describes the outcome of the first. Say what would happen if the first sentence were not true. Begin with *si* and combine the sentences into a single conditional sentence.

√ Check your answers in key 29.22 at the back of the workbook.

29.23-29.25 Observation and activation: Past conditional

Up to now you have been using the **present conditional**: if X were true right now, Y **would** happen. But speculation and hypothesizing are not limited to the present, and as you might expect there is also a **past conditional**, illustrated in chart 29.23. The past conditional refers to nonexistent conditions and hypothetical outcomes in the past: if X had been true back then, Y **would have** happened.

The past conditional is a compound tense like the *passé composé* or the pluperfect. Recall that the condition that introduces the **present conditional** is expressed by a verb in the **imperfect**. The past condition that introduces a past conditional is in the pluperfect: "si j'avais su. . . ." The past conditional is made up of the past participle of the verb and an auxiliary (*avoir* or *être*). The auxiliary is in the present conditional: ". . . j'aurais loué une voiture."

• Complete the sentences you hear in exercise 29.24 with the appropriate verb in the past conditional.

• In 29.25, you see several pairs of sentences containing facts about the story of Robert and Mireille. In each pair, the second sentence is a consequence of the first. Speculate what the outcome would have been for the story if the action expressed in the first sentence of each pair had not taken place. Use the pluperfect and past conditional, as in the example.

√ Check your answers in key 29.25 at the back of the workbook.

29.26 Activation: Dialogue between Robert and Mireille

Listen to the conversation between Robert and Mireille and memorize Mireille's lines, imitating and repeating as usual.

TOWARD FREE EXPRESSION

29.27 Words at large

Proceed as usual. (If necessary, refer to lesson 27 for directions.)

29.28, 29.29 Role-playing and reinvention of the story

In 29.28, Robert and Mireille are discussing Mireille's dream car. Imagine their dialogue.

In 29.29, imagine an encounter between the young Swede and the man in black.

• Suggested written assignment. Write a version of the meeting between the Swede and the man in black in 29.29. Write 50-75 words. Send this assignment to your instructor (see the course syllabus for details).

OPTIONAL EXERCISE FOR WRITING PRACTICE

Listen again to exercise 29.12 on the audio recording and write out the audio cues you hear.

Check what you have written against the printed text in the study guide.

SELF-TESTING EXERCISES

• Complete and check exercises 29.30 and 29.31 as usual.

SUMMARY QUIZ

Consult the course syllabus or check with your instructor for information about completing and handing in summary quiz 29.

LESSON 30
All manner of transportation IV

<u>The story</u>

The next day, Robert has not slept too well. He asks about Provins and about car rentals. The hotelkeeper sends him to a Shell station run by a friend. There, Robert, who does not want to waste time weighing the relative merits of different cars, settles on an inexpensive Peugeot 205. When the necessary paperwork has been done and Robert is behind the wheel, he gets directions to Fontainebleau, which he has been told is not far from Provins. The directions seem rather complicated, but the garage man says there are signs everywhere and Robert can't possibly get lost. Of course he doesn't know him as well as we do.

In the meantime, Mireille arranges with Uncle Guillaume to borrow one of his cars. It seems she really is going to Provins to visit a friend, Colette.

Robert seems to be following the directions successfully. By 11:30, elated, he is near his destination. But when next we see him, at about 2, he is hopelessly lost somewhere in Burgundy, about 300 kilometers from Paris. He has spent hours in hot pursuit of a sports car just like the one from Chartres, with a blonde in it who could have been Mireille. By the time Robert realizes his mistake, the wine country holds him tightly in its thrall.

<u>Notes on culture and communication</u>

● **La Bourgogne.** Burgundy ranks with Bordeaux and Champagne as one of the most prestigious wine-growing regions in France. The best Burgundies, red and white, have a combination of power and finesse surpassed by no other wines in the world. Burgundy's finest vineyards lie in villages strung out along a few narrow hillsides from Dijon to south of Beaune: Gevrey-Chambertin, Morey St.-Denis, Chambolle-Musigny, Vougeot, Vosne-Romanée, Nuits St.-Georges, Aloxe-Corton, Beaune, Pommard, Volnay, Meursault, Puligny-Montrachet, Chassagne-Montrachet, and Santenay are the principal townships.

Further south, between Macon and Lyon, the vineyards of the Beaujolais region produce well-known and popular red wines, of which the best carry the name of the village or vineyard slope where they are produced: from north to south, St.-Amour, Juliénas, Chénas, Moulin-à-Vent, Fleurie, Chiroubles, Morgon, Brouilly, and Côtes-de-Brouilly.

• **Getting lost in France.** "No way to make a mistake . . . you can't get lost!" That's what they tell Robert when he starts out, and, for most people anyway, it is accurate advice. The maps available in France are so remarkably complete, accurate, and easy to read that it is virtually impossible to lose your way. The autoroutes, national highways, departmental roads, even the *chemins vicinaux* or local roads are shown on the maps, and as you drive you find they are all well-marked. Most maps show not only the roads but dangerous curves, beautiful views, hazardous mountain passes, interesting tourist attractions, historic sites, and so forth. You can even get maps of the Sentiers de Grande Randonnée, a system of paths blazed all over France, that let you hike even in the most rural areas without getting lost.

Content and learning objectives of lesson 30

This lesson illustrates ways in which French speakers express concern about others, express impossibility, and describe geographical locations. It also shows how they talk about lending, borrowing, and returning borrowed items.

The following points are highlighted in lesson 30 (you should concentrate on the section marked with a √):

- Indefinite expressions
- Forms of the present indicative, review

√ • Past participles in -*é* and -*u* (30.18-30.20)

ASSIMILATION OF THE TEXT

30.1-30.4 Text work-up, aural comprehension, and oral production

Proceed as usual in these sections. (Refer to lesson 28.1-28.4 for directions, if necessary.) Work with the text of lesson 30 in the textbook, as in previous lessons.

TOWARD COMMUNICATION

30.5, 30.6 Observation and activation: Pronunciation; Quality of vowels (review)

The words in pairs in 30.5 differ in pronunciation from each other by their vowel sounds. Since all that is different is the vowel, it is crucial to pronounce the vowel correctly so your listeners won't think you're talking about the climate—"C'est l'air!" (/ɛ/)—when in fact you're telling them it's time to go—"C'est l'heure!" (/œ/).

• Repeat the words and expressions you hear in 30.6, taking care (1) to avoid letting the /r/ sound at the end color the vowel in the middle, (2) not to create a diphthong by slipping and sliding from one vowel sound to another, and (3) to pronounce a clear French /r/, compressing the back of your mouth as if to make a *yuchhh!* sound and letting your tongue touch the base of your lower teeth.

30.7, 30.8 Observation and activation: Solicitude; *qu'est-ce que vous avez?*

Robert has just stumbled down to the hotel lobby after a sleepless night spent worrying about whom Mireille is really going to see in Provins. Chart 30.7 shows how to express concern over people in such states, and the kind of answer to expect. Notice that the last question, in the negative, is answered *Si!* to indicate that nothing is wrong.

• In exercise 30.8, various people aren't in top form. Ask them what's wrong. Respond as quickly as you can.

Audio cues (for reference):
30.8 Activation orale: Sollicitude; qu'est-ce que vous avez?

1. Vous n'avez pas l'air en forme!
2. Tu n'as pas l'air en forme!
3. Robert n'a pas l'air en forme!

4. Robert n'avait pas l'air en forme!
5. Tes parents n'avaient pas l'air en forme!
6. Tes parents n'ont pas l'air en forme!

30.9, 30.10 Observation and activation: Indefinite expression + *de*; *c'est ce que nous avons de moins cher*

When your budget tells you to rent a Peugeot 205 but the garage offers you a Citroën CX, you naturally ask for something less expensive. You do not know what else they have, so you use an expression like *rien*, *quelque chose*, or *ce que*—one that does not refer to anything specific (an **indefinite** expression). The indefinite expression is followed by *de* and the appropriate adjective (*cher*, *grand*, *petit*, and so forth), as chart 30.9 demonstrates.

• In 30.10, you are the salesman. The customer asks for something other than what you have. Say you don't have anything like what your customer wants. The customer will use the indefinite expression *rien de*. Answer with the indefinite expression *ce que* + verb + *de*.

Audio cues (for reference):
30.10 Activation orale: Expression indéfinie + de

1. Vous n'avez rien de plus grand?   5. Ils n'ont rien de plus grand?
2. Vous n'avez rien de moins grand?   6. Vous n'avez rien de moins cher?
3. Vous n'avez rien de plus petit?   7. Il n'y a rien de moins cher?
4. Ils n'ont rien de plus petit?   8. On ne fait rien de plus grand?

30.11, 30.12 Observation and activation: Cardinal points

In France, all roads lead to Paris. Chart 30.11 names four French cities and regions that are located at each of the cardinal points of the compass in relation to the capital. These four principal points can of course be combined to refer to any intermediary sector of the compass: *nord-est*, *sud-ouest*. Notice that in these combined forms *nord* and *sud* come first.

• In exercise 30.12, mark the location of the places mentioned by writing the number of each in the proper sector of the diagram.

√ Check your answers in key 30.12 at the back of the workbook.

30.13, 30.14 Observation and activation: Impossibility; *il n'y a pas moyen*

The car rental agent, no judge of character, is so sure his directions to Fontainebleau are clear that he tells Robert there is no way he can get lost. He uses the expression *il n'y a pas moyen* with *de* and an infinitive. Notice that the impersonal *il y a* and the third person reflexive pronoun *se* make what he says applicable not just to Robert, but to anyone: "Il n'y a pas moyen de se perdre."

• In exercise 30.14, answer that what is mentioned in the questions you hear is impossible, using *il n'y a pas moyen de* + infinitive.

Audio cues (for reference):
30.14 Activation orale: Impossibilité; il n'y a pas moyen

1. Est-ce qu'on peut se perdre?   4. Est-ce qu'on peut sortir de l'autoroute?
2. Est-ce qu'on peut se tromper?   5. Est-ce qu'on peut faire demi-tour?
3. Est-ce qu'on peut attraper l'autoroute?

30.15, 30.16 Observation and activation: Lending and borrowing

Expressions that refer to the cycle of borrowing, lending and returning are presented in chart 30.15, using Mireille and her doting Uncle Guillaume as examples. Notice that all of the verbs in these expressions are used with *à* and an indirect object: "Elle rend la voiture **à son oncle**" ⇒ "Elle **lui** rend la voiture."

• In exercise 30.16, questions are asked about what usually happens in situations where some people have and some have not. Decide what would most likely happen in each situation, and answer accordingly, choosing between *emprunter* and *prêter*.

30.17   Activation: Forms of the present indicative (review)

• You are Robert, bound for Provins. Repeat the rental agent's directions for getting there, as in the example. (But please do **not** imitate Robert's tendency to forget what he has just heard.)

This exercise will give you practice in switching from one form of a verb (the *vous* form) to another (the *je* form). Remember that in many verbs there is a consonant sound in the plural that is absent in the singular: *vous suivez*, *je suis*.

Audio cues (for reference):
30.17 Activation orale: Formes du présent de l'indicatif (révision)

1. Vous êtes en bas de Boulevard Raspail.
2. Vous remontez le boulevard jusqu'à Denfert-Rochereau.
3. Vous voyez un lion sur la place.
4. Vous prenez l'avenue Général Leclerc.
5. Vous la suivez jusqu'à la porte d'Orléans.
6. Vous ne pouvez pas vous tromper.

30.18-30.20   Observation and activation: Compound tenses and past participles (review)

When you want to use a verb in a compound tense (such as the *passé composé*, the pluperfect, the past conditional), two questions await you.

The first is: Which auxiliary to use? Fortunately, the choice is limited: *avoir* or *être*. And the guidelines for choosing one or the other are straightforward and familiar. (Not entirely familiar? Review workbook and study guide materials for lesson 22.21 and 22.22).

The second question is: What is the past participle of the verb? Here you must depend on familiarity, if not downright **memorization**.   Chart 30.18 places side by side examples of past participles in -*é* and -*u*. The -*é* category is composed of verbs whose infinitives all look alike (they end in

-er), with two exceptions: *naître* and *être*. The -u category contains verbs whose infinitives are very dissimilar. These are the ones you will need to get more familiar with. Exercises 30.19 and 30.20 will help you do so.

• Before beginning 30.19, read the infinitives printed in the left-hand column of the chart to familiarize yourself with their location on the grid. Then listen to the past participles in -u and mark the corresponding infinitive on the grid.

√ Check your answers in key 30.19 at the back of the workbook.

• In exercise 30.20, confirm the details of Robert's trip to Burgundy using the *passé composé*. Notice that the sentences you hear are in the immediate future, which gives you the necessary **infinitives** to work with.

Audio cues (for reference):
30.20 Activation orale: Temps composés; participes passés en -é et -u

1. Vous allez voir que Robert va aller au garage Shell!
2. Vous allez voir qu'il va louer une voiture!
3. Il va attraper l'autoroute.
4. Maintenant vous allez voir qu'il va vouloir sortir de l'auto route.
5. Il va voir une Alpine.
6. Il va croire que c'est Mireille.
7. Il ne va pas savoir que faire.
8. Il va se lancer à la poursuite de l'Alpine.
9. Il va s'arrêter à Beaune.
10. Il va descendre de la voiture.
11. Il va boire un verre de Bourgogne.
12. Ça va lui plaire!
13. Il va tenir à goûter tous les vins de Bourgogne.
14. Il va se perdre.
15. Il va revenir à Paris très tard.
16. Il va rendre la voiture le lendemain.

30.21   Activation: Dialogue between Robert and the rental agent

Listen to the conversation between Robert and the car rental agent and memorize Robert's lines, imitating and repeating as usual.

• **Suggested oral assignment.** Record the dialogue between Robert and the rental agent in 30.21. Identify each character before you give his line. Send this assignment to your instructor (see the course syllabus for details).

TOWARD FREE EXPRESSION

30.22 Words at large

Proceed as usual. (If necessary, refer to lesson 27 for directions.)

30.23, 30.24 Role-playing and reinvention of the story

In 30.23, Robert is asking you how to get to Provins. Answer him (out loud), using the suggestions in the workbook as a point of departure.

In 30.24, the scene shifts to Mireille's house. The telephone rings; it is the man in black. He has tracked her down at last. Imagine their dialogue.

OPTIONAL EXERCISE FOR WRITING PRACTICE

Listen again to exercise 30.20 on the audio recording and write out the audio cues you hear.

Check what you have written against the printed text in the study guide.

SELF-TESTING EXERCISES

Complete and check exercises 30.25, 30.26, and 30.27 as usual.

SUMMARY QUIZ

Consult the course syllabus or check with your instructor for information about completing and handing in summary quiz 30.

LESSON 31
All manner of transportation V

The story

While Robert undertakes a study of the fine wines of Burgundy, Mireille goes to get Uncle Guillaume's car. Its battery is dead, so the garageman, unflappable, lends her a rented car that has just come in. It starts beautifully. We soon learn, however, that it has no brake fluid. Soon after that problem is remedied, the car runs out of gas. Then, near Mireille's destination, Provins, the left front tire blows out. Naturally, the spare is flat. Luckily for Mireille, a cyclist offers to have a tow truck sent. Later, both tires repaired, she runs into a rainstorm. Can you guess how well the windshield wipers work? Once at her friend Colette's, Mireille thinks to check the headlights before it gets dark. Not surprisingly, they don't work. On the return trip she must swerve to avoid a skidding cyclist and gets into a fender-bender. What a day! Let's hear it for trains!

At about 11 p.m. she calls Robert's hotel. No answer at his room and his key is at the desk; Robert is still out. Where is our wandering boy? Out among the vineyards of Burgundy, that's where, pursuing his research. His mind may no longer be 100 percent clear, but science's loss is music's gain.

Content and learning objectives of lesson 31

This lesson shows ways in which French speakers talk about owing and paying, discuss driving and traffic signals, and refer to various parts of an automobile.

The following points are highlighted in lesson 31 (you should concentrate on sections marked with a √):

- Nouns in *-age*
- √ Past participles in *-i*, *-is*, *-it*, and *-rt*, review (31.19-31.24)
- √ Agreement of past participles, review (31.25-31.26)

ASSIMILATION OF THE TEXT

31.1-31.4 Text work-up, aural comprehension, and oral production

Proceed as usual in these sections. (Refer to lesson 28.1-28.4 for directions, if necessary.) Work with the text of lesson 31 in the textbook, as in previous lessons.

TOWARD COMMUNICATION

31.5, 31.6 Observation and activation: Pronunciation; initial vowels

In English, vowel sounds at the beginning of words tend to get more energy than they do in French. There is more tension in the vocal cords, more "punch," in the first sound of *uncle*, for example, than in the first sound of its French counterpart, *oncle*. When the nasal vowel of *uncle* is first pronounced, it is already at its most intense, while the attack in French is less explosive, more gradual.

• Repeat the words and expressions you hear in 31.6, letting your throat and vocal cords relax fully before you begin each word.

31.7, 31.8 Observation and activation: Closures; *porte, portière, portail*

The things you open and close to get into and out of a house, a car, a garden, and a cathedral are not called by the same name in French. The words that refer to them are related, however, as chart 31.7 shows.

• In the mini-detective story in 31.8, fill in the clues, using *porte*, *portière*, or *portail*, as appropriate.

√ Check your answers in key 31.8 at the back of the workbook.

31.9, 31.10 Observation and activation: Nouns in -*age*

You saw in lesson 29 that the result of the action of *freiner* is *le freinage*. Chart 31.9 assembles several words in -*age* that bear a similar relation to an infinitive in -*er*. (The examples in 31.9 all refer to handling an automobile, but there are -*age* words in virtually every field of activity.)

• Once you have studied the commentary in 31.9 and are familiar with the way in which each infinitive and noun is used, complete the sentences in 31.10 with the noun or infinitive that is called for by the context.

√ Check your answers in key 31.10 at the back of the workbook.

31.11-31.13 Observation and activation: Money matters; payments

The service station attendant won't take Mireille's money for filling her brake-fluid reservoir, but for the rest of us it is usually necessary to settle up. Chart 31.11 sets forth the most common and useful expressions for asking how much, where, and when to pay, and for talking afterwards about what a great (or lousy) deal you got.

Before beginning the exercises, review the forms of *devoir* (lesson 16.10). You saw in lesson 16 that *devoir* refers to situations involving obligation ("je **dois** aller à Chartres"). Used with money, it refers to financial obligation ("combien est-ce que je vous **dois**?").

Note also in chart 31.11 the forms of the verb *payer* in the present and the *passé composé*. *Payer* behaves like *essayer* (see lesson 16.31).

• In exercise 31.12, you will hear a series of amounts owed and amounts paid. Calculate the difference between the two, determine whether each is an underpayment or an overpayment, and decide who still owes whom what, using *devoir*.

• In 31.13, write the appropriate forms of *payer* (infinitive, present indicative, *passé composé*, future, and so forth) according to the context.

√ Check your answers in key 31.13 at the back of the workbook.

31.14, 31.15 Observation and activation: Traffic lights

Mireille has a good excuse for going through a red light: she has no brakes. Under normal conditions, though, the French obey traffic signals, and chart 31.14 presents basic words and expressions for referring to them. You saw *feu* used in lesson 11 to ask someone for a light ("Pardon, Mademoiselle, est-ce que vous avez du **feu**?"). *Un feu* is also what burns in a fireplace. Note that the verb used to describe disregarding a red light is *brûler*.

Note the color of caution in the French system: *un feu* **orange**.

• In exercise 31.15, you will hear phrases spoken in various driving situations. Decide which traffic light is probably associated with each situation, and mark your answer on the grid in your workbook.

√ Check your answers in key 31.15 at the back of the workbook.

31.16-31.18 Observation and activation: Anatomy of an automobile; *arrière, avant, droite, gauche*

Like a compass, a car has four cardinal points; naming the location of a flat tire or a crumpled door is a matter of combining the terms given in chart 31.16. Notice that two of the basic terms, *avant* and *arrière*, do not agree with nouns, while the other two, *droit* and *gauche*, are regular adjectives that do agree.

• In exercise 31.17, you will hear a series of sentences that refer to areas of a car. Identify each area on the schematic chart in your workbook and write the corresponding letter in the numbered space.

• In 31.18, complete the sentences with the appropriate words, drawing on car terminology you have learned in the lesson.

√ Check your answers in keys 31.17 and 31.18 at the back of the workbook.

31.19-31.24 Observation and activation: Compound tenses and past participles (review)

Our review of past participles began in lesson 30 with two groups of participles: those that end in -*é* and those that end in -*u*. Participles in -*é* correspond, with only one or two exceptions, to infinitives in -*er*. Participles in -*u*, however, do not reflect a single category of infinitives.

Chart 31.19 adds participles ending in -*i* and -*is*. Chart 31.22 adds participles ending in -*it* and -*rt*. Like participles ending in -*u*, no ending corresponds reliably to any one group of infinitives. They must therefore be memorized.

• Exercises 31.20, 31.21, 31.23 and 31.24 will help you memorize these past participles. Look for the correct past participle and write it in the space provided.

√ Check your answers in keys 31.20, 31.21, 31.23, and 31.24 at the back of the workbook.

31.25, 31.26 Observation and activation: Agreement of past participles (review)

The past participles you have just been studying show agreement in the same ways all participles do. Participles agree with **preceding direct objects**

in the cases of verbs conjugated with *avoir* and reflexive verbs. They agree
with **subjects** in the case of nonreflexive verbs conjugated with *être*. (See
lesson 22 for a review.)

Notice that in the case of past participles in *-é*, *-u*, and *-i*, agreement
is not reflected in speech; it is purely a matter of spelling. (The past
participle in "Il les a invitées" is pronounced in exactly the same way as in
"il m'a invité"). But in the case of participles that end in a consonant (*-is*,
-it, *-rt*), adding an *-e* to the feminine forms will change the pronunciation of
the consonant. There is no /t/ sound at the end of the participle in "Elle a
ouvert la portière." But a /t/ sound is added when it agrees with a feminine
pronoun: "elle l'a ouver**t**e."

• In exercise 31.26, answer yes to each question, replacing nouns with
pronouns and using the appropriate past participle. Pay close attention to
the direct object in each sentence (is it feminine?) and to the form of the
past participle (does it end in a consonant sound?).

Audio cues (for reference):
31.26 Activation orale: Accord des participes passés (révision)

1. Tu as conduit la Matra?
2. Tu as pris la voiture ce matin?
3. Tu as pris le train ce matin?
4. Vous avez ouvert le capot?
5. Vous avez ouvert la porte?
6. Vous avez ouvert la portière?

7. Tu as écrit la lettre pour ta mère?
8. Tu as fait la vaisselle?
9. Tu as mis la voiture au garage?
10. Tu as mis le contact?
11. Tu as déjà conduit l'Alpine?

31.27 Activation: Dialogue between Mireille and the cyclist

Listen to the conversation between Mireille and the cyclist and memorize
Mireille's lines, imitating and repeating as usual.

TOWARD FREE EXPRESSION

31.28 Words at large

Proceed as usual. (If necessary, refer to lesson 27 for directions.)

31.29, 31.30 Role-playing and reinvention of the story

In 31.29, Mireille is explaining her car problems to the garage mechanic.
Imagine the dialogue.

In 31.30, Mireille has picked up the two hitchhikers who pushed her to the service station. Imagine their adventures.

● **Suggested written assignment.** Write a version of the adventures of Mireille and the hitchhikers in 31.30. Write about 75 words. Send this assignment to your instructor (see the course syllabus for details).

SELF-TESTING EXERCISES

Complete and check exercises 31.31 and 31.32 as usual.

SUMMARY QUIZ

Consult the course syllabus or check with your instructor for information about completing and handing in summary quiz 31.

LESSON 32
Residences I

The story

Thursday evening. Dinner with Mireille's family. As always, Robert must ask directions. When he finds the building, the concierge tells him he must climb to the fifth floor (*quatrième étage*) because the elevator is out of order.

The apartment door is opened for him by Mireille's friend Colette. Marie-Laure greets her "cowboy" boisterously but agrees that he did well not to bring his horse upstairs. Robert meets Mireille's parents. Finally, Mireille comes in, greets Robert, and asks Marie-Laure to turn off the TV. Robert notices the weatherman, who is just then in the process of announcing the weather. It's the same guy who helped him find Mireille's street a half-hour ago!

M. Belleau shows Robert the view, which, except for an unobstructed vista of the Tour Montparnasse, an architectural monstrosity, is really splendid. When her father excuses himself to attend to the apéritifs, Mireille explains to Robert that her parents have invited Hubert, a childhood friend. Hubert is a true aristocrat, but he loves to exaggerate the aristocratic role, and he's very amusing. At least she finds him amusing. How will Robert find him? A threat? That seems at least a good possibility.

Notes on culture and communication

• **La Tour Eiffel.** The Eiffel Tower was built by Gustave Eiffel (1832-1923), a civil and aeronautic engineer specializing in metal constructions, for the Universal Exposition of 1889 in Paris. (A few years earlier, Eiffel had designed the inner framework of the Statue of Liberty.) In spite of the fact that it was criticized for many years, the Eiffel Tower is now considered the very symbol of Paris.

• **La Tour Montparnasse.** The Montparnasse office building is the highest skyscraper in Paris. It was built in the early 1970s under President Georges Pompidou (1911-1974), in the heart of the old Montparnasse district. It has been called an eyesore and blamed for disfiguring Paris by wrecking the harmony of its skyline.

• **Getting invited home to dinner.** Americans often complain that the French do not invite outsiders into their homes. This is an area of cultural difference between Americans and French, and evidence for it is clear in this episode. Americans are so informal that on the spur of the moment they may invite strangers in for a meal. The French say they cannot do sufficient honor to a guest on the spur of the moment. Indeed, the Belleau family has gone to considerable trouble to receive Robert properly. The meal has been discussed and planned, and Robert invited, well in advance. Two guests his age, friends of Mireille, have also been invited to make Robert feel at home as well as to avoid the impression that the family is looking Robert over. The very proper Hubert has sent roses to Mme Belleau, and they have been displayed to greatest advantage in a place where he will see them when he enters the apartment. Finally, the substantial meal that is served almost certainly took a large part of Mme Belleau's day to prepare.

Content and learning objectives of lesson 32

This lesson will familiarize you with ways in which French speakers ask for and give directions. It also presents basic vocabulary for referring to various aspects of housing.

The following points are highlighted in lesson 32 (you should concentrate on the section marked with a √):

- Expressing strangeness: *drôle de*
- Operations involving parts of the body, review
- *Eteindre, s'éteindre*
- *Passé composé*, review
√ • Two different aspects of the past: imperfect and *passé composé* (32.16–32.20)

ASSIMILATION OF THE TEXT

32.1–32.3 Text work-up, aural comprehension, and oral production

Proceed as usual in these sections. (Refer to lesson 28.1–28.3 for directions, if necessary.) Work with the text of lesson 32 in the textbook, as in previous lessons.

TOWARD COMMUNICATION

32.4 Observation and activation: Pronunciation: /ɔ̃/, /ɑ̃/

The four nasal vowels in French were introduced in lesson 4. Section 32.4 reviews two of them.

● Repeat the words and expressions you hear, paying close attention to the difference between the two nasal vowels. For /ɑ̃/, open your mouth without rounding your lips. For /ɔ̃/, the mouth is less open and the lips are rounded.

32.5, 32.6 Observation and activation: Asking and giving directions

Thanks to Robert's knack for losing his way, lesson 32 is rich in expressions for asking and giving directions. The most useful of these are grouped together in chart 32.5.

● In exercise 32.6, you will hear a series of requests for directions, followed by answers. You will hear each question and answer once. Then the question will be repeated. Give the appropriate directions.

Audio cues (for reference):
32.6 Activation orale: Pour demander son chemin

1. La rue de Vaugirard, s'il vous plaît?
2. Est-ce que vous pourriez m'indiquer la rue de Vaugirard?
3. C'est par ici?
4. C'est par là?
5. Le quai de Grenelle, s'il vous plaît?
6. C'est loin d'ici?

32.7, 32.8 Observation and activation: Habitats

Mireille's friend Colette lives in a single-family house in Provins, but Mireille and her parents and most other inhabitants of Paris live in apartments. Chart 32.7 shows how to refer to various aspects of housing: type of building, floor number and general location of the apartment, and the various rooms that make it up.

Notice that the street level of a building has its own name (*rez-de-chaussée*); the upper floors are numbered beginning with the next story (*premier étage*). Many apartment buildings in Paris and throughout France have a central courtyard. Apartments that look out on the street usually have more light and a better view, but they tend to be noisier; apartments that look out on the courtyard are generally quieter, but darker.

The size of a house or an apartment is reckoned in terms of the number of *pièces*. Notice that *la salle de bain* is for bathing and washing up; toilets are located in a separate space in most French homes. Toilets, bathrooms, and kitchens are not usually counted as *pièces*.

• Complete the *dictée* in 32.8 with the words and expressions you hear relating to housing.

√ Check your answers in key 32.8 at the back of the workbook.

32.9, 32.10 Observation and activation: Strangeness; *drôle de*

Hubert's self-parody of an aristocrat amuses Mireille; she finds him funny. She finds him funny in another way, too: "C'est un drôle de type," she says, referring not to his talents as a comic but to his eccentric behavior, to the fact that he's unlike most other people. As chart 32.9 shows, the expression *drôle de* can be used with a noun to refer to anything that strikes you as slightly odd: people, things, situations.

• In exercise 32.10, you will be asked if you have noticed various people and things. Say yes, they're odd, using *drôle de* and the noun you hear. Remember that the **indefinite article** you use (*un, une, des*) will depend on who or what strikes you as odd.

Audio cues (for reference):
32.10 Activation orale: Etrangeté; drôle de

1. Tu as vu ce type?   4. Tu as vu ce bonhomme?
2. Tu as vu cette fille?   5. Tu as vu cette salle de bain?
3. Tu as vu ces gens?   6. Tu as vu cette voiture?

32.11, 32.12 Observation and activation: Operations involving parts of the body (review)

Watching Robert get up in lesson 25 ("il se brosse les dents," etc.), you saw how tooth-brushing and nail-cutting and other routines of grooming are expressed with a reflexive verb and a noun preceded by the **definite** article.

As he arrives at the Belleaus', Robert demonstrates how this pattern can be used for other kinds of activities involving parts of the body. Always conscientious, always obedient, Robert sees a sign telling him to wipe his feet, and he complies: "il s'essuie les pieds."

• In exercise 32.12, you are Marie-Laure. Mme Belleau is asking whether you have completed various grooming routines. Answer yes, using reflexive verbs and the definite article with parts of the body. Notice that the verbs are in the *passé composé*.

Audio cues (for reference):
32.12 Activation orale: Opérations sur les parties du corps (révision)

1. Et tes pieds, tu les as lavés?
2. Et tes dents, tu les a brossées?
3. Et tes ongles, tu les as coupés?

4. Et tes mains, tu les as lavées?
5. Et tes mains, tu les as essuyées?
6. Et tes cheveux, tu les as brossés?

32.13, 32.14 Observation and activation: Blackout; *éteindre, s'éteindre*

Marie-Laure is constantly being told to switch off the TV: "éteins la télé!" *Eteindre* refers in general to the act of turning off or extinguishing light sources or light- or heat-producing devices (televisions, lights, cigarettes, fires).

The verb is used reflexively when these devices go off or go out by themselves, as Robert discovers hall lights do in Paris apartment buildings: "la lumière **s'éteint**." Chart 32.13 shows the forms of *éteindre* in the present and gives its past participle.

• Complete the *dictée* in 32.14 with forms of *éteindre* or *s'éteindre*, as appropriate.

√ Check your answers in key 32.14 at the back of the workbook.

32.15 Activation: *Passé composé* (review)

This soul-searing page from Robert's personal journal is reproduced word for word as it came into the Authors' hands. Not so much as a name has been changed to protect the innocent. To keep Robert's revelations from idle curiosity-seekers, however, most of the *passés composés* have been deleted.

• Reconstruct the document by supplying the missing *passés composés*. Notice that the verb you are to use in each incomplete sentence appears in the preceding complete sentence. Remember that for each *passé composé* you write you must check that you have (1) the correct auxiliary; (2) the correct past participle; (3) the correct agreement, if appropriate. (If you need to review agreement and the use of auxiliaries, turn to the relevant sections of lesson 22.)

√ Check your answers in key 32.15 at the back of the workbook.

32.16-32.20 Observation and activation: Two aspects of the past; imperfect and *passé composé*

Robert's walk down the Boulevard Saint-Michel can be looked at from two different points of view. The walk is an event, one of the things Robert did that day. It is a **point** on the story line we are following, located between leaving the hotel and noticing the student demonstrators. Chart 32.16 shows how from this perspective Robert's walk can be expressed using the *passé composé*. "Il s'est promené" is one event in a chronological progression of events.

At the same time, Robert's walk down the Boul' Mich' is also a process, an activity with a certain temporal and psychological **duration**, an action that we can talk about not as an event but as a flow. The second chart in 32.16 shows how from this perspective Robert's walk can be considered as a segment on the line of time, and expressed using the imperfect. "Il se promenait" focuses on the walk in progress, the walk as an ongoing activity rather than a completed action, whereas "il s'est promené" merely tells us that the walk took place.

During the course of Robert's walk, something else happened: "il a vu les manifestants." This event is expressed by means of the *passé composé*. "Il se promenait . . . il a vu les manifestants" indicates that the walk was in progress when Robert noticed the demonstrators. The actions of taking a walk and seeing the demonstrators took place at the same time, but the action of *voir* is seen as a **point** in the flow of action expressed by *se promener*.

Chart 32.17 presents another example of these two perspectives on actions that occur during the same period of time. An action that is seen as extending over a period of time ("nous **habitions**") is combined with another action seen as a single point within this period of time: "Mireille **est née**."

When verbs in the *passé composé* and the imperfect are used together:

• The verb in the imperfect will often set the stage or serve as background for the action of the verb in the *passé composé*.

• The verb in the imperfect answers the questions, "**What were things like? What was going on?**" at the time being referred to. The verb in the *passé composé* answers the question, "**What happened next?**"

• The verb in the imperfect is often used to express a condition, situation, feeling, or attitude that underlies the event you want to report. The verb in the *passé composé* expresses the event.

Chart 32.18 shows the relationship between the *passé composé* and the imperfect in graphic form.

• In exercises 32.19 and 32.20, determine which verb refers to an event and which describes a condition and rewrite the sentences in the past, using the *passé composé* in the first instance and the imperfect in the second.

√ Check your answers in keys 32.19 and 32.20 at the back of the workbook.

Note. Do these exercises carefully and check them thoroughly. If you have made errors, review charts 32.16, 32.17, and 32.18 and the above commentary until you are confident you understand why each verb is in the imperfect or *passé composé*.

32.21   Activation: Dialogue between Robert and the concierge

Listen to the conversation between Robert and the concierge and memorize the concierge's lines, imitating and repeating as usual.

TOWARD FREE EXPRESSION

32.22   Words at large

Proceed as usual. (If necessary, refer to lesson 27 for directions.)

32.23, 32.24   Role-playing and reinvention of the story

In 32.23, M. Belleau invites Robert onto the balcony to admire the view. Imagine their dialogue.

In 32.24, Robert is asking for information from the concierge at the Belleaus' apartment building. Imagine their conversation.

• **Suggested oral assignment.** Record a version of Robert's dialogue with the concierge in 32.24. Identify each speaker before you give his or her lines. Send this assignment to your instructor (see the course syllabus for details).

SELF-TESTING EXERCISES

• Complete and check exercises 32.25 and 32.26 as usual.

SUMMARY QUIZ

Consult the course syllabus or check with your instructor for information about completing and handing in summary quiz 32.

LESSON 33
Residences II

<u>The story</u>

Hubert is every bit as advertised: formal, very polite, even courtly. At the dinner table, when Hubert mentions the wines of Burgundy, Robert has a chance to show the results of his recent study. Then the conversation turns to Provins, the nearby provincial town where Colette lives, and to the advantages of being in the country yet within an hour of Paris. Hubert makes a rather ghastly play on the words Provins, Provence, and province; the critical Marie-Laure is silenced by her mother.

Then it happens. M. Belleau asks Hubert how things are in the construction business. Hubert says that his uncles, who run what is evidently a family concern, are putting up nothing but low-rent housing for workers. Playing his aristocratic role to the hilt, he takes the view that "those people" were no more unhappy a hundred years ago when they lived in crowded hovels with no modern conveniences. The Belleaus don't take him seriously. But Robert explodes self-righteously. He says he doesn't think Hubert would be so happy without his many luxuries, and that today's workers have every right to the same comforts as the descendants of their medieval oppressors (does the shoe fit, Hubert?).

Mme Belleau nimbly changes the subject. She seizes on the word "medieval" and asks if anyone has seen the Carolingian manuscripts on exhibit at the Petit Palais museum. Well played, Madame!

<u>Notes on culture and communication</u>

• **Paris, la Province, la campagne.** The distinction between Paris and the provinces has always been strong in France. It reflects traditional tensions between the different French regions—each with its own traditions and history, each attached to its provincialism and aspiring to autonomy—and the determination of the national government (whether royal, imperial, or republican) to centralize the nation around its capital. To live in the provinces, even if one's home is in a city or town, means to live closer to the countryside than one would in Paris. And that is why Colette prefers Provins to Paris.

• **Chez soi derrière les haies, les murs, la grille.** Houses and yards in France, unlike their American counterparts, are generally enclosed by hedges,

48

walls, and railings, and do not open onto the neighbors' properties. This aspect of residential design exemplifies a typical feature of the French national character: individualism. It may not be so much that good fences make good neighbors, as Robert Frost put it, as that the French need fences to feel truly at home.

● **Manners, morals, and social behavior.** At the Belleaus', Robert is confronted with a number of cultural problems that may partly explain his ill-temper in this episode. First, he seems unaware that in France, as in most of Europe, friendship free of sexual overtones is frequent between men and women. He saw Hubert kiss Mireille on both cheeks when they met in the courtyard of the Sorbonne, so he assumed that their feelings toward each other were stronger than friendship. Now he sees them greet each other warmly once again, and jealousy gnaws at him all evening.

He is also turned off because Hubert exhibits aristocratic manners and mannerisms. The all-American boy is offended by what he considers snobbish and phony. This feeling is aggravated by his realization that Mireille and her family find Hubert very amusing. So when Hubert launches into his upper-class patter about the working classes, Robert inappropriately loses his cool, creating a most uncomfortable social situation that causes embarrassment to everyone present.

Finally, the situation is made even worse for Robert by his feeling of inadequacy in French table manners. He notices that a person sitting at dinner never puts his hands below the table but politely keeps his wrists on the edge of the table when the hands are not in use. But he does not change his American habit of transferring his fork back and forth from hand to hand after cutting his meat and before raising a bite to his mouth. (The French keep the fork in the left hand both for cutting and for feeding.) Robert's not-quite-conscious awareness of these cultural differences contributes a note of frustration to his self-righteousness and jealousy.

Content and learning objectives of lesson 33

This lesson illustrates ways in which French speakers talk about manners, retort to critics, and disagree with the opinions of others. It also shows how they thank others for acts of generosity or thoughtfulness.

The following points are highlighted in lesson 33 (you should concentrate on sections marked with a √):

- Need and exigency: *Il (me) faut* + nouns
- Lack of self-control: *s'empêcher de*
- Protest: *si on ne peut plus..., il n'y en a que pour..., pas si...que ça*
- Time: *en une heure*

√• Irregular imperatives: *être*, *avoir*, *vouloir*, *savoir* (33.22, 33.23)
√• Imperfect and *passé composé*, review and extension (33.24, 33.25)

ASSIMILATION OF THE TEXT

33.1-33.4 Text work-up, aural comprehension, and oral production

Proceed as usual in these sections. (Refer to lesson 28.1-28.4 for directions, if necessary.) Work with the text of lesson 33 in the textbook, as in previous lessons.

TOWARD COMMUNICATION

33.5 Activation: Pronunciation; nasal vowels /ã/ and /ɛ̃/ (review)

In the preceding lesson you saw a review of the difference in pronunciation between /ɔ̃/ (*dont*) and /ã/ (*dans*). Section 33.5 contrasts /ã/ (*vent*) and another of the nasal vowels, /ɛ̃/ (*vin*).

• Repeat the words and expressions you hear, paying particular attention to the difference between the two nasal vowels. For /ã/, the mouth falls open and the lips are not rounded. For /ɛ̃/, the mouth is less open, and the lips are well spread.

33.6 Observation: Bad manners

As part of the process of socializing their irrepressible ten-year-old and teaching her how to behave like an adult, the Belleaus are occasionally obliged to scold her in the presence of non-family members. Chart 33.6 shows some of the ways in which one can reprimand an unruly child in public. No responses are given because, as everyone knows, well-brought-up children **never** talk back to their parents. (The same cannot be said of sisters; in her squabbles with Mireille, Marie-Laure is always ready to answer back in her best preteen style.)

33.7, 33.8 Observation and activation: Out of control; *s'empêcher de*

One of Marie-Laure's strategies for dealing with nagging parents is to tell them she just can't help doing whatever it is that is irritating them. She uses *s'empêcher de* with an infinitive, as chart 33.7 demonstrates. This expression can also be used to indicate a real lapse of self-control, as in Robert's outburst at the Belleaus's dinner table.

• In certain of the sentences in exercise 33.8, the behavior of a number of people is questioned. Say they can't help themselves, using *s'empêcher de* in the present tense. In other sentences, you will be told that certain individuals shouldn't have acted as they did. Say they couldn't help themselves, using *s'empêcher de* in the *passé composé*.

Audio cues (for reference):
33.8 Activation orale: Manque de contrôle; s'empêcher de

1. Pourquoi tu te moques des gens comme ça?
2. Tu n'aurais pas dû intervenir.
3. Pourquoi il se gratte comme ça?
4. Pourquoi vous riez comme ça, vous deux?
5. Pourquoi Robert intervient-il?
6. Il n'aurait pas dû intervenir comme ça.
7. Marie-Laure n'aurait pas dû se moquer de Robert.
8. Robert et Hubert n'auraient pas dû se disputer comme ça.

33.9, 33.10 Observation and activation: Protest; *si on ne peut plus . . .*

Jean-Pierre Bourdon and Marie-Laure Belleau, those two misbehavers, react to criticism in the same way. When someone disapproves of their actions (Jean-Pierre, on the prowl, has cut in line; Marie-Laure has made a rude comment at the table), they respond defensively, making it sound as though what they were doing was the commonest, most innocent human pastime imaginable. From Marie-Laure's point of view, to chide her for cracking her idea of a joke is tantamount to banning laughter altogether: "si on ne peut plus rire, maintenant!"

• In exercise 33.10, react defensively to the objections you hear, using *si on ne peut plus. . . .*

Audio cues (for reference):
33.10 Activation orale: Protestation; si on ne peut plus...

1. Marie-Laure, ne te moque pas des gens comme ça.
2. Arrête de rouspéter! Ce n'est pas poli.
3. Arrête de faire des jeux de mots absurdes.
4. Arrête de blaguer!
5. Ne discute pas!
6. Oh, là, le resquilleur! Pas de resquille!

33.11, 33.12 Observation and activation: Satisfaction/dissatisfaction

The expressions in chart 33.11 are used to indicate that even though some things cannot be changed, people are no better off or less well off because of them. No matter how bratty Marie-Laure is, we still love her. The fact that Uncle Guillaume is well-to-do doesn't mean he's any happier.

• In 33.12 you will hear about various people's advantages or disadvantages. Say that these don't make them happier or unhappier.

Audio cues (for reference):
33.12 Activation orale: Satisfaction/insatisfaction

1. Tonton Guillaume a deux voitures pour lui tout seul.
2. Tante Georgette n'a qu'un vélo.
3. Tonton Guillaume va au restaurant tous les jours.
4. Tante Georgette ne va jamais au restaurant.
5. Tonton Guillaume voyage partout dans le monde.
6. Tante Georgette reste chez elle.
7. Tonton Guillaume a un magnifique appartement.
8. Tante Georgette n'a qu'un petit appartement sous le toit.
9. Tonton Guillaume a beaucoup d'amis et de relations.
10. Tante Georgette n'a que Fido.
11. Les Belleau n'ont que des filles.
12. Mireille et Cécile n'ont pas de voiture.

33.13 Observation: Thank-yous (review and expansion)

In lesson 24, you saw ways of thanking a host or hostess at the end of a social function. Chart 33.13 presents ways of thanking people for a specific act of generosity or thoughtfulness, and gives the appropriate responses. As in most situations involving the politeness factor, the ritual requires a bit of exaggeration on either side. Madame Belleau thanks Hubert for his *magnifique bouquet* of a measly half-dozen roses; the more she builds up his gift, the more he belittles its importance, saying it was nothing, really.

Note that one hears both "Merci **de** votre magnifique bouquet!" or, as Madame Belleau says, "Merci **pour** votre magnifique bouquet!" Recall, too, that while *je vous en prie* can be used to respond to an expression of thanks, as here, it can also be used to react politely when people say they're sorry or ask you to excuse them: "Oh, pardon!" —"Je vous en prie!" (see lesson 20.11).

33.14, 33.15 Observation and activation: Restriction, exclusivity; *il n'y en a que pour . . .*

When Hubert, doggedly playing his hereditary role, suggests that workers get all the attention these days, he uses *il y a* with the restrictive expression *ne . . . que* that you saw in lesson 26.

● In exercise 33.15, complain about various people who expect everything to be done for them, using *il n'y en a que pour. . . .*

Audio cues (for reference):
33.15 Activation orale: Restriction, exclusivité; il n'y en a que pour...

1. Il faut tout faire pour elle.
2. Il faut tout faire pour les jeunes.
3. Il faut tout faire pour les hommes.

4. Il faut toujours s'occuper d'eux.
5. Il faut toujours s'occuper des vieux.
6. Il faut toujours s'occuper de Fido.

33.16, 33.17 Observation and activation: Disagreement; *pas si . . . que ça*

Robert, offended by Hubert's comments about the working class, challenges his statements by implying that they are exaggerated. Hubert seems too certain that workers were happy living in substandard housing; Robert isn't so sure they were. And Robert doesn't think Hubert would be as happy as all that if **he** were obliged to live that way. The expression Robert uses, *pas si . . . que ça*, suggests that the other person's assertions or presumptions overstate the case.

● In exercise 33.17, disagree with the statements and questions you hear by saying that they overstate the case, using *pas si . . . que ça*.

Audio cues (for reference):
33.17 Activation orale: Désaccord; pas si...que ça

1. Tu es content?
2. Tante Georgette est rouspéteuse.
3. Robert est grand?
4. Il paraît que Marie-Laure est moqueuse!

5. Elle est insupportable, cette Marie-Laure!
6. Votre villa est loin?
7. Ça doit être ennuyeux, la campagne...
8. Il est infect, ce taudis!

33.18, 33.19 Observation and activation: As time goes by; *en une heure*

One reason Colette likes living in Provins is that she can get to Paris quickly: "Je suis à Paris en une heure." *En* and an expression of time are used to indicate the amount of time it takes to complete an action.

• In 33.19, you will be asked if various activities took a long time. Say that they took only two minutes, using the appropriate form of the verb and *en*, followed by the expression of time (*deux minutes*).

Audio cues (for reference):
33.19 Activation orale: Le temps qui passe; en une heure

1. Il t'a fallu longtemps pour faire ça?
2. Il lui a fallu longtemps pour faire ça?
3. Il vous a fallu longtemps pour faire ça?
4. Il vous a fallu longtemps pour finir?
5. Il t'a fallu longtemps pour venir?
6. Vous avez mis longtemps pour venir?
7. Vous avez mis longtemps pour trouver la maison?
8. Tu as mis longtemps pour lire ça?
9. Il lui a fallu longtemps pour écrire ça?
10. Il t'a fallu longtemps pour comprendre?

33.20, 33.21 Observation and activation: Necessity; *il me faut* + noun

In lesson 5 you saw how *il faut* is used with infinitives to indicate necessity or obligation: "il faut inventer une histoire." There the attention was focused on an action that needed to be accomplished: "il faut **inventer**." Chart 33.20 shows how *il faut* can be used to say that someone needs something, with the attention focused on the thing that is needed: "il leur faut **tout le confort moderne**." Notice that when *il faut* is used in this way, the party in need is identified by an indirect object pronoun: "il **leur** faut."

• In exercise 33.21, you will be asked whether people want certain material comforts. Say yes, they have to have them, using *il faut* and the indirect object pronoun.

Audio cues (for reference):
33.21 Activation orale: Nécessité; il me faut + nom

1. Tu veux deux chambres?
2. Vous voulez l'eau courante maintenant?
3. Vous voulez le chauffage central maintenant?
4. Vous voulez l'électricité maintenant?
5. Vous voulez le téléphone maintenant?
6. Ils veulent un téléviseur?
7. Ils veulent deux salles de bains?
8. Comment? Ils veulent un ascenseur?
9. Comment? Ils veulent des domestiques?

33.22, 33.23 Observation and activation: Commands; irregular imperatives
(*être, avoir, vouloir, savoir*)

Silver-tongued Hubert likes to use language elegantly, presumably as a reflection of the refined circles he frequents. At the Belleaus' dinner table he seems to favor expressions containing irregular imperatives. These imperatives are not common in everyday speech, and they lend to what he says a tone of high refinement that is a little bit pompous, especially since he is only asking for the salt. (Two of his imperatives—*sachez* and *veuillez*— are almost never heard colloquially, and are considered quite pretentious.)

• In exercise 33.23, you will hear people accused of various short-comings. Tell them to shape up, using the imperative. Decide whether the statements you hear address the other person as *tu* or *vous*, and use the corresponding form of the imperative.

Audio cues (for reference):
33.23 Activation orale: Impératif irrégulier

1. Tu n'as pas de patience!
2. Vous n'avez pas de patience!
3. Vous n'êtes jamais à l'heure!

4. Vous ne savez pas ça!
5. Tu n'as pas de courage!
6. Tu n'es pas obéissant!

33.24 33.25 Observation and activation: Time gone by; the imperfect and the
passé composé (review and extension)

You saw in lesson 32 how the *passé composé* and the imperfect are used to describe actions in the past from two very different points of view.

The **passé composé** expresses past actions as points on the line of time, as events that mark the progress of the story. Verbs in the *passé composé* answer the question, "What happened next?"

The **imperfect** expresses past action as a process, a flow; it examines action from the point of view of its duration, its extension in time. Verbs in the imperfect answer the questions, "What was going on at the time? What were things like?"

It is important to remember that these tenses **both** refer to the past. Whether you use one or the other will depend on how you look at the actions you are describing. This is especially true when you want to establish a relationship between two or more past actions.

Chart 33.24 sets forth the possibilities:

a. "Robert **est tombé** d'un balcon quand il **avait** dix ans." Used together, the **passé composé** and the **imperfect** indicate an action that takes place in the context of another. The action of falling is in the *passé composé* because it is an event that occured within a situation expressed by the imperfect (Robert was ten).

b. "Quand Robert **avait** dix ans, il **voulait** être pompier." An **imperfect** used with another **imperfect** indicates two situations that are simultaneous.

c. "Quand Robert **est tombé** du balcon, on **l'a emmené** à l'hôpital." A **passé composé** used with another **passé composé** indicates two successive actions, the second occurring after the first.

• In 33.25, rewrite the story of Robert and Mireille's meeting in the past tense, changing each of the verbs you see in the present tense to the *passé composé* or the imperfect, as appropriate.

√ Check your answers in key 33.25 at the back of the workbook.

33.26 Activation: Dialogue between Robert and Colette

Listen to the conversation between Robert and Colette and memorize Colette's lines, imitating and repeating as usual.

TOWARD FREE EXPRESSION

33.27 Words at large

Proceed as usual. (If necessary, refer to lesson 27 for directions.)

33.28, 33.29 Role-playing and reinvention of the story

In 33.28, you are Hubert in a series of discussions at dinner, then Robert giving full rein to your outrage at Hubert's attitudes. Play the scenes out loud.

In 33.29, imagine a conversation between Robert and a new guest at dinner.

• **Suggested written assignment.** Write out a version of the dinner conversation between Robert and the new guest in 33.29. Write 75 words. Send this assignment to your instructor (see the course syllabus for details).

OPTIONAL EXERCISES FOR WRITING PRACTICE

Listen again to exercises 33.21 and 33.23 on the audio recording and write out the audio cues you hear.

Check what you have written against the printed text in the study guide.

SELF-TESTING EXERCISES

Complete and check exercises 33.30, 33.31, and 33.32 as usual.

SUMMARY QUIZ

Consult the course syllabus or check with your instructor for information about completing and handing in summary quiz 33.

LESSON 34
Residences III

The story

Answering Robert's question about rents in the neighborhood, M. Belleau explains that he and his wife bought their apartment about twenty years ago. He goes on to talk about the co-op system. Hubert agrees that property is a fine thing, and he mentions a lot of domains that his family **used** to own. But these days, taxes are so damnably high, and of course it's impossible to find enough good servants.

M. Belleau goes on, unpretentiously, about a little peasant cottage that they bought when it was in terrible condition and that the whole family worked on. Now, all fixed up and with running water and electricity, it's a pleasant country home. They made a garage out of the barn.

Mme Belleau tells Robert that a lot of city-dwellers are buying and refurbishing old peasant houses. Robert doesn't like the idea of gentrification chasing the peasants from their homes, but Mireille assures him that most of the places are abandoned ruins anyway.

Marie-Laure answers the doorbell: it's a nun selling raffle tickets on a sixteenth-century priory. The little girl has no compunctions about sending her away. Don't the Belleaus already have a summer house? And with all the taxes and the lack of servants, one's enough. In any event, she is convinced that this was no real nun. Convinced by what? By the "sister's" abundant moustache. No mere shadow on the upper lip, it's a luxuriant adornment. Bizarre, bizarre!

Notes on culture and communication

• **Une chaumière et un coeur.** *Une chaumière* is a small, humble cottage with a thatched roof. The phrase, "Une chaumière et un coeur," a home and a sweetheart, refers to the proverbial ideal of owning a modest house and sharing with a loved one an idyllic life of rustic happiness.

• **Les familles françaises sont-elles fermées?** Just as French homes are usually enclosed (see lesson 33), French families tend to protect their privacy and are generally less open to strangers than American families. Although the French are courteous, they are formal with people they do not know. This occasionally makes it difficult for more gregarious Americans to meet

French people and make French friends, and it gives some the impression that although the French are constantly kissing each other they are "cold" with outsiders. Nothing could be further from the truth. The fact is that the French value individualism and privacy over instant familiarity, and they take friendship very seriously. Although less numerous and perhaps harder to establish, their friendships often prove deeper and steadier than the acquaintanceships that are a product of more superficial contacts.

• **Peasants, farmers, and class distinctions.** Robert's ill-tempered attack on Hubert is made even more inappropriate by his lack of understanding of France today. Robert expresses pity for the poor peasants who have been expelled from their homes, but the truth is that the word *paysan* no longer evokes a social class except in history books. A farmer today is called an *agriculteur* or *cultivateur. Paysan* is used only by politicians to arouse archaic class feelings or as a swearword hurled at bad drivers or, as Mme Belleau uses it, to mean old-fashioned and simple.

Class distinctions, furthermore, are not so clearly defined as they once were. The Belleaus' grandparents might have been horrified at the thought of actually working manually on an old house, but M. Belleau explains with pride how his whole family pitched in and did the house over without professional help. Besides, the owners of the old house were probably delighted to unload it. Small farms are no longer viable, and are frequently combined into a larger, economically efficient operation. Most peasants became either big farmers or turned to another way of making a living. Finally, the style and culture of farmers today differ less and less from those of city people.

Content and learning objectives of lesson 34

Lesson 34 shows ways in which French speakers talk about building and remodeling residences and refer to the time it takes to complete an action. It also illustrates how they refer to renting versus ownership.

The following points are highlighted in lesson 34 (you should concentrate on sections marked with a √):

- *Il faut* + expression of time + *pour*
- Adopting behaviors: *faire l'idiot, faire le maçon*, etc.
- Nouns in *-age*, review and extension
- Verbs with vowel changes, review and extension
- √ Transformations: *rendre* + adjectives (34.16, 34.17)
- √ Causative *faire* (34.20-34.23)
- Imperfect and *passé composé*, review

ASSIMILATION OF THE TEXT

34.1-34.4 Text work-up, aural comprehension, and oral production

Proceed as usual in these sections. (Refer to lesson 28.1-28.4 for directions, if necessary.) Work with the text of lesson 34 in the textbook, as in previous lessons.

TOWARD COMMUNICATION

34.5 Activation: Pronunciation; the vowels /a/ and /ã/ (review)

Mireille's little play on words ("on a transformé la **grange** en **garage**") gives us a good excuse to review pronunciation of the nasal /ã/ (*grange*) and the nonnasal /a/ (*garage*).

• Repeat the words and expressions you hear, distinguishing carefully between the two vowels. Remember that although words containing /ã/ have an *n* or *m* after the *a* in writing, the *n* or *m* is not pronounced as a separate sound. In pronouncing *chambre*, for instance, go straight from the /ã/ sound to the /b/ sound; in *avantages*, go straight from /ã/ to /t/.

Remember, too, that the nonnasal sound *a* is pronounced /a/ even when it does not fall at the end of a rhythmic group: *la chambre*.

34.6-34.9 Observation and activation: The time it takes

You saw *mettre* used to express the amount of time something requires in lesson 29: "**Nous** avons mis deux ans pour la rendre habitable;" "**les Belleau** ont mis deux ans. . . ."

Chart 34.6 presents two alternate expressions that emphasize the time requirements of a job: **it** took two years.

Like the expression with *mettre*, "nous avons mis deux ans", the expression with *prendre*, "ça nous a **pris** deux ans," and the expression with *falloir*, "il nous **a fallu** deux ans," often suggest that the operation seemed difficult or long. In the two latter expressions, note that the party whose time was taken is referred to by an **indirect object** pronoun: "ça **lui** a pris trois jours;" "il **leur** a fallu deux ans."

• In exercise 34.7, you will hear how long it took various people to do various things. Say they needed that much time, using the appropriate indirect object pronoun and *il faut* in the *passé composé*. Note that although

"il leur a fallu deux ans pour rendre la maison habitable" is a more challenging response, "il leur a fallu deux ans" is perfectly acceptable.

Audio cues (for reference):
34.7 Activation orale: Le temps qu'il faut

1. Ça leur a pris deux ans pour rendre leur maison habitable.
2. Ça lui a pris 3 heures pour aller chez les Courtois à pied.
3. Ça leur a pris 2 jours pour nettoyer tout l'appartement.
4. Ça te prend une heure pour aller à Chartres?
5. Ça nous a pris 3 semaines pour repeindre la maison.
6. Ça vous a pris trois mois pour installer l'eau courante?

• In 34.8, people needed a certain amount of time to complete various
activities. Say that's how long it took them, using *ça a pris* and the
appropriate indirect object pronoun. As above, a briefer response such as "ça
lui a pris une heure" is perfectly acceptable in this context.

Audio cues (for reference):
34.8 Activation orale: Le temps qu'il faut

1. Il lui a fallu une heure pour aller à Chartres en train.
2. Il m'a fallu une heure pour réparer la porte.
3. Il nous a fallu 2 mois pour réparer le toit.
4. Il leur a fallu 5 secondes pour finir le fois gras!
5. Il te faut toujours une heure pour comprendre.
6. Il vous a fallu 3 mois pour moderniser la cuisine?

• In 34.9, it took people a certain amount of time to do something. Say
that's how much time they spent at it, using *mettre*. Here again, you may
answer using a shorter version, such as "ils ont mis cinq secondes."

Audio cues (for reference):
34.9 Activation orale: Le temps qu'il faut

1. Ça leur a pris cinq secondes pour finir le foie gras.
2. Ça nous a pris un an pour trouver de bons domestiques.
3. Ça m'a pris 6 mois pour transformer la grange en garage.
4. Ça va lui prendre deux heures pour remplacer cette vitre.
5. Ça vous prend une journée pour remplacer 4 tuiles?
6. Ça leur a pris une semaine pour nettoyer la façade.

34.10, 34.11 Observation and activation: Behavior; *faire l'idiot, le maçon, etc.*

To make their country house livable on a modest budget, the Belleaus
were obliged to do much of the work themselves, acting as masons and

carpenters: "ils ont fait les maçons, les charpentiers." *Faire* and a noun preceded by a **definite article** is used to speak of assuming a role that isn't one's natural or usual role. When Marie-Laure is acting like a jerk, Mireille uses *faire* to tell her to snap out of it: "Ne **fais** pas l'idiote!

    • In exercise 34.11, stress that the activities you hear about don't reflect people's usual behavior, using *faire* and the appropriate definite article and noun.

Audio cues (for reference):
34.11 Activation orale: Comportements

1. Ils ne sont pas menuisiers, mais ils ont travaillé comme des menuisiers.
2. Elle n'est pas idiote, mais elle parle comme une idiote.
3. Il n'est pas bête, mais il rit bêtement.
4. Elle n'est pas sourde, mais elle fait comme si elle n'entendait pas.
5. Je ne suis pas plombier, mais j'ai réparé les robinets.
6. Il n'est pas chauffeur professionnel, mais il conduit la voiture du patron.
7. Nous ne sommes pas gardiens, mais nous gardons leur maison.

34.12, 34.13 Observation and activation: Nouns in -*age* (review and extension)

    You saw in lesson 31 a series of nouns in -*age* referring to an activity: *freiner* ⇒ *le freinage*. Chart 34.12 extends the series. Note that *le gardiennage* is what *le gardien* or *la gardienne* does.

    • In exercise 34.13, figure out from the context what activity is involved and write in the noun in -*age* that expresses it. Note that the related infinitive or noun will not necessarily appear in the context; you will have to infer it.

    √ Check your answers in key 34.13 at the back of the workbook.

34.14, 34.15 Observation and activation: Rental and ownership

    Chart 34.14 reviews basic terms that apply to housing: ownership versus rental and the kinds of expenses that each involves.

    • In exercise 34.15, paragraph 1 contrasts the situation of Mme Dupin who rents a house and M. Lemercier who owns one. Complete each paragraph with appropriate expressions referring to renting or ownership, as appropriate.

    √ Check your answers in key 34.15 at the back of the workbook.

34.16, 34.17 Observation and activation: Transformation; *rendre* + adjective

With two years of effort the Belleaus transformed their country house: they made it livable. The verb *rendre* is used with an adjective to express the change that results from an activity or situation, as chart 34.16 shows.

• In exercise 34.17, you will hear a series of statements, each referring to an action followed by an outcome. Describe the change that the outcome represents, using *rendre* in the *passé composé* or the future, as appropriate.

34.18, 34.19 Observation and activation: Verbs with vowel changes (review and extension)

You saw in lesson 26 that verbs like *acheter* and *se promener* have an /ɛ/ before a closed syllable that changes to /ə/ before an open syllable. That pattern extends to the other verbs in chart 34.18 as well.

Note that all these verbs act like *acheter* and *promener:* in writing, the /ɛ/ sound is written as *è*.

• In exercise 34.19, answer yes to the questions you hear. Note that the *vous* form of the question contains an /ə/ sound; your answer should contain an /ɛ/ sound.

Audio cues (for reference):
34.19 Activation orale: Verbes à changement vocalique

1. Vous emmenez Minouche en voyage?
2. Vous vous promenez?
3. Vous enlevez le foie gras?

4. Vous achetez un appartement?
5. Vous emmenez Robert à Chartres?
6. Vous vous levez?

34.20-34.23 Observation and activation: Delegation; causative use of *faire*

The Belleaus acted as their own masons and carpenters in fixing up their country house, but they had to have certain kinds of work, such as electrical wiring and laying in the water main, done by professionals. The charts in 34.19 show how *faire* is used with an infinitive to refer to activities you have done by others. (Since you are causing others to do them, this use of *faire* is known as **causative**.)

Notice that when you are delegating the work, and are therefore the subject of *faire*, the persons who do it are introduced by *par:* "nous **avons fait** amener l'eau **par** des ouvriers." Notice, too, that when the work that gets done is represented by a pronoun, there is no agreement with the past participle of *faire* in a compound tense: "ils ont fait amener **l'eau**" ⇒ "ils **l'**ont fait amener." This is true because, strictly speaking, the feminine noun *eau*, and its pronoun *l'*, are the object of *amener*, not of *faire*.

   • In exercise 34.21, answer yes to the questions you hear, using the causative *faire* (in the present, future, or *passé composé*, as appropriate), and an object pronoun.

Audio cues (for reference):
.34.21 Activation orale: Délégation; sens causatif du verbe faire

1. Vous avez fait repeindre votre chambre?
2. Vous avez fait retapisser votre salle à manger?
3. Vous avez fait remplacer votre baignoire?
4. Vous faites amener l'eau courante?
5. Vous faites moderniser votre cuisine?
6. Vous avez fait transformer votre grange?
7. Vous ferez mettre l'électricité?
8. Vous avez fait réparer votre voiture?

   • In 34.22, you will be asked whether various things had to be done to the house. Say yes, and add that you did them, using causative *faire*.

Audio cues (for reference):
34.22 Activation orale: Délégation; sans causatif du verbe faire

1. Il fallait amener l'eau?
2. Il fallait mettre l'électricité?
3. Il fallait remplacer la douche?
4. Il fallait installer le gaz?
5. Il fallait repeindre la façade?
6. Il fallait réparer le toit?
7. Il fallait tout refaire!

   • In exercise 34.23, specify who has been called upon to do various jobs, using causative *faire* in the present or *passé composé*, as appropriate. Choose from among the alternatives printed in the workbook.

Audio cues (for reference):
34.23 Activation orale: Délégation; sens causatif du verbe faire

1. Les Belleau ont amené l'eau eux-mêmes?
2. Vous avez repeint votre chambre vous-même?
3. Vous réparez le mur de la grange vous-même?
4. Tu répares ta voiture toi-même?
5. Vous avez installé votre salle de bains vous-même?
6. Vous avez mis l'électricité vous-même?
7. Tu nettoies ta chambre toi-même?
8. Vous avez réparé le toit vous-même?

34.24 Activation: Time gone by; imperfect and *passé composé* (review)

• Exercise 34.24 contains the final episode of our retelling of Robert and Mireille's meeting, begun in lesson 32. Rewrite the sentences in the past, using the *passé composé* and the imperfect, as appropriate. You may want to review lesson 33.24 briefly before you begin.

√ Check your answers in key 34.24 at the back of the workbook.

34.25 Activation: Dialogue between Mme Belleau and Marie-Laure

Listen to the conversation between Mme Belleau and Marie-Laure and memorize Marie-Laure's lines, imitating and repeating as usual.

TOWARD FREE EXPRESSION

34.26 Words at large

Proceed as usual. (If necessary, refer to lesson 27 for directions.)

34.27, 34.28 Role-playing and reinvention of the story

In 34.27, you are M. Belleau, then Hubert, talking about residences owned by the family. Imagine the monologue of each character, out loud.

In 34.28, imagine a new version of the episode of Marie-Laure and the moustached nun.

• **Suggested oral assignment.** Record a version of Marie-Laure's conversation with the nun in 34.28. In each exchange, say one sentence for each character. Identify the characters before you say their lines. Send this assignment to your instructor (see the course syllabus for details).

OPTIONAL EXERCISES FOR WRITING PRACTICE

Listen again to exercises 34.21 and 34.23 on the audio recording and write out the audio cues you hear.

Check what you have written against the printed text in the study guide.

SELF-TESTING EXERCISES

Complete and check exercises 34.29, 34.30, and 34.31 as usual.

SUMMARY QUIZ

Consult the course syllabus or check with your instructor for information about completing and handing in summary quiz 34.

LESSON 35
Residences IV

The story

The dinner at the Belleaus's is still underway. Mireille is talking about the country house when the doorbell rings again. This time, Marie-Laure reports that it was the nun's brother; he had the same moustache. He asked her if she had an older sister who looked like a movie actress, and of course Marie-Laure, being Marie-Laure, said no. Mireille is outraged. This could have been opportunity knocking. For a long time she dreamed of living the glamorous life of a star: Hollywood, exciting roles, travel, staying in deluxe hotels. But now she's so attached to that modest house in Dreux. . . .

The talk turns to building materials. Nearly all French houses are made of brick, concrete block, or stone. The Belleau place in the country, built out of native stone, is hundreds of years old and Mireille expects her great-grandchildren to enjoy it. The French like things that last.

Paris is teeming with students, many of them foreign. Robert learns that French families sometimes take foreign students in as boarders, because they want their children to meet people of other nationalities, or because they are widowed or retired and have an apartment that is too big. He asks about his chances with the Belleau family. Nice try, but no dice. The apartment is too small (only seven rooms, counting the kitchen and bathroom), Mme Belleau is neither widowed nor retired, and Mireille needs no help finding foreign friends. She has lots of them, including (note the gender) . . . a Swedish fellow.

Notes on culture and communication

• **Independence and family ties.** Mme Belleau considers Parisian college students are lucky because they can live at home. Many American students do not want to go to college in their home town because they don't want to remain so close to their parents. And often if they do decide to go to a local university they move out of home to live in a dormitory or fraternity so they can get the "full experience" of living with other students in the college atmosphere. There is a sharp difference between French and American family life in the emphasis placed on independence training. From early childhood, American children are made to feel that society wants them to be as independent as possible from their family. Grateful and loving, certainly, but independent. French families place more emphasis on staying together until the children form their own households, and even after marriage family relations remain rather tight by American standards. In recent years, with students more often forming living relationships without being married, the clash of the two attitudes has caused some conflict in French families—but, of course, the more modern way usually wins out.

Content and learning objectives of lesson 35

This lesson shows how French speakers refer to various habitats in the city, the suburbs, and the country. It gives basic vocabulary for talking about building materials and taking different meals. It also shows how to talk about the beginning and evolution of an action, and how to express need.

The following points are highlighted in lesson 35 (you should concentrate on sections marked with a √):

- *Commencer à* (35.15, 35.16)
- Intensives: *joliment*, *drôlement*, *c'est fou ce que* . . . , etc..
- Indirect questions *ce que c'est*, *qui c'est*
- √ *En* and the present participle (35.17, 35.18)
- √ Negative *ni . . . ni . . .* (35.21, 35.22)
- Verbs of evolution in *-ir: vieillir*, *grossir*, etc.
- Need: *avoir besoin de*

ASSIMILATION OF THE TEXT

35.1-35.4 Text work-up, aural comprehension, and oral production

Proceed as usual in these sections. (Refer to lesson 28.1-28.4 for directions, if necessary.) Work with the text of lesson 35 in the textbook, as in previous lessons.

TOWARD COMMUNICATION

35.5 Activation: Pronunciation; the semivowel /j/ (review)

- Repeat the words and expressions you hear, paying particular attention to the /j/ sound.

35.6   Observation: *Prendre des repas, prendre pension*

Section 35.6 extends the use of *prendre* with meals to boarding arrangements: *prendre pension ou demi-pension.*

35.7   Observation: Habitat

Chart 35.7 lists various kinds of living quarters, arranged by location (big city, suburb/small city, countryside) and by approximate relative cost in terms of rent or taxes. Thus, the taxes on a private château or townhouse would be about 50 times greater than the rent on a working-class dwelling; the only housing that is completely free is under a bridge (city) or in a cave (countryside).

Note that *hôtel* is used to refer to two quite different kinds of habitats: Le Home Latin is *un hôtel*; a private townhouse in a fashionable part of the city is *un hôtel particulier.*

35.8, 35.9   Observation and activation: Building materials

The French, as Robert learns, prefer to construct their houses *en dur:* out of bricks, stone, or cement blocks. Chart 35.8 shows how to say what a dwelling is built of using *en.* (More generally, *en* may be used to refer to what any object is made of: "C'est un oeuf **en** chocolat").

• In exercise 35.9, you will be asked whether various objects are made of certain substances. Say they are, using *en.*

Audio cues (for reference):
35.9 Activation orale: Matières

1. C'est du bois, votre table, là?
2. C'est de la tuile, votre toit, là?
3. C'est de la pierre, cette grange, là?

4. C'est de la brique, ce mur, là?
5. C'est de l'ardoise, ce toit, là?
6. C'est du chocolat, cet oeuf?

35.10-35.12   Observation and activation: Intensives

It is sometimes useful to make one's point with special emphasis, as a means of impressing or convincing others. Take the statement "c'est lourd." It can be made more intense by being cast as an exclamation: "c'est lourd!" And if an intensive expression is added, it really makes people sit up and take notice: "c'est **joliment** lourd!"

Chart 35.10 shows how various intensives are used with adjectives and verbs.

Chart 35.11 presents *tellement* separately. *Tellement* could be called a double-duty intensive. First, like the other intensive expressions it draws attention by its very presence. Second, the listener expects some conclusion to follow it (as in "je suis **tellement** fatiguée **que je ne peux pas venir**"); of course, when *tellement* is used in an exclamation, no conclusion is given, and the listener is left hanging.

• In exercise 35.12, answer the questions you hear with an exclamation, using the intensive *drôlement*. The challenge is to determine the part of the sentence (here, an **adjective**) that needs to be stressed and add *drôlement* in front of it.

Audio cues (for reference):
35.12 Activation orale: Intensifs

1. Elle était en si mauvais état que ça, votre maison?
2. Les murs sont si épais que ça?
3. C'est si lourd que ça, la tuile?
4. Elle est vieille, votre maison?
5. C'est si joli que ça, l'ardoise?
6. C'est long, de retapisser une pièce?

35.13, 35.14 Observation and activation: *Ce que c'est / qui c'est*

You have seen how to use *Qu'est-ce que c'est?* and *Qui est-ce?* to ask the identity of things and people. *Qu'est-ce que c'est?* and *Qui est-ce?* are **direct questions**—that is, they are used to ask someone else directly for the information you seek.

Chart 35.13 presents equivalent expressions for **indirect questions**. *Ce que c'est* and *qui c'est* are used to refer to unnamed things or people, but not in direct question form. Notice they are the direct objects of verbs; they are not used alone.

• In exercise 35.14, complete the indirect questions you see. Essentially you have to determine whether the question is about a thing (in which case you will use *ce que c'est*) or a person (use *qui c'est*).

√ Check your answers in key 35.14 at the back of the workbook.

35.15, 35.16 Observation and activation: Beginnings; *commencer à*

You have seen a number of verbs that are used with an infinitive, for example, "Robert **va** accompagner Mireille," "il **veut** accompagner Mireille," "il **peut** accompagner Mireille," and so forth. Chart 35.15 shows that *commencer*, too, can be followed by an infinitive; when it is, the infinitive is usually preceded by *à* (occasionally it is preceded by *de*).

• In exercise 35.17, you will be asked whether certain things are happening. Say they are beginning to, using *commencer à*.

Audio cues (for reference):
35.16 Activation orale: Commencement; commencer à

1. Eh bien, on dirait qu'il pleut!
2. Tu as mal à la tête?
3. Dis donc, on dirait que tu grossis!
4. Je trouve qu'elle vieillit.

5. Les gens rouspètent?
6. Vous avez faim?
7. Mireille s'ennuyait?
8. Hubert agace Robert?

35.17, 35.18 Observation and activation: Cause and occasion; *en* + present participle

Getting a touch softheaded at the ripe old age of eighteen, Mireille waxes lyrical about home and hearth. As she gets older, she says, she begins to understand the charm of having a little house of one's own: "en vieillissant, je commence à comprendre."

Mireille says *en vieillissant* to justify her newfound insight. The process of growing older and her understanding go hand in hand; *en vieillissant* and *je commence à comprendre* are associated in time. In addition, there is often a suggestion of cause and effect, a hint that growing older is what makes understanding possible.

As chart 35.17 states, *vieillissant* is a **present participle**—a form of the verb *vieillir* that is not conjugated, like the past participle and the infinitive. The present participles of verbs end in *-ant*, and are invariable (they do not show agreement with objects or subjects). The stem of the present participle is the same as that of the *nous* form of the present indicative (except in the case of *avoir*, *être*, and *savoir*, as the chart demonstrates).

• In exercise 35.18, state what happened in the various situations you hear described, establishing a link between events using *en* and present participles.

√ Check your answers in key 35.18 at the back of the workbook.

35.19, 35.20 Observation and activation: Evolution

Chart 35.19 groups together verbs of change and development. Notice that each of these verbs corresponds to the feminine form of an adjective. Notice, too, that the conjugation of all of them follows the pattern of *finir:* there is a double *s* in the stem of the plural forms of the present indicative (*nous vieillissons*, etc.). This double *s* is of course also present in the imperfect (*je vieillissais*, etc.) and the present participle (*vieillissant*), both of which have the same stem as the *nous* form of the present.

• In exercise 35.20, complete the answers by stating the appropriate change or evolution. (Use verbs that correspond to the adjectives in italics.)

√ Check your answers in key 35.20 at the back of the workbook.

35.21, 35.22 Observation and activation: Negation; *ni . . . ni . . .*

When Robert asks whether the Belleau family might be looking for a student lodger, Mme Belleau says no, and gives her reasons: the apartment is not big enough, she is neither widowed nor retired, Mireille needs no help meeting foreigners, and so forth. Note that in her first statement, "nous n'avons pas un grand appartement," which contains a single negation, Mme Belleau uses the regular negation *ne . . . pas*. In her statement about not being widowed or retired, which contains **multiple** negations, she uses a different negative expression, *ne . . . ni . . . ni. . . .*

This expression is used to refer negatively to more than one item in a list of similar items. Like the other negative expressions you have seen, it is introduced by *ne* placed in front of the verb: "Robert **n'a ni** frères **ni** soeurs" (the list could go on indefinitely: "**ni** cousins, **ni** cousines, **ni** tantes," and so forth).

When the multiple nouns being negated are indefinite ("Est-ce que Robert a **des** frères et **des** soeurs?"), there is no article between *ni* and the noun: "Non, Robert n'a ni frères ni soeurs." When they are definite ("Vous connaissez **le** père et **la** mère de Robert?), the definite article is used with *ni:* "Non, nous ne connaissons ni **le** père ni **la** mère de Robert."

• In exercise 35.22, give negative answers to the questions you hear, using *ni . . . ni. . . .*

Audio cues (for reference):
35.22 Activation orale: Négation; ni...ni...

1. Aimez-vous les pieds de porc et la tête de veau?

2. Vous prenez du café ou du thé le matin?

3. Est-ce que Robert a des frères et des soeurs?

4. Est-ce que Mme Belleau est veuve et retraitée?

5. Vous connaissez le père et la mère de Mireille?

6. Mireille connaît la Bourgogne et la Provence. Et vous?

7. Mireille connaît la Bretagne et le Pays Basque. Et Robert?

8. Le toit de la maison des Belleau est en chaume ou en ardoise?

35.23, 35.24 Observation and activation: Need; *avoir besoin*

Mme Belleau says Mireille has made plenty of foreign friends and needs
no help in that department: "elle n'**a** pas **besoin** qu'on lui trouve des amis."
The charts in 35.23 show 1) that *avoir besoin* is used to express need with a
noun (*argent*) or an infinitive (*gagner*), both introduced by *de*, or a full
clause introduced by *que* (*qu'on lui trouve des amis*); and 2) that when *avoir
besoin* is followed by a partitive noun, the noun is introduced by *de* alone,
with no definite article.

• In exercise 35.24, you will be asked whether you need certain things.
Say you do, using *avoir besoin*.

Audio cues (for reference):
35.24 Activation orale: Nécessité, avoir besoin

1. Il te faut de l'argent?

2. Il te faut un peu d'argent?

3. Il te faut 50F?

4. Il te faut un peu de temps?

5. Qu'est-ce qu'il te faut? Une heure?

6. Il te faut des vacances?

7. Qu'est-ce qu'il te faut? Un mois de vacances?

8. Il te faut un congé?

9. Qu'est-ce qu'il te faut? Un an de congé?

35.25 Activation: Dialogue between Mme Belleau and Marie-Laure

Listen to the conversation between Mme Belleau and Marie-Laure and
memorize Marie-Laure's lines, imitating and repeating as usual.

TOWARD FREE EXPRESSION

35.26 Words at large

Proceed as usual. (If necessary, refer to lesson 27 for directions.)

35.27, 35.28 Role-playing and reinvention of the story

In 35.27, Mireille, Robert, and Hubert are discussing the Belleaus' country house. Reconstruct their conversation.

In 35.28, describe your ideal house.

• **Suggested written assignment.** Write a description of your ideal house, as in 35.28. Write 75 words. Send this assignment to your instructor (see the course syllabus for details).

OPTIONAL EXERCISES FOR WRITING PRACTICE

Listen again to exercises 35.9 and 35.24 on the audio recording and write out the audio cues you hear.

Check what you have written against the printed text in the study guide.

SELF-TESTING EXERCISES

Complete and check exercises 35.29-35.32 as usual.

SUMMARY QUIZ

Consult the course syllabus or check with your instructor for information about completing and handing in summary quiz 35.

LESSON 36
Entertainment I

The story

At last the meal is over. Mme Belleau asks if anyone wants herb tea; M. Belleau takes orders for after-dinner drinks. Then the crowd begins to thin out. Marie-Laure is sent to bed, Colette rushes off to catch her train back to Provins, M. and Mme Belleau retire. It's 11:00 and, they explain, they are used to going to bed early. A little later, Hubert takes his leave.

It's a bit late to go to the movies now, so Mireille suggests a matinee tomorrow. They consult the *Pariscope*, a weekly entertainment guide. They reject Chinese, Japanese, and Yugoslavian films—Robert wants to understand more than subtitles convey—and must pass up an X-rated American film. Mireille finally notices that they're looking at last week's *Pariscope* anyway. They consult the Minitel (a telephone-linked computer network), find an acceptable French film (an oldie but goodie), and agree to meet at 1:30 tomorrow afternoon. Mireille gives Robert such clear and simple directions that he can't possibly go wrong.

There's a switch in the hall that keeps the lights on for just two minutes, barely enough time to get downstairs. They press the button and then waste about a minute and 59 seconds discussing the device. Naturally, as soon as Mireille closes the door the light goes out, leaving Robert to curse the darkness.

Notes on culture and communication

• **Une matinée.** Despite the reference to morning in its name, *une matinée* refers to the **afternoon** performance of a show (concert, theater, cinema, ballet, etc.).

• **La minuterie.** A light switch with a built-in timer, *la minuterie* allows the lights in a public place, such as a staircase or the entrance hall of an apartment building, to be turned on for a given number of minutes. Then it turns them off automatically. This energy-saving device has been a feature of French buildings for decades, and is found nearly everywhere. (Conserving energy, which is relatively expensive in France, goes hand in hand with the French sense of thrift.)

• **Terms of endearment.** The most difficult skill to learn in the communication of any culture is to know the proper terms of affection and to use them in the right situation. M. Belleau says goodnight to Marie-Laure and adds, *ma poule*. (What American father would ever call his young daughter "chicken" as a term of affection?) Mme Belleau calls Mireille *ma cocotte*, "my hen." When Hubert tells Mireille goodnight, he too draws on barnyard imagery, calling her *mon canard*, "my duck." But he would never call Mme Belleau *ma cocotte*, which can also mean, more suggestively, something like "tart" or "cutie." The best solution to the problem for a foreigner is simply to avoid using such terms until you have witnessed so many instances of their use that you fully understand the circumstances that make them appropriate.

In general, Hubert, for all his pomposity, is an ideal guide to proper usage. The socially acceptable locutions pour out of him naturally. Learn by heart his goodnight speech to Madame Belleau, and you'll never be at a loss when the time comes to take leave of your hostess. But do not copy Robert, who doesn't stand up at once when Madame Belleau gets up to say goodnight. It's not his fault, of course: although he knows the language almost perfectly (thanks to his French mother), he has never been to France before, is not entirely at ease with French culture, and does not always know exactly how to behave.

Content and learning objectives of lesson 36

This lesson will familiarize you with ways in which French speakers talk about habits, and about being tired and going to bed, and how they say goodnight.

The following points are highlighted in lesson 36 (you should concentrate on sections marked with a √):

   • The word family *lumière, allumer, illuminer*
   • Conjugation of verbs like *éteindre*
√• Indefinites + *de* + adjective (36.14-36.16)
√• The subjunctive: formation (36.17-36.23)
   • Se mettre en congé/prendre congé

ASSIMILATION OF THE TEXT

36.1-36.4 Text work-up, aural comprehension, and oral production

Proceed as usual in these sections. (Refer to lesson 28.1-28.4 for directions, if necessary.) Work with the text of lesson 36 in the textbook, as in previous lessons.

TOWARD COMMUNICATION

36.5 Observation and activation: Pronunciation; the vowel /y/ and the semi-vowel /ɥ/ (review)

• Repeat the words and expressions you hear, distinguishing carefully between the vowel /y/ (*musique*) and the semivowel /ɥ/ (*cuisine*).

36.6-36.8 Observation and activation: Light; *allumer, éteindre; peindre*

You saw in lesson 32 how *éteindre* refers to the act of extinguishing light- or heat-emitting objects. *Allumer* is the action that gets them glowing in the first place, as section 36.6 illustrates.

Notice the similarity among the words *lumière, allumer,* and *illuminer.*

Chart 36.7 shows the forms of *éteindre* and another of several verbs that follow the same pattern, *peindre.*

• In exercise 36.8, read the sentences you see, saying aloud and writing down the appropriate form of *éteindre* or *allumer* for each incomplete sentence.

√ Check your answers in key 36.8 at the back of the workbook.

36.9, 36.10 Observation and activation: A matter of habit; *avoir, prendre une habitude*

Robert, Mireille, and Hubert are used to going to bed late, but M. and Mme Belleau have taken to going to bed early, and after dinner M. Belleau mentions this recent habit of theirs as they say goodnight: "Nous avons pris l'habitude de nous coucher tôt." Chart 36.9 shows how various related expressions with *habitude* are used to refer to getting into, being used to, and getting out of habits.

• In exercise 36.10, you will be asked whether various people engage in various activities. Say yes, they do regularly, using *avoir l'habitude.*

Audio cues (for reference):
36.10 Activation orale: Question d'habitude; avoir, prendre une habitude

1. Tu te couches tôt tous les soirs?
2. Les Belleau passent le weekend à la campagne?
3. Mireille va au Luxembourg?

4. Colette vient souvent à Paris?
5. Tu vas au cinéma tous les samedis soirs?
6. Mireille fait du karaté le samedi matin?

36.11, 36.12 Observation and activation: *Il se fait tard; c'est l'heure d'aller au lit*

The oldest and youngest Belleaus go off to bed first. M. and Mme Belleau say goodnight because they are early risers, and Marie-Laure is told to say goodnight because she is a growing girl and needs her sleep. Marie-Laure is generally much more interested in what Mireille and her friends are up to than in going to bed, and must occasionally be reminded several times. Section 36.11 contains the expressions the Belleaus use most often to get her going.

Among the examples in 36.11 are two that contrast the styles of two different generations. Tante Amélie, a more elderly member of the family, has a kindly, somewhat formal way of encouraging Marie-Laure to retire for the night. Tonton Guillaume, the bachelor-about-town and her favorite uncle, speeds her along just as affectionately but more briskly, humorously adopting a brusque sort of military slang.

• Complete the dictation exercise in 36.12, writing what is needed to complete the four short texts about going to bed. As in all dictations, you should make certain you **understand** what is being said before writing anything down.

√ Check your answers in key 36.12 at the back of the workbook.

36.13 Observation: *Se mettre en congé; prendre congé*

Chart 36.13 contrasts two functions of *congé:* to refer to a leave of absence or a vacation, and to refer to a departure.

36.14-36.16 Observation and activation: Designation; indefinite + *de* + adjective (review)

In lesson 30, you saw indefinite expressions like "Est-ce que vous avez **quelque chose de** moins cher?" used to refer to something whose precise identity is unknown or not specified. Chart 36.14 extends the list of indefinite expressions. In addition, the chart focuses on the use of *de* + adjective to narrow down the indefinite aspect of the expression. (An expression like *something* is very vague, very indefinite. An expression like *something interesting*, on the other hand, is more specific; it designates at least the general category of unknowns that we are dealing with.)

• In certain of the phrases for exercise 36.15, you will be told how strange, interesting, extraordinary, etc. something is. Agree that it is strange, interesting, etc. using *quelque chose de* with the appropriate adjective. In other phrases, you will be asked if various people are nice or smart. Say they are, using *quelqu'un de* with an adjective. Remember that *quelqu'un* is a **masculine** word, no matter whom you're referring to.

Audio cues (for reference):
36.15 Activation orale: Détermination; indéfini + de + adjectif

1. Tiens, c'est curieux...
2. Il est sympathique?
3. C'est intéressant.
4. Ça, c'est bizarre.
5. Ça, c'est extraordinaire.

6. Tu vas voir, c'est facile.
7. Elle est sympathique?
8. Il est gentil?
9. Elle est intelligente?

• In 36.16, you will again be asked whether people and things are interesting, intelligent, nice, and so forth. Say no, using *personne de* or *rien de* and the appropriate adjective.

Audio cues (for reference):
36.16 Activation orale: Détermination; indéfini + de + adjectif

1. Ils font des choses intéressantes?
2. Il y a des gens intéressants, dans ton cours d'italien?
3. Tu fais des choses fascinantes?
4. Tu vois des choses intéressantes?
5. Robert fait des choses extraordinaires?
6. Robert et Mireille se disent des choses intelligentes?
7. Il y a des gens fascinants, ici?
8. Il y a des gens sympathiques, ici?
9. Tu as rencontré des gens intéressants?
10. Tu as rencontré des gens sympathiques?

36.17-36.23 Observation and activation: Introduction to the subjunctive

"Il faut que je **descende** en deux minutes!" says Robert incredulously at the top of the stairs. Notice that he has not yet gone downstairs, nor is he in the process of going downstairs. He does not even say that he is going to go downstairs. If he were indicating that he had done, were doing, or were going to do so, he would have expressed those actions in the indicative, since they would refer to actual reality.

But Robert does not use the indicative, because he is saying something different. In his sentence, the act of going downstairs in two minutes is expressed in the **subjunctive**: *que je descende*. It is not represented as actual, but rather as the projected outcome of some necessity: *il faut*. (It has some of the unreality about it that sentences in the conditional have: "Si je voulais, je **descendrais** en deux minutes." In both cases—conditional and subjunctive—the action of *descendre* is not presented as actually taking place.) Here, what Robert presents as actual is the **necessity** of going downstairs (*il faut* is in the indicative). But the **action** of going downstairs is not presented as actual (*descende* is in the subjunctive.) Note that the action might very well happen later; in fact, it does. But this is not what Robert is saying.

As the examples in chart 36.17 show, while the **indicative** expresses the actual unfolding of action, the **subjunctive** is used to refer to actions that are not presented as actual. The subjunctive is subordinated to a main verb. It is linked to this main verb by the conjunction *que*.

The subjunctive is a **mood**, like the indicative, the conditional, and the imperative—that is, it is one way of using a verb to achieve a communicative purpose (the **indicative** indicates, the **conditional** describes a hypothetical outcome, the **imperative** is used to give an order). The subjunctive is used to refer to actions without presenting them as actual. Note that the subjunctive is very common in everyday French, more common than in everyday English. And, as chart 36.18 shows, it is easy to form.

Chart 36.18 gives the forms of the present subjunctive in regular verbs. The stem of the three singular forms and the *ils/elles* form of the subjunctive is the same, for most verbs. It is the same as the stem of the *ils/elles* form of the present indicative. The *nous* and *vous* forms of the subjunctive are identical to the equivalent forms of the imperfect.

• In exercise 36.19, you will be asked why people aren't doing various things. Say they've got to do them, using *il faut* and the subjunctive. Notice that the verbs you hear are all in the *ils* form of the indicative, which is identical to the *ils/elles* form of the subjunctive.

Audio cues (for reference):
36.19 Activation orale: Formation du subjonctif; formes régulières

1. Pourquoi est-ce qu'ils ne disent rien?
2. Pourquoi est-ce qu'ils ne viennent pas?
3. Pourquoi est-ce qu'ils ne descendent pas?
4. Pourquoi est-ce qu'ils ne partent pas?
5. Pourquoi est-ce qu'ils ne comprennent pas?
6. Pourquoi est-ce qu'ils ne boivent rien?
7. Pourquoi est-ce qu'ils ne voient pas un docteur?

8. Pourquoi est-ce qu'ils n'attendent pas?

9. Pourquoi est-ce qu'ils ne suivent pas un cours de cinéma?

10. Pourquoi est-ce qu'ils ne finissent pas?

● In 36.20, various people are doing certain things. Tell someone you know well enough to call *tu* to do likewise, using *il faut* and the subjunctive.

Audio cues (for reference):

36.20 Activation orale: Formation du subjonctif; formes régulières

1. Ils disent où ils vont.

2. Ils viennent.

3. Ils descendent au Home Latin.

4. Ils partent.

5. Ils me comprennent, eux!

6. Ils attendent.

7. Ils suivent des cours.

● In 36.21, you will hear a person reproached for not doing a number of things. Tell that person to shape up. Use *il faut* and the subjunctive. Notice that the verbs you hear are in the *vous* form of the imperfect, which is identical to the *vous* form of the subjunctive you will have to use.

Audio cues (for reference):

36.21 Activation orale: Formation du subjonctif; formes régulières

1. Pourquoi n'écoutiez-vous pas?

2. Vous ne vous serviez jamais de votre voiture?

3. Vous ne veniez jamais à Paris?

4. Vous ne preniez jamais le métro?

5. Vous n'alliez jamais à la fac?

6. Vous ne travailliez pas?

7. Vous ne buviez pas d'eau?

● In 36.22, you will hear a series of commands. Insist that they be obeyed, using *il faut* and the *tu* form of the subjunctive.

Audio cues (for reference):

36.22 Activation orale: Formation du subjonctif; formes régulières

1. Descends!

2. Pars maintenant!

3. Prends un congé!

4. Dis au revoir!

5. Bois quelque chose!

6. Réponds!

7. Dis quelque chose!

8. Viens!

9. Apprends tes leçons!

10. Finis ton travail!

11. Conduis prudemment!

12. Rends-moi mon argent!

● In 36.23, you will hear another series of commands. Insist that they be obeyed, using *il faut* and the *vous* form of the subjunctive.

Audio cues (for reference):
36.23 Activation orale: Formation du subjonctif; formes régulières

1. Descendez!
2. Sortez!
3. Partez!
4. Prenez de l'essence!
5. Souvenez-vous!
6. Répondez-moi!

7. Dites quelque chose!
8. Buvez quelque chose!
9. Venez avec nous!
10. Apprenez vos leçons!
11. Suivez un cours de maths.
12. Finissez vos devoirs!

36.24 Activation: Dialogue between Mireille and Robert

Listen to the conversation between Mireille and Robert and memorize Robert's lines, imitating and repeating as usual.

• **Suggested oral assignment.** Record the dialogue between Mireille and Robert in 36.24. Send this assignment to your instructor (see the course syllabus for details).

TOWARD FREE EXPRESSION

36.25 Words at large

Proceed as usual. (If necessary, refer to lesson 27 for directions.)

36.26, 36.27 Role-playing and reinvention of the story

In 36.26, Robert and Mireille are talking about movies and about the *minuterie*. Imagine their dialogues.

In 36.27, Hubert has overstayed his welcome at the Belleaus' and appears determined to stay as long as Robert does. Imagine their three-way conversation with Mireille.

OPTIONAL EXERCISES FOR WRITING PRACTICE

Listen again to exercises 36.21, 36.22, and 36.23 on the audio recording and write out the audio cues you hear.

Check what you have written against the printed text in the study guide.

SELF-TESTING EXERCISES

Complete and check exercises 36.28 and 36.29 as usual.

SUMMARY QUIZ

Consult the course syllabus or check with your instructor for information about completing and handing in summary quiz 36.

LESSON 37
Entertainment II

The story

This time the couple gets together after only a minor delay (it might have been a permanent delay but for a certain anonymous driver's good brakes) and heads for the cinema. Once there, they buy tickets. Mireille remembers to show her student ID, which entitles her to a discount. While they wait for the place to open, the ever-frugal Mireille expresses regret that they didn't come on Monday, when tickets are cheaper.

Inside, an usher helps them find seats, gives the tickets back to Robert, and thanks him rather coldly. Mireille explains that she expected a tip. Robert, who didn't know that this is customary, gets cross with Mireille for not filling him in earlier.

Finally, the screen comes alive, but what's this? A series of commercials, ending in an ad for chocolate bonbons. At that point the lights come on and the ushers circulate, peddling that very product. Robert is impatient. This isn't what he came to see.

When the lights dim again, Robert asks Mireille to explain anything he may not understand. His talking irritates a (rather crabby) neighbor. The film is about a near-extramarital affair that ends in fidelity, connubial bliss, and the like. As Aunt Georgette says: "All's well that ends well." (Georgette? I thought that was someone else.)

Notes on culture and communication

• **Le cinéma est moins cher le lundi.** To encourage people to go to the movies on Monday, a slow day, tickets are sold at 30% off the regular price.

• **Les ouvreuses.** In France, whether at the movies, the theater, a concert, or the opera, ushers accompany the audience to their seats and expect a tip in return. (In one of her books, the American novelist Mary McCarthy relates an episode that recalls Robert's blunder: "Did you know that you're supposed to tip the usher in a French movie house? I didn't know and got hissed at by the woman the other day when I went to see an Antonioni flick. . . . The picture was half over before I finally grasped what my big crime of omission had been. Then it was too late to rectify it.")

84

● **Advertising at the movies and on TV.** The French have advertising at the movies as well as on television, although there is much less advertising on television than in the United States. In addition, they prefer to show a whole string of ads one after the other and then run the movie or television program without interruption. This is in sharp contrast to the American practice of breaking up TV shows every three or four minutes—always at the most exciting moment—to show advertising spots. One result of this bunching of ads before and after programs is that French TV ads tend to be more imaginative and more interesting than American TV ads. The attention of viewers must be captured by the sheer quality of the advertisement, since they are not obliged to sit through the ad in order to see the balance of a program.

Content and learning objectives of lesson 37

This lesson shows ways in which French speakers refer to people's approximate ages and how they express repeated and reverse action.

The following points are highlighted in lesson 37 (you should concentrate on sections marked with a √):

- Different uses of *coup*
- Time: *en deux minutes/dans deux minutes*
- Verbs with vowel changes: *jeter*, *acheter*, review
√ ● Position of direct and indirect object pronouns (37.19-37.22)
√ ● Irregular subjunctives (37.23-37.26)
- The past subjunctive

ASSIMILATION OF THE TEXT

37.1-37.4 Text work-up, aural comprehension, and oral production

Proceed as usual in these sections. (Refer to lesson 28.1-28.4 for directions, if necessary.) Work with the text of lesson 37 in the textbook, as in previous lessons.

TOWARD COMMUNICATION

37.5, 37.6 Observation and activation: Pronunciation; consonant linking

Recall that most syllables in French are **open**: they end on a vowel sound. That is a fundamental feature of French speech. Recall also that the rhythm of spoken French is based on the little knots of words called

rhythmic groups, each group forming a meaningful unit and ending with a very slight stress.

The end of a rhythmic group in spoken French coincides with a break between two written words. The divisions between spoken syllables, however, do not necessarily reflect their distribution in written words, as the sample sentence in 37.5 illustrates. All of the **spoken** syllables (except the last) in *c'est une habitude idiote* are open, but not a single one of the words as **written** ends in a vowel sound.

What happens is this: in order to form as many open syllables as possible, some syllables are made to straddle two words, borrowing a consonant from the preceding word (syllable 2 in the example) or a vowel from the following word (syllable 6 in the example). That is, if a word ending with a consonant sound is followed by a word beginning with a vowel sound, the consonant sound of word 1 will link up with the vowel sound of word 2. You already know one form of this phenomenon as **liaison**. In *liaison*, a written consonant that would not be pronounced if it fell at the end of a rhythmic group is pronounced and linked to the vowel sound that begins the following word; such is the case with *c'est une* in the example.

Such linking is not limited to *liaison*, however. It also occurs with words ending in a consonant that is usually pronounced; such is the case with *une ha*bitude in the example. This kind of linking is called **consonant linking**.

• Repeat the rhythmic groups you hear in exercise 37.6 as you look at their written versions in the workbook. Make sure you do not stop between words; consonant linking will help you keep going.

37.7, 37.8 Observation and activation: Ages

Estimating other people's ages, like guessing their weight, is best done in round figures. You saw in lesson 15 how the ending *-aine* is added to common numbers to produce approximations. Chart 37.7 shows how to use these approximate numbers to refer to ages.

• In exercise 37.8, you will hear estimates of people's ages. Agree with each estimate, using an approximate expression in *-aine*.

Audio cues (for reference):
37.8 Activation orale: Ages

1. Ce monsieur doit avoir près de cinquante ans.
2. L'ouvreuse doit avoir près de 40 ans.
3. Ce jeune cadre doit avoir près de 30 ans.
4. M. Belleau doit avoir près de 50 ans.

5. Tante Georgette doit avoir près de 60 ans.

37.9, 37.10 Observation and activation: Repetitions and returns; *re-*

The charts in 37.9 show how the prefix *re-* (*r-* in front of a vowel) is used in two related but different circumstances: (1) to refer to an action that is repeated ("Robert part et **re**part," "il téléphone, puis **re**téléphone") and (2) to indicate a return to where one started ("Il part, puis il **re**vient," "le garçon a **r**apporté la côtelette à la cuisine," "Mireille ferme les yeux puis elle les **r**ouvre").

• In exercise 37.10, people will argue that they have already done the things you asked them to do. Don't take any back talk; tell them to do them again, adding *re-* (or *r-*) to the verb you hear, and using the imperative form.

Audio cues (for reference):
37.10 Activation orale: Répétitions et retours en arrière; re-

1. Tu veux que je fasse la vaisselle? Mais je l'ai déjà faite!
2. Tu veux que je mette cette robe? Mais je l'ai déjà mise hier!
3. Des légumes? Mais j'en ai déjà pris!
4. Que je téléphone à Tante Georgette? Mais je lui ai déjà téléphoné tout à l'heure!
5. Mon devoir de maths? Mais je l'ai déjà fait!
6. Mais je l'ai déjà lu, cet Astérix!

37.11, 37.12 Observation and activation: *Coups*

Chart 37.11 gives some of the many dozens of expressions in French that use the word *coup*. Any decisive, energetic movement can be called *un coup*, from *un coup de pied* to *un coup d'état*. The kind of *coup* is indicated by *de* and a noun.

• In exercise 37.12, determine from the context of the sentences you see what kind of *coup* is being referred to, and complete with the appropriate noun.

√ Check your answers in key 37.12 at the back of the workbook.

37.13-37.16 Observation and activation: As time goes by; *en deux minutes, dans deux minutes* (review)

You saw in lesson 28 how *dans* and an expression of time are used to refer to the future ("elle va partir **dans** une heure"). It says how long from now the action will take place. You have also seen (lesson 33) how *en* and an expression of time are used to specify the time it takes to complete an action (Colette: "je suis à Paris **en** une heure"). Chart 37.16 contrasts the two expressions.

• In exercise 37.14, you will hear the time at which various events are going to take place, and the current time. Make a quick calculation and say how many minutes from now each event is going to happen, using *dans*.

Audio cues (for reference):
37.14 Activation orale: Le temps qui passe; dans deux minutes

1. Il est 10h moins 5, et le train part à 10h!
2. La pièce de théâtre commence à 8h. Il est 8h moins 20.
3. Le concert commence à 7h. Il est 7h moins le quart.
4. L'exposition Renoir ouvre à midi. Il est midi moins 12.
5. Le concert commence à 6h. Il est 6h moins 8.
6. Le film commence à 9h 20. Il est 9h 10.
7. La séance commence à 9h. Il est 9h moins le quart.

• In 37.15, people have only a limited amount of time to complete certain actions. Ask if they must complete them within that time, using *en*.

Audio cues (for reference):
37.15 Activation orale: Le temps qui passe; en deux minutes

1. Robert a seulement deux minutes pour descendre.
2. Ils ont seulement 1 mois pour tout repeindre.
3. Colette a seulement 10 minutes pour aller à la gare.
4. Marie-Laure a une heure pour faire tous ses devoirs.
5. Je n'ai qu'une demi-heure pour déjeuner.

37.17, 37.18 Observation and activation: Verbs with vowel changes; *jeter*, *acheter* (review)

You saw in lessons 26 and 34 how verbs like *appeler* and *se lever* have a different vowel sound in the stem depending on whether the ending produces a stem vowel in an open syllable (= one that ends in a vowel sound: *vous* **appe***lez*) or a closed syllable (= one that ends in a consonant sound: *j'*appelle). In the first case, the stem vowel is /ə/ (as in *me*); in the second, it is /ɛ/ (as in *mais*).

The sound of the vowel in the closed syllable is the same from verb to verb; what changes is the spelling. In the case of *acheter*, *mener* and family (*amener*, *emmener*, *promener*, *se promener*, and so forth), and *lever* and company (*se lever*, *enlever*, etc.) it is written as *è* (*j'achète*). In the case of *appeler* and *jeter* there is no accent mark on the *e;* rather the consonant is doubled (*je jette*).

• In exercise 37.18, answer the questions with the appropriate form of the verb you hear. Note that in the questions the stem vowel is in an open syllable (*promenez*) and is pronounced like the /ə/ of *me*. In your answers it will be in a closed syllable (*promène*), pronounced like the /ɛ/ of *mais*.

Audio cues (for reference):
37.18 Activation orale: Verbes à changement vocalique

1. Qu'est-ce que vous faites? Vous vous promenez?
2. Pour les programmes des spectacles, qu'est-ce que vous achetez, Pariscope?
3. Vous vous levez toujours à 7h?
4. Vous vous appelez vraiment Robert?
5. Qu'est-ce que vous faites de vos vieux Pariscopes? Vous les jetez?

37.19-37.22 Observation and activation: Position of personal pronouns (review and extension)

Recall that direct and indirect objects can be expressed as pronouns. When they are, the pronouns come before the verb (before the auxiliary, in the case of the *passé composé*). Occasionally there will be both a direct and indirect object pronoun, and the question arises: Since both pronouns come before the verb, which one comes first? Chart 37.19 gives the answer.

• In exercise 37.20, you will be asked what has happened to various things, and whether you have seen Rohmer's latest film. Say yes, replacing the direct object nouns with pronouns. (So far, so good; there is only one pronoun to place in front of the verb.)

Audio cues (for reference):
37.20 Activation orale: Place des pronoms personnels

1. L'ouvreuse a pris les tickets?
2. L'ouvreuse a rendu les tickets?
3. Tu as ton ticket?
4. Ils ont leurs tickets?
5. Mireille a trouvé son Pariscope?
6. Tu as vu le dernier film de Rohmer?

• In 37.21, you will be asked whether people have been shown or given various things. Say they have, replacing the indirect object nouns with pronouns. (Still only one pronoun to put before the verb.)

Audio cues (for reference):
37.21 Activation orale: Place des pronoms personnels

1. L'ouvreuse t'a rendu les tickets?

2. Pardon, Madame, vous m'avez rendu mon ticket?

3. La caissière t'a rendu la monnaie?

4. Pardon, Mademoiselle, vous m'avez rendu la monnaie?

5. L'ouvreuse a rendu son ticket à Robert?

6. Est-ce que la caissière a donné les tickets à Robert et Mireille?

8. Tu as montré ta carte à la caissière?

• In 37.22, you will see a series of sentences that contain both a direct and indirect object; replace both objects with pronouns. (This is where it gets interesting. Refer to chart 37.19 to figure out which pronoun should come first. The best way to master this problem of pronoun sequence is to practice until the two pronouns come out automatically in the right order.)

√ Check your answers in key 37.22 at the back of the workbook.

37.23-37.26 Observation and activation: Irregular subjunctives; *aller, pouvoir, savoir, avoir, être*

The verbs you see in chart 37.23 have irregular subjunctive forms. The **endings** of the subjunctive in these verbs are perfectly regular, but the subjunctive **stem** does not follow the general pattern for formation of subjunctive stems (see lesson 36.18).

The stems of *pouvoir* and *savoir* stay the same through all persons of the subjunctive. *Avoir* and *être* add a semivowel sound, /j/ (written as *y*), in the *nous* and *vous* forms. (You saw other examples of this in lesson 16.31). Note that the stem of *aller* is perfectly regular in the *nous* and *vous* forms.

Since these five verbs are among the most commonly used verbs in French, it is worthwhile learning their subjunctive forms thoroughly.

• In exercise 37.24, people are setting lofty goals for themselves. Say you have to do the same, using *il faut* and the *nous* form of the verb you hear.

Audio cues (for reference):

37.24 Activation orale: Subjonctifs irréguliers

1. Il faut que j'aille à la bibliothèque.

2. Il faut que j'aille acheter un Pariscope.

3. Il faut que je puisse comprendre!

4. Il faut que j'aie plus de patience.

5. Il faut que je sache à quelle station descendre.

6. Il faut absolument que je sois à l'heure.

• In 37.25, people don't or can't do certain things. Say they really ought to do them, using *il faudrait* and the subjunctive.

Audio cues (for reference):
37.25 Activation orale: Subjonctifs irréguliers

1. Nous ne savons pas où Mireille habite.
2. Tu ne peux pas venir?
3. Il ne sait pas conduire?
4. Tu ne sais pas conduire?
5. Vous ne pouvez pas venir?
6. Ils ne peuvent pas venir?

7. Vous ne savez pas où ils sont?
8. Je ne peux pas dormir.
9. Tu ne vas pas voir Trash?
10. Vous n'allez pas à Chartres?
11. Il ne va pas à Chartres?

• In 37.26, you will be asked whether you think various things are possible or true. Say no, you're afraid they aren't, using *j'ai peur que* and the subjunctive.

Audio cues (for reference):
37.26 Activation orale: Subjonctifs irréguliers

1. Tu crois qu'il va bien?
2. Tu crois que c'est ouvert?
3. Tu crois que nous avons le temps d'y aller?
4. Tu crois que c'est cher?

5. Tu crois que ce sera en japonais?
6. Tu crois qu'il est libre ce soir?
7. Tu crois qu'elle sera là?
8. Tu crois que ça ira, ici?

37.27, 37.28 Observation and activation: The past subjunctive

Mireille tells Robert it is too bad they could not have gone to the movies on a Monday because ticket prices are lower then: "C'est dommage que nous n'ayons pas pu venir lundi." She uses the subjunctive because she is saying not that they actually did or didn't go on Monday (there would be no point in that—Robert knows they didn't go), but that she wishes they had. And because this possibility of going or not going is a matter of the past, she uses the past subjunctive.

The past subjunctive is made up of the subjunctive of the auxiliary and the past participle of the verb. In terms of the choice of *avoir* or *être* and the agreement of the past participle, the past subjunctive functions like any other compound tense.

• In exercise 37.28, people have done various things that you think are good, wonderful, stupid, and so forth. Say it's good, wonderful, stupid, etc. that they've done them, using the past subjunctive.

Audio cues (for reference):
37.28 Activation orale: Subjonctif passé

1. Vous avez raté votre train? Ah, c'est bête!
2. Vous n'êtes pas venu hier? C'est dommage.
3. Vous avez perdu votre ticket? Ah, c'est bête.
4. Vous avez su venir tout seul? C'est formidable!
5. Vous avez osé prendre le métro tout seul? C'est extraordinaire!
6. Vous avez eu des difficultés à suivre le film? C'est tout à fait normal.
7. Vous êtes allé au cinéma avec Mireille? C'est bien.
8. Vous avez pu acheter Pariscope? C'est bien.

37.29 Activation: Dialogue between Mireille and Robert

Listen to the conversation between Mireille and Robert and memorize Robert's lines, imitating and repeating as usual.

TOWARD FREE EXPRESSION

37.30 Words at large

Proceed as usual. (If necessary, refer to lesson 27 for directions.)

37.31, 37.32 Role-playing and reinvention of the story

In 37.31, Robert and Mireille are discussing the practice of tipping ushers. Imagine their dialogue.

In 37.32, reinvent Robert and Mireille's afternoon at the movies.

• **Suggested written assignment.** Write a version of Mireille's and Robert's afternoon at the movies in 37.32. Write 75 words. Send this assignment to your instructor (see the course syllabus for details).

DOCUMENT

At the end of the textbook chapter for lesson 27 you will find a poem for reading practice by the filmmaker Jean-Luc Godard (b. 1930).

Godard was one of the founders of French "new wave" cinema with his film *A Bout de souffle* (*Breathless*, 1960). The *nouvelle vague* sought to take filmmaking out of the realm of entertainment and mass consumption and elevate it to the status of painting or literature. Godard, who is a film critic and theoretician as well as a filmmaker, states his views in a playful way in this poem, published in one of the leading journals of film criticism. For Godard, cinema emerges from the interplay of spontaneous creation (*Je joue, Tu joues, Nous jouons*) and serious intellectualizing (*savoir . . . Penser et parler*), the impulsive playfulness of children tempered by the rules and definitions of adults. The result is a mirror in which we see ourselves, the world, and life itself.

OPTIONAL EXERCISES FOR WRITING PRACTICE

Listen again to exercises 37.10, 37.14, and 37.28 on the audio recording and write out the audio cues you hear.

Check what you have written against the printed text in the study guide.

SELF-TESTING EXERCISES

Complete and check exercises 37.33, 37.34, and 37.35 as usual.

SUMMARY QUIZ

Consult the course syllabus or check with your instructor for information about completing and handing in summary quiz 37.

LESSON 38
Entertainment III

The story

Our protagonists decide to take a walk after the film. Mireille wants Robert to see Montparnasse, the artists' and intellectuals' neighborhood. A moment of panic: Robert can't find his passport. At Mireille's suggestion, he runs back to his room, where he finds it in the pocket of his seersucker jacket. They resume their walk, noting studios and cafés once frequented by famous artists and thinkers.

They talk about the film they have just seen, and we learn that while Robert prefers "serious" films full of political and philosophical discussions, for Mireille those are too static. Action, not words, is the soul of cinema. The silents just may be the greatest films of all. It's not that she is against color, but there are some superb movies in black and white.

They pass a Rodin statue of Balzac, which Marie-Laure once mistook for a cow, note one or two landmarks of a more personal nature, and then cross to the Right Bank. Here, among many other things, Mireille points out the Church of the Madeleine, where her mother would like her to get married. Robert wants to approach the obelisk on the Place de la Concorde and try his hand at deciphering some of the hieroglyphics, but the traffic is even more impenetrable than the inscriptions.

On the quiet paths along the Champs-Elysées, a loudmouthed soldier is amused by Robert's jacket and makes a disparaging remark to his companion. Mireille, our aspiring Black Belt in karate, promptly sends the soldier sprawling in the dust, explaining to an astonished Robert that she needed the exercise. Now she has worked up a thirst and would like to stop for a drink. That's OK with Robert, who's a bit shaken himself.

Notes on culture and communication

• **Montparnasse, Montmartre, St.-Germain-des-Prés.** Montparnasse became the hub of artistic bohemian life between World War I and World War II, after Montmartre, which had been the cradle of cubism and the favorite haunt of many painters at the turn of the century, and before St. Germain-des-Prés (see lesson 29), which took over as the heart of existentialism and jazz in the years immediately after World War II. From its cosmopolitan and bohemian golden age in the 1920s and 1930s, Montparnasse still has many

94

literary cafés and artists' studios, as well as numerous theaters, movie houses, and nightclubs.

   • **Charlot** is the nickname given by the French to the famous American moviemaker Charlie Chaplin (1889-1977).

   • **L'Obélisque de la Place de la Concorde.** The obelisk that occupies the center of the Place de la Concorde was erected there in 1836, after having been brought from Luxor, Egypt, in 1831.

   • **Garçon-boucher.** The two soldiers make fun of Robert and compare him to a butcher's boy because of his seersucker jacket. In France the butcher's traditional uniform is a blue seersucker shirt worn under a long white apron.

   • **Cinema and the French.** Mireille is keenly interested in movies, as most French students are. They take movies seriously, read intellectual movie magazines like *Cahiers du Cinéma*, and hold the creators of movie classics like Griffith and Eisenstein in great esteem. It comes to Americans as something of a surprise that Europeans respect Charlie Chaplin as a visionary artist and not, as many Americans have traditionally believed, merely a funny clown.

Content and learning objectives of lesson 38

   In this lesson, you will find ways in which French speakers express surprise and call for restraint.

   The following points are highlighted in lesson 38 (you should concentrate on sections marked with a √):

   • *C'est là que*, *c'est . . . où* with places
   √• Position of *jamais*, *toujours*, *souvent* (38.13-38.16)
   √• Position of direct and indirect object pronouns (38.17-38.18)
   √• Verbs in *-yer* (38.19-38.21)
   • Subjunctive of *faire*
   √• Irregular subjunctives (38.22-38.25)

ASSIMILATION OF THE TEXT

38.1-38.4 Text work-up, aural comprehension, and oral production

   Proceed as usual in these sections. (Refer to lesson 28.1-28.4 for directions, if necessary.) Work with the text of lesson 38 in the textbook, as in previous lessons.

TOWARD COMMUNICATION

38.5, 38.6 Observation and activation: Pronunciation; consonant linking (review and extension)

You saw in lesson 37 how syllables straddle words in French, the consonant sound at the end of a word linking up with a following vowel sound. You will see from the examples in 38.5 and 38.6 that it is the last **spoken** consonant sound at the end of a word—not necessarily the last **written** consonant letter—that links up with the following vowel sound. In "c'est une habitude idiote," the example in lesson 37, the last consonant sound you say in each word is also the last one you see. But in "Robert et Mireille," the *t* of *Robert* is not pronounced at all; the last consonant you say is /r/, and it is this /r/ that links up with the /e/ of *et*.

• Repeat the phrases you hear as you read their written versions in the workbook.

38.7-38.9 Observation and activation: Surprise (review and extension); calling for restraint

Robert is discovering that Mireille is a woman of strong convictions. She is surprised by Robert's taste for talky movies, and she makes it clear that she doesn't share his preference: "Quelle idée!" Chart 38.7 groups together this and other expressions that can be used to indicate surprise at what someone has said.

Surprise can be mixed with other reactions. *Comme c'est bizarre!*—like *Quelle idée!*—suggests **disapproval** as well as surprise. Expressions like *Vous m'étonnez!* and *Sans blague!* suggest surprise combined with **skepticism** at what others say. *Ça alors!*, *Pas possible!*, and *Ce n'est pas vrai!* can also be used when you are astonished or amazed by some event—a chance encounter, for instance. (In this context they are considerably stronger than *Tiens!*)

Robert also finds out that Mireille is a woman of decisive action. When she dispatches the soldier it is Robert's turn to be astonished, and he suggests that she has overreacted: "Tu y vas un peu fort!" Chart 38.8 contains further expressions for urging restraint.

• In exercise 38.9, decide whether the phrases you hear express surprise or recommend restraint, and mark the appropriate space on the grid.

√ Check your answers in key 38.9 at the back of the workbook.

38.10-38.12 Observation and activation: Indicating places; *c'est là que, c'est . . . où*

As Robert and Mireille pass by a garage on the Boulevard Raspail, Robert points to it and identifies it as the garage where he rented a car on his ill-fated mission to Provins. The charts in 38.10 show how a place can be singled out as the setting for a particular action, using *c'est là que* as Robert does, or using a noun and *où*.

Note that these are **demonstrative** expressions: they direct people's attention to what you are talking about.

• In exercises 38.11 and 38.12, play tour guide and point out where various events take place, combining the two sentences you hear into one, as in the examples.

Audio cues (for reference):
38.11 Activation orale: Indication de lieu; c'est là que, c'est...où

1. Ça, c'est l'Assemblée Nationale. On y prépare les projets de loi.
2. Ça, c'est le Quatorze-Juillet-Parnasse. On y a vu l'Amour l'après-midi.
3. Ça, c'est l'Institut d'Art et d'Archéologie. J'y suis un cours d'art grec.
4. Voilà Le Luxembourg. Marie-Laure va y jouer tous les jours.
5. Ça, c'est la Closerie des Lilas. Robert y a déjeuné l'autre jour.

38.12 Activation orale: Indication de lieu; c'est là que, c'est...où

1. Tu vois cette maison? J'y suis né.
2. Tu vois cette bibliothèque? Mireille y travaille tous les jours.
3. Tu vois ce cinéma? Nous y avons vu l'Amour l'après-midi.
4. Tu vois ce garage? Robert y a loué une voiture.
5. Tu vois ce restaurant? Robert et Mireille y sont allés ensemble.
6. Tu vois cette maison? Mireille y est née.

38.13-38.16 Observation and activation: Position of *jamais, toujours, souvent*

Jamais, *toujours*, and *souvent* are commonly used words that express frequency. Chart 38.13 shows how they behave in the present and the *passé composé*. They are placed after the verb in the present and in other **simple** tenses where there is only one verb form (the imperfect, the future, the conditional). They come between the auxiliary and the past participle in the *passé composé* and other **compound** tenses (the pluperfect, the past conditional).

• In exercises 38.14, 38.15, and 38.16, answer by saying that the events referred to occur never, always, or often. Some of the questions you hear will be in the *passé composé;* be sure to answer them in the *passé composé.*

Audio cues (for reference):
38.14 Activation orale: Place de jamais

1. Tu vas au cinéma quelquefois?
2. Tu as entendu parler de la <u>Ruée vers l'Or</u>?
3. Tu fumes quelquefois?
4. Vous allez en ville quelquefois, vous deux?

5. Robert déjà est venu en France?
6. Tu es déjà allé à la Closerie des Lilas?
7. Le professeur se trompe quelquefois?

38.15 Activation orale: Place de toujours

1. Mireille déjeune avec ses parents?
2. Mireille a voulu être actrice?
3. Mireille travaille chez elle?
4. Robert a passé ses vacances en Amérique du Sud?

5. Robert a parlé français avec sa mère?
6. M. Belleau rentre à la maison à midi?
7. Tonton Guillaume fait des cadeaux à Marie-Laure?

38.16 Activation orale: Place de souvent

1. Tu vas au cinéma quelquefois?
2. Tu as entendu parler de la <u>Ruée vers l'Or</u>?
3. Vous allez à la bibliothèque quelquefois, vous deux?
4. Tu vas en ville quelquefois?
5. Les Belleau vont à la campagne quelquefois?
6. Mireille a téléphoné à Colette quelquefois?
7. Tonton Guillaume apporte des cadeaux à Marie-Laure?
8. Tu es allée à la Closerie des Lilas?

38.17, 38.18 Observation and activation: Position of the pronouns *le, la, les, lui, leur*

You saw in lesson 37.19 that when there are two objects to be expressed as pronouns (a **direct** object and an **indirect** object), and when the indirect object pronoun is *me, te, nous,* or *vous,* the indirect object pronoun is placed before the direct object pronoun.

Chart 38.17 shows what happens when the indirect object pronoun is *lui* or *leur:* the order is inverted.

• Answer the questions in exercise 38.18, deciding which object nouns you hear are direct and which are indirect, and expressing both as pronouns in your answer. (If you need to review the distinction between direct and indirect objects, return to lesson 18.27.)

Audio cues (for reference):
38.18 Activation orale: Place des pronoms le, la, les, lui, leur

1. Robert a demandé son numéro de téléphone à Mireille?
2. Vous prêtez votre voiture à votre nièce?
3. Vous prêtez vos voitures à vos nièces?
4. Robert a montré à Mireille le garage où il a loué une voiture?
5. Vous recommandez ce garage à vos clients?
6. L'ouvreuse a rendu les billets à Robert et Mireille?
7. Mme Courtois a donné son adresse à Robert?

38.19–38.21 Observation and activation: Verbs in -*yer* (review and extension)

You know from the example of *s'ennuyer* in lesson 15 that verbs whose infinitives end in -*yer* have an extra semivowel sound, /j/ (written *y*), in the stem of the *nous* and *vous* forms of the present. Chart 38.19 shows that the semivowel sound is present in all the forms of the imperfect (to be expected, since the stem of the imperfect is the same as that of the *nous* form of the present) and in the *nous* and *vous* forms of the subjunctive, as well as in the past and present participles.

We can generalize about this /j/ sound and say that it occurs:

a) in forms where the syllable that carries the main stress comes immediately after the stem (as happens in *essay*er, *essay*é, *essay*ant, *essay*ais, and so forth);

b) when the stem is followed by the syllable /i/ (*essay*ions, *essay*iez).

The /j/ sound does **not** occur when the principal stress is on the last syllable of the stem itself (*essaie, essaies, essaient*) or where there is a mute *e* between the stem and the stressed syllable, as occurs in the future (*essaierai, essaierons*, and so on).

• In exercise 38.20, you will hear a series of commands in the *vous* form, followed by two statements in the *nous* form. Restate each sentence, changing *vous* to *tu* and *nous* to *je*, and replacing the verb forms that contain a /j/ sound with forms that do not.

Audio cues (for reference):
38.20 Activation orale: Verbes en -yer

1. Appuyez sur le bouton.
2. Essayez!
3. Payez!
4. Nettoyez tout!
5. Essuyez tout!

6. Tutoyez-le!
7. Nous n'employons jamais ces
   mots-là.
8. Nous nous ennuyons.

• In 38.21, you will be asked whether or not you are washing the windows, trying, paying for the program, and so forth. Ask why you should, using the conditional.

Audio cues (for reference):
38.21 Activation orale: Verbes en -yer

1. Vous ne nettoyez pas les vitres?
2. Vous n'essayez pas?
3. Vous ne payez pas le programme?

4. Vous ne vous ennuyez pas?
5. Vous ne me croyez pas?
6. Vous ne me tutoyez pas?

38.22-38.25 Observation and activation: Irregular subjunctives; *faire*

Chart 38.22 adds the verb *faire* to the list of verbs with irregular subjunctive stems, familiar to you from lesson 37.

• In exercise 38.23, you will hear that various people aren't doing certain things. Your reaction is that they ought to shape up. Say they'd better do them, using *il faudrait* and the subjunctive.

Audio cues (for reference):
38.23 Activation orale: Subjonctif irrégulier; faire

1. Il ne fait pas attention!
2. Elles ne font pas d'exercise.
3. Nous ne faisons pas d'exercise.
4. Eh, vous deux, vous ne faites pas votre travail?
5. Je ne fais pas d'exercice.

• In 38.24, various people are not being patient, going to the Courtois's, being on time, and so forth. Tell them to be patient, go to the Courtois's, be on time, etc., using *il faudrait que* and the subjunctive.

Audio cues (for reference):
38.24 Activation orale: Subjonctifs irréguliers

1. Tu n'as pas de patience!
2. Robert ne va pas chez les Courtois.
3. Tu n'es pas à l'heure.
4. Vous n'allez pas à Chartres?

5. Tu ne fais pas la sieste?
6. Vous n'avez pas le temps?
7. Robert ne sait pas le japonais?
8. Robert et Mireille ne vont pas au cinéma ensemble?

• In 38.25, retell details of the story according to your own tastes and preferences, using the subjunctive.

√ Check your answers in key 38.25 at the back of the workbook.

38.26 Activation: Dialogue between Mireille and Robert

Listen to the conversation between Mireille and Robert and memorize Robert's lines, imitating and repeating as usual.

• **Suggested oral assignment.** Record the dialogue between Mireille and Robert in 38.26. Send this assignment to your instructor (see the course syllabus for details).

TOWARD FREE EXPRESSION

38.27 Words at large

Proceed as usual. (If necessary, refer to lesson 27 for directions.)

38.28 Role-playing and reinvention of the story

In 38.28, Robert and Mireille are walking from Montparnasse to the Place de la Concorde. Imagine their dialogue.

In 38.29, it turns out that the two soldiers on furlough that Robert and Mireille meet behind the Petit Palais are not soldiers at all. They are actually . . . . Imagine who.

OPTIONAL EXERCISES FOR WRITING PRACTICE

• Listen again to exercises 38.18 and 38.21 on the audio recording and write out the audio cues you hear.

√ Check what you have written against the printed text in the study guide.

SELF-TESTING EXERCISES

• Complete and check exercises 38.30–38.33 as usual.

SUMMARY QUIZ

Consult the course syllabus or check with your instructor for information about completing and handing in summary quiz 38.

LESSON 39
Entertainment IV

The story

At Fouquet's, where they are seated having a drink, Robert asks Mireille to tell him about theater in Paris. There is a tremendous variety, ranging from the great publicly supported houses like the Comédie Française to tiny experimental places seating barely a hundred; from classical tragedies to silly farces; from the traditional to the most *avant* of the *avant-garde*.

Robert is about to order another round of refreshments when Mireille and Hubert catch sight of each other. Mireille's acknowledgment of the coincidence comes in the form of a line from an Ionesco comedy. Hubert invades their table unceremoniously. Then Jean-Pierre, our would-be ladies' man, recognizes Mireille from the Luxembourg gardens. Ionesco again, and another invasion.

Hubert heartily agrees with Robert's negative reactions to the practice of tipping ushers and to the presence of commercials in the cinema. Of course, Hubert states his opinions in an exaggerated way. Mireille is much more tolerant and reasonable. (Obviously she can enjoy Hubert without agreeing with him.)

Now here's the man in black again! Will we ever know who he is, or does that kind of disclosure occur only in fiction? To quote the well-known philosopher Marie-Laure Belleau: "Mystery . . . and gumdrops."

Notes on culture and communication

• **Fouquet's** is an old and rather distinguished café-restaurant on the Champs-Elysées, about two miles from the Latin Quarter. It is rarely frequented by students, which is why Hubert is surprised to run into Mireille and Robert there. (You will notice, by the way, that some French speakers pronounce the -*t*'s at the end of *Fouquet's*, and others don't.)

• **Les Cafés-théâtres.** Cafés-théâtres are small theatre workshops in the cabaret style that present unconventional plays, satiric comedies, and humorous one-man or one-woman shows.

• **Les Salles subventionnées.** National theaters are subsidized by the state and generally specialize in productions of plays from the classic repertory.

• **Le Théâtre de boulevard.** Since the nineteenth century, the tradition of popular comedy and light entertainment has flourished in theatres located along the Paris boulevards.

• **"Comme c'est curieux, comme c'est bizarre! Et quelle coïncidence!"** is the leitmotiv of Eugène Ionesco's absurdist comedy, *The Bald Soprano* (*La Cantatrice chauve*, 1950). (See the document for lesson 39 in the textbook).

Content and learning objectives of lesson 39

This lesson shows ways in which French speakers express restriction, necessity, and obligation. It also shows how they state reservations.

The following points are highlighted in lesson 39 (you should concentrate on sections marked with a √):

√• *Falloir* and the subjunctive (39.10-39.11)
√• Irregular subjunctives: *aller*, *falloir*, *valoir*, *vouloir* (39.12-39.13)
√• Subjunctive with expressions of doubt (39.16, 39.17)
• *Ça fait* + infinitive
• Position of object pronouns, recapitulation

ASSIMILATION OF THE TEXT

39.1-39.4 Text work-up, aural comprehension, and oral production

Proceed as usual in these sections. (Refer to lesson 28.1-28.4 for directions, if necessary.) Work with the text of lesson 39 in the textbook, as in previous lessons.

TOWARD COMMUNICATION

39.5 Observation and activation: Pronunciation; *liaison* and consonant linking (recapitulation)

Section 39.5 brings together examples of two categories of consonant-vowel linking you have seen:

a) *liaison*, where a written consonant that would not be pronounced if it fell at the end of a rhythmic group is pronounced and linked to the vowel sound of the following word (*des /z/histoires*);

b) the linking that occurs between a consonant sound that is always pronounced at the end of a word and the vowel sound at the beginning of the next word (*avec* /k/*Hubert*, *une* /n/*histoire* /r/*idiote*).

• Repeat the words and expressions you hear as you look at their written versions in the workbook.

39.6-39.8 Observation and activation: Restriction; *ne . . . que* (review)

In lesson 26, you saw how *ne . . . que* expresses restriction by specifying an exception to an overall situation of absence or lack. At dinner with Jean-Denis, Cécile isn't hungry. She can't go to a restaurant without eating anything, however, so she says she will only have an omelette: "Je **ne** veux **qu'**une petite omelette." Chart 39.6 provides new situations for understanding and using this negative expression.

About France, Robert has no reservations, or almost none: "Je **ne** fais **que** de très légères réserves." One of the reservations he does have is shared wholeheartedly by Jean-Pierre: tipping ushers in movie houses. The only thing ushers are good for, says Jean-Pierre, is getting in the way: "Elles **ne** servent **qu'**à déranger les gens."

Note that a restriction expressed with *ne . . . que* may itself be put in the negative. If someone asks you whether the Comédie Française produces only tragedies ("Ils **ne** jouent **que** des tragédies?"), you can say no, there is more to it than that: "Ils **ne** jouent **pas que** des tragédies, ils jouent aussi des comédies, des drames."

• In exercise 39.7, you are asked about various kinds of restricted behavior. Answer by insisting there is more to it than that, using *ne . . . que*.

Audio cues (for reference):
39.7 Activation orale: Restriction; ne...que

1. Vous allez voir seulement des films français?
2. Vous aimez seulement le théâtre d'avant-garde?
3. Vous parlez seulement l'anglais?
4. Est-ce que les ouvreuses servent seulement à déranger?
5. Tu lis seulement des pièces classiques?
6. Tu connais seulement des Américains ici?
7. Vous allez voir seulement des films doublés?

• In 39.8, you are asked about open-ended, unrestricted behavior. Admit that in reality the situation is much more limited, using *ne . . . que*.

Audio cues (for reference):
39.8 Activation orale: Restriction; ne...que

1. Tu as vu beaucoup de pièces d'Arrabal?	4. Tu as deux voitures?
2. Tu as vu tous les films de Rohmer?	5. Tu as visité tous les musées de la ville?
3. Tu as lu toutes les pièces d'Anouilh?	6. Tu as rencontré tous les amis de Mireille?

39.9 Activation: Forms of the subjunctive (review)

You saw in the restaurant scene in lesson 25 how Tante Georgette, a woman of strong convictions and an independent turn of mind, is fond of the imperative. It should come as no surprise that she also has a natural affinity for the subjunctive. In 39.9, Mireille is reporting to her parents about a recent visit to Georgette. All verbs in the subjunctive have been removed from her account. Your challenge is to put them back in.

• Write the appropriate subjunctive forms of each verb printed in *italics* in the blank spaces that follow that verb.

√ Check your answers in key 39.9 at the back of the workbook.

39.10, 39.11 Observation and activation: Necessity, obligation

From lesson 36 on, you have seen the verb *falloir* used with the subjunctive to express obligation or necessity. The most common form of *falloir* is the present tense, *il faut*. (Recall that, as an impersonal expression, *falloir* is conjugated exclusively in the third person singular.) But *falloir* is seen in other tenses as well: future, conditional, imperfect, and *passé composé*, all used with the present subjunctive, as chart 39.10 demonstrates.

• In exercise 39.11, you will hear a series of actions described as obligatory. Agree that they must be done, using *falloir* and the subjunctive.

Audio cues (for reference):
39.11 Activation orale: Nécessité, obligation

1. Il faudra que vous fassiez les courses, ce soir.
2. Il faut que vous ameniez Minouche chez le vétérinaire?
3. Il faudrait que vous voyiez la dernière pièce d'Anouilh!
4. Il faut que tu ailles à ton cours de karaté samedi?
5. Il faut que nous achetions les tickets à l'avance?
6. Il faut que j'aille chez Tante Georgette ce soir?

39.12, 39.13 Observation and activation: Irregular subjunctives; *aller, falloir, valoir, vouloir* (review and extension)

In lesson 37.23, you saw that the *nous* and *vous* forms of the subjunctive of *aller* had a different stem from the other forms. Chart 39.12 groups *aller* with two other verbs whose subjunctive forms follow the same pattern. Notice that in the *nous* and *vous* forms these three verbs actually act like the majority of regular verbs: the *nous* and *vous* forms of the subjunctive are identical to the corresponding forms of the imperfect.

The chart also contains the solitary subjunctive form of *falloir*.

• In exercise 39.13, you will hear that various people will certainly not want to do certain things or go certain places, and that something is surely not very expensive. Say you would be surprised if they did want to do them or did want to go, or if it were very expensive, using *ça m'étonnerait que* and the subjunctive.

Audio cues (for reference):
39.13 Activation orale: Subjonctifs irréguliers; aller, falloir, valoir, vouloir

1. Tante Georgette n'ira sûrement pas au cinéma.
2. Il ne voudra sûrement pas voir ça.
3. Vous ne voudrez sûrement pas voir ça.
4. Ils ne voudront sûrement pas sortir.
5. Je ne voudrai sûrement pas y aller.
6. Ils n'iront sûrement pas aux Folies-Bergère.
7. Vous n'irez sûrement pas jusque là.
8. Tu n'iras sûrement pas mieux.
9. Je n'irai sûrement pas mieux.
10. Ça ne vaut sûrement pas très cher.

39.14, 39.15 Observation and activation: Reserve; *on ne peut pas dire que*

Robert has asked Mireille about the Comédie Française: "Est-ce que c'est bien?" Mireille's first response is very positive: "Oh oui, très bien!" Then she decides to temper her enthusiasm, adding a reservation lest Robert get the impression that the Comédie Française is at the cutting edge of theatrical innovation and experimentation in France. What the Comédie Française does can't exactly be called *avant-garde*, she says, using the subjunctive: "On ne peut pas dire que ce **soit** du théâtre d'avant-garde."

• In exercise 39.15, you will be asked whether certain things are true. Express a reservation in each case, using *on ne peut pas dire que* and the subjunctive.

Audio cues (for reference):
39.15 Activation orale: Réserve; on ne peut pas dire que

1. C'est du théâtre d'avant-garde?
2. Ça fait penser?
3. Ça vaut la peine?
4. Robert connaît bien Paris?
5. Elle est jolie, cette fille?
6. Vous allez souvent au théâtre?

39.16, 39.17 Observation and activation: Doubt

The subjunctive is often used to project attitudes or desires onto an action in a way that calls its reality into question. One of the most frequent of these attitudes is skepticism. Mireille tells Robert to go to the Folies-Bergère if what he wants is mindless enjoyment, but she doubts it will be worth his while: "Je doute que ça **vaille** la peine." Chart 39.16 presents this and other common expressions of doubt, all used with the subjunctive.

• In exercise 39.17, you will be asked whether you think various things are true and whether they will happen. Express doubt that they are true or will happen, using *je doute que* and the subjunctive.

Audio cues (for reference):
39.17 Activation orale: Doute

1. Vous pensez que ça vaut la peine?
2. Vous pensez que c'est du théâtre d'avant-garde?
3. Vous croyez que ça me plaira?
4. D'après vous, il y a plus de cent places dans ce théâtre?
5. C'est une salle subventionnée?
6. Vous pensez que la pièce sera un triomphe?
7. Ils ont beaucoup de monde, d'après vous?
8. Vous pensez que les Belleau iront voir ça?

39.18, 39.19 Observation and activation: Effects; *ça fait* + infinitive

Trying to characterize various types of theatre for Robert, Mireille describes the lightweight *théâtre de boulevard* in terms of its effect on its audience: "Ça ne fait pas beaucoup penser!" Chart 39.18 illustrates this use of *ça fait* and an infinitive to refer to the broad effects of things.

• In exercise 19.19, determine the principal effect of what is referred to in each of the sentences you hear, and add a comment that states this effect, using *ça fait* and the appropriate infinitive from the list printed in your workbook.

39.20-39.21 Observation and activation: Position of object pronouns (recapitulation)

Chart 39.20 brings together material on the position of direct and indirect object pronouns that you saw in lessons 37 and 38.

• Complete exercise 39.21, expressing each of the objects in the sentences you see as pronouns.

√ Check your answers in key 39.21 at the back of the workbook.

39.22 Activation: Dialogue between Hubert and Robert

Listen to the conversation between Hubert and Robert and memorize Robert's lines, imitating and repeating as usual.

TOWARD FREE EXPRESSION

39.23 Words at large

Proceed as usual. (If necessary, refer to lesson 27 for directions.)

39.24, 39.25 Role-playing and reinvention of the story

In 39.24, reconstitute a discussion between Robert and Mireille about theatre.

In 39.25, Hubert meets the man in black. Imagine their exchange.

• **Suggested written assignment.** Write out a version of Hubert's encounter with the man in black in 39.25. Write seventy-five words. Send this assignment to your instructor (see the course syllabus for details).

DOCUMENT

At the end of the textbook chapter for lesson 39 you will find an excerpt from *La Cantatrice chauve* by Eugène Ionesco for reading practice.

Ionesco is, with Samuel Beckett, the leading figure in a movement known as the Theatre of the Absurd that flourished between the Second World War and the 1960s. Rejecting traditional notions of plot, character, and dramatic structure, practitioners of the Theatre of the Absurd sought to express a sense of bewilderment and despair produced by the accelerating future-shock of the twentieth century. One of their ancestors in the French theatre is Alfred Jarry, whose *Ubu Roi* is excerpted in the document for lesson 40.

In *La Cantatrice chauve*, his first play, Ionesco exposes the dislocated dialogue and mindless banality of everyday communication. The result, on the stage, is hilariously funny, although the play has also been read as a somber commentary on the meaninglessness of life. Ionesco himself claimed to be reaching for a pure comic style similar to that of the Marx Brothers.

OPTIONAL EXERCISES FOR WRITING PRACTICE

• Listen again to exercises 39.7 and 39.15 on the audio recording and write out the audio cues you hear.

√ Check what you have written against the printed text in the study guide.

SELF-TESTING EXERCISES

Complete and check exercises 39.26 and 39.27 as usual.

SUMMARY QUIZ

Consult the course syllabus or check with your instructor for information about completing and handing in summary quiz 39.

LESSON 40
Entertainment V

The story

Jean-Pierre has a theory about the man in black's eyes: he's using them
to send signals in Morse code. The blink of one eye is a dot, the blink of
both is a dash. Wait, he's listening! Let's talk about something else.

(Jean-Pierre's Morse seems a bit rusty: he gets Z right, but U is two
dots and a dash, not one dot and a dash, and T is a single dash, not a single
dot. But no matter.)

The conversation turns to theater and cinema. Robert and Jean-Pierre
are enthusiastic about the permanence of film, its spectacular possibilities, its
power over time and space. Hubert and Mireille speak in favor of the
legitimate theater. They prefer the interplay between actors and audience
and the need, given much more limited resources, for the exercise of imagination on both sides of the footlights. Jean-Pierre, a populist when it comes
to art, likes the fact that the dialogue of foreign films can be dubbed into
other languages. Mireille considers dubbing an atrocity; Robert, too, prefers
original versions, with subtitles for Japanese films (his Japanese, like
Jean-Pierre's Morse, is a bit rusty.)

Jean-Pierre is in the midst of a pretty good defense of music-hall
performances—they're not all girlie shows—when Mireille interrupts to ask if
the M. in B. is still listening. He's gone, and in his place there is a nun,
also in black of course, who seems, at least to Jean-Pierre, to be sending
signals in Morse code with her headgear.

Notes on culture and communication

• **Les Cinémathèques.** The *cinémathèques* at Chaillot and Beaubourg are
film libraries that collect and screen old films.

Content and learning objectives of lesson 40

This lesson shows how French speakers express criticism, indifference,
appreciation, and emphasis.

111

The following points are highlighted in lesson 40 (you should concentrate on the section marked with a √):

√ • *Personne*, *rien* as subjects and objects (40.14-40.16)
  • The future and object pronouns, review
  • The conditional, review
  • Pronouns, *y*, and *en*

ASSIMILATION OF THE TEXT

40.1-40.4 Text work-up, aural comprehension, and oral production

Proceed as usual in these sections. (Refer to lesson 28.1-28.4 for directions, if necessary.) Work with the text of lesson 40 in the textbook, as in previous lessons.

TOWARD COMMUNICATION

40.5, 40.6 Observation and activation: Pronunciation; general character of consonants in French

The examples in 40.5 and 40.6 illustrate the tense, rapid nature of French consonant sounds compared to those of English. This is particularly noticeable in clusters of two or more consonant sounds (*théâtre*, *monstre*): the consonants are pronounced in swifter succession than in English. English tends to avoid clusters like these at the end of words, and in the English words that correspond to the examples in 40.6 the clusters are broken up by a vowel sound. (Notice that this gives the English versions one more syllable than the French versions.)

• Repeat the words and expressions you hear, stressing the final vowel sound slightly, then pronouncing the final consonant sounds very rapidly.

40.7, 40.8 Observation and activation: Headgear

Chart 40.7 introduces the terms for a few common head-coverings worn by people in various regions and walks of life.

• In exercise 40.8, determine which kind of headgear is mentioned in each of the sentences you hear, and conclude from that whom the sentence is about, marking the appropriate box.

√ Check your answers in key 40.8 at the back of the workbook.

40.9-40.12 Observation and activation: Criticism, studied indifference, appreciation

The examples in sections 40.9, 40.10, and 40.11 set forth three kinds of common expressions:

Section 40.9 illustrates some of the ways in which French speakers express criticism.

Section 40.10 contains expressions that call for pretended indifference.

Section 40.11 gives expressions of enthusiastic approval.

• In exercise 40.12, decide whether what you hear refers to criticism, apparent indifference, or appreciation, and mark the appropriate box.

√ Check your answers in key 40.12 at the back of the workbook.

40.13 Observation: Emphasis

You saw intensives used in lesson 35 as a means of emphasizing what you have to say, thereby attracting or keeping the attention of others. The expressions in chart 40.13 review and extend the use of intensifying expressions.

40.14-40.16 Observation and activation: *Personne, rien* as subjects and direct objects (review)

In lesson 20, you saw *rien* used as the negative of *quelque chose* and *personne* used as the negative of *quelqu'un*. *Personne* and *rien* can be either **subjects** or **objects** of the verb, as the charts in 40.14 illustrate. In either case, of course, they are used with *ne*.

• In exercise 40.15, determine whether the objects of the questions you hear are things or people (listen for *quelque chose* or *qu'est-ce que*, indicating things, or *quelqu'un*, indicating people). Then answer negatively, using *ne . . . rien* when the question is about a thing and *ne . . . personne* when it is about a person.

Audio cues (for reference):
40.15 Activation orale: Personne, rien, sujets et objets directs

1. Tu vois quelque chose?
2. Tu attends quelqu'un?
3. Robert fait quelque chose?
4. Qu'est-ce qu'elle dit?

5. Tu vois quelqu'un?
6. Qui est-ce que tu attends?
7. Qu'est-ce que tu fais?

● In 40.16, decide whether the subjects of the questions you hear are people (listen for *quelqu'un* or *qui est-ce qui*) or things (listen for *quelque chose* or *qui est-ce qui*). Then answer negatively, using *personne* when the question is about a person and *rien* when it is about a thing.

Audio cues (for reference):
40.16 Activation orale: Personne, rien, sujets et objets directs

1. Quelqu'un fait de l'oeil à Mireille?
2. Quelque chose est cassé?
3. Quelqu'un téléphone à Mireille?
4. Quelque chose te fait peur?

5. Qui est-ce qui te parle?
6. Qu'est-ce qui te plaît?
7. Qu'est-ce qui marche?
8. Qui est-ce qui t'attend?

40.17 Activation: The future and object pronouns (review)

Whether you know it or not, next year you will take a year off and go to France. Your experiences there will parallel Robert's in the most curious way. Look into the crystal ball and foresee your adventures.

● Base your account on the sentences you hear in exercise 40.17. Change the forms of the verbs you hear to say what will happen, using the future. By all means change the facts of the story to suit your own preferences if you wish.

40.18 Activation: The conditional (review)

If you had the time and the means, you would take a year off and go to France. Your experiences would probably be very similar to Robert's. Imagine what would happen.

● You will hear the same sentences you heard in 40.17. Change the forms of the verbs you hear to say what would happen, using the conditional. As before, feel free to reinvent the story as you go along.

40.19 Activation: Pronouns, *y*, and *en*

• Each of the questions in 40.19 is preceded by a quotation in *italics*. Answer the question out loud, basing your response on what you learn from the quotation. Express nouns as pronouns, using *y* and *en* also where appropriate. As you answer, write your response in the space provided.

√ Check your answers in key 40.19 at the back of the workbook.

40.20 Activation: Dialogue between Mireille and Hubert

Listen to the conversation between Mireille and Hubert and memorize Hubert's lines, imitating and repeating as usual.

TOWARD FREE EXPRESSION

40.21 Words at large

Proceed as usual. (If necessary, refer to lesson 27 for directions.)

40.22–40.24 Role-playing and reinvention of the story

In 40.22, Mireille, Robert, Hubert, and Jean-Pierre are discussing the theatre. Reconstruct their conversation.

In 40.23, you are in possession of new information about the man in black. Divulge what you know.

In 40.24, the man in black visits a psychiatrist. Imagine the session.

• **Suggested oral assignment.** Record a version of the man in black's interview with the psychiatrist in 40.24. Say ten to twelve sentences. Send this assignment to your instructor (see the course syllabus for details).

OPTIONAL EXERCISES FOR WRITING PRACTICE

• Listen again to exercises 40.15 and 40.16 on the audio recording and write out the audio cues you hear.

√ Check what you have written against the printed text in the study guide.

DOCUMENT

At the end of the textbook chapter for lesson 40 you will find an excerpt from *Ubu Roi* by Alfred Jarry for reading practice.

As a young man, Jarry was a precocious poet and novelist, and an ambitious innovator. The play *Ubu Roi*, his best-known work, caused an uproar when it appeared in 1896 at the Théâtre de l'Oeuvre, then the leading experimental theatre in Paris. A mixture of mock epic, farce, burlesque, and parody (certain elements are based on Shakespeare's *Macbeth*), peopled by grotesque characters, full of violent and vulgar language, *Ubu Roi* has been seen as a savage attack on the dominant artistic, moral, and social conventions of its time. It had a liberating effect on the theater of the early twentieth century, opening the way for various surrealistic and absurdist experiments.

SELF-TESTING EXERCISES

Complete and check exercises 40.25, 40.26, and 40.27 as usual.

SUMMARY QUIZ

Consult the course syllabus or check with your instructor for information about completing and handing in summary quiz 40.

LESSON 41
A matter of chance I

The story

Getting the check from an inattentive waiter is a long process. Then the tray is overturned and all the glasses on it smash on the sidewalk. Jean-Pierre, who is not very well-bred, says a no-no. Hubert's response is more restrained. Mireille says that, on the contrary, since it was all ordinary glass, they are destined to have good luck.

Later, after Hubert (elegantly) and Jean-Pierre (inelegantly) have both departed, Robert thinks about taking Mireille's hand, but he chickens out of this daring maneuver. Seeing a sign for the national lottery, he asks her if anyone ever wins it. She's never won it, but that's probably because she's never bought a ticket. Robert could use a fresh pot of money (living in France is proving to be expensive). Some of the lottery profits go to charitable causes, and besides, they should take advantage of the good luck that broken glass is supposed to bring. They buy a ticket whose digits add up to nines. Because of several coincidences (Mireille's age, her address, the price of the drinks at Fouquet's, the number of couples he counted holding hands), Robert thinks this is a good omen.

Robert wants Mireille to keep the ticket, but she insists, in spite of his tendency to misplace things (including himself), that he hold on to it. In any case they mustn't forget to look at the list of winners in Thursday's paper to see, says Robert, not **if** but **how much** they have won.

Notes on culture and communication

• **La Loterie nationale.** The French national lottery was inaugurated in 1933.

• **Les Ailes brisées, les Gueules cassées.** Crushed wings and broken faces are military slang expressions for veterans who have had their limbs or faces mutilated.

<u>Content and learning objectives of lesson 41</u>

This lesson will familiarize you with ways in which French speakers express indifference and condescension, speak about making a living, and refer to good and bad luck.

The following points are highlighted in lesson 41 (you should concentrate on sections marked with a √):

- *Tenter* versus *tendre*
- √ Position of *rien* and *personne* in compound tenses (41.15, 41.16)
- The subjunctive with expressions of preference
- √ The subjunctive with conditional expressions (41.19–41.21)
- Verb forms, review

ASSIMILATION OF THE TEXT

41.1–41.4 Text work-up, aural comprehension, and oral production

Proceed as usual in these sections. (Refer to lesson 28.1–28.4 for directions, if necessary.) Work with the text of lesson 41 in the textbook, as in previous lessons.

TOWARD COMMUNICATION

41.5, 41.6 Observation and activation: Pronunciation; general characteristics of French consonants

Compared to their English counterparts, French consonants are tenser, shorter, and give the impression of being more precise. Speakers of American English often have the impression that the French speak **faster** than they do. Partly this is due to the universal fact that anyone speaking a language you don't understand thoroughly seems to be speaking very fast. But it is due also to the fact that most French speakers articulate their sounds very precisely: their vowel sounds are constant, not diphthongized (lesson 18), and their consonant sounds have a crisp, clear quality.

- Repeat the words and expressions you hear, saying each syllable as distinctly as you can. Be careful not to linger over any individual sound.

41.7, 41.8 Observation and activation: Condescension

Robert is sincere and well meaning, but he hasn't yet learned all there is to learn about French culture. While Mireille appreciates the fresh perspective he brings to things she that she takes for granted, she occasionally finds what he says overenthusiastic or downright naïve. In such circumstances, she is apt to tease him playfully, using one of the expressions in chart 41.7.

• In exercise 41.8, listen and repeat Mireille's (somewhat patronizing) replies.

41.9, 41.10   Observation and activation: Indifference; *n'importe*

As long as the last two digits add up to nine, Robert doesn't care which lottery ticket Mireille picks: "Prends **n'importe quel** billet." Although it is important that she choose a ticket, the specific one she selects is of little consequence. Chart 41.9 illustrates how *n'importe* can be used with expressions like *où*, *quand*, and *comment* to indicate that the speaker has no specific preference.

Notice that when there is a choice among possible items in a category ("**Quel numéro** est-ce qu'on va prendre?"), the person responding may repeat the noun ("Prends **n'importe quel numéro**") or replace it with a pronoun ("Prends **n'importe lequel**").

Expressions like *peu importe!* and *ça m'est égal*, shown at the bottom of the chart, can be used alone to indicate indifference.

• In exercise 41.10, you will be asked which actions you prefer to take in various situations. Say it doesn't matter which, using *n'importe* and *quoi* when the question is about things (*qu'est-ce que*), *où* when it is about places, *quand* when it is about times, *qui* when it is about people, and *lequel*, *laquelle*, *lesquels*, or *lesquelles* when you hear *quel* used with a noun.

Audio cues (for reference):
41.10 Activation orale: Indifférence; n'importe

1. Qu'est-ce qu'on va faire?
2. Quel numéro est-ce qu'on va prendre?
3. Quel journal est-ce qu'on va acheter?
4. Qu'est-ce qu'on va dire?

5. Où est-ce qu'on va aller?
6. Quand est-ce qu'on va partir?
7. Qui est-ce qu'on va inviter?

41.11   Observation: *Tenter, tendre*

Certain forms of the verbs *tenter* and *tendre* are close enough in sound to be mistaken for each other. Chart 41.11 reveals the differences between them.

Tenter, an -*er* verb, has a consonant sound, /t/, at the end of the singular forms, and its past participle ends in -*é*.

Tendre is an -*re* verb, and although the singular forms end in a *d* in writing, there is no /d/ **sound** at the end of these forms. The past participle ends in -*u*.

The two forms that are the most likely to cause confusion are the forms of the future, where the only difference you will hear is the consonant sound of the stem: /t/ in *tentera*, /d/ in *tendra*. (Recall that the written *e* at the end of the stem of *tentera* is an unstable /ə/ sound that is barely pronounced in everyday speech; see lesson 24.5).

41.12 Observation: *Gagner sa vie, gagner à la loterie*

The verb *gagner* has two related but separate functions. It can refer to making money or making a living. In this context, *gagner* is used with a direct object: *gagner* **10.000F**, *gagner* **sa vie**.

Gagner can also refer to winning in a game or a contest; in this context it is often used with an object introduced by *à*: *gagner* **à la loterie**, *gagner* **à la belote**.

41.13, 41.14 Observation and activation: Good and bad luck

The examples in chart 41.13 are divided into two parallel sets of expressions that refer to good and bad luck. Tante Amélie, who belongs to an earlier generation and whose French is more refined than Marie-Laure's, uses *chance* and *malchance* to talk about luck. Marie-Laure uses the more colloquial expression *veine*.

Among the things considered to bring good or bad luck in the French cultural system is broken glass. If, as Robert discovers, you break an object made of ordinary glass (as opposed to crystal), that is good luck. Section 41.13 attributes this traditional superstition to Tante Amélie, but, as Jean-Pierre's comments prove, it is shared by the younger generation as well.

• In exercise 41.14, Mireille has borrowed Tonton Guillaume's car to go to Provins. You will hear about various things that happen to her. Determine whether each is lucky or unlucky, and mark the corresponding box on the grid.

√ Check your answers in key 41.14 at the back of the workbook.

41.15, 41.16 Observation and activation: Position of *rien* and *personne* in compound tenses

You saw in lesson 40 that the negative words *personne* and *rien* can be either subjects or objects. When they are direct objects of a verb in the *passé composé*, they are positioned differently in the sentence, as chart 41.15 shows.

Rien comes **before** the past participle: "Je n'ai **rien vu**."

Personne is placed **after** the past participle: "Je n'ai **vu personne**."

• In exercise 41.16, you will be asked whether you have done various things involving persons or things. Say no, answering with *personne* when the question you hear contains *quelqu'un*, with *rien* when it contains *quelque chose*. Pay particular attention to the position of *personne* and *rien* in relation to the past participle.

41.17, 41.18 Observation and activation: Preference and the subjunctive

You saw in lesson 36 that the subjunctive can be used to project constraints and attitudes: "**Il faut que** tu comprennes ça;" "**j'ai peur que** tu sois déçu." Chart 41.17 shows a number of ways in which the subjunctive can be used to express **preference** for a particular action or outcome. Note that the verb in the subjunctive is introduced by *que*.

• In exercise 41.18, you will hear a series of commands urging action of various kinds. The sentences in your workbook restate each command in terms of preference. Respond out loud, using the appropriate form of the subjunctive, and write that form in the corresponding space in the workbook.

√ Check your answers in key 41.18 at the back of the workbook.

41.19-41.21 Observation and activation: Conditions and the subjunctive

Robert tells Mireille to take any lottery ticket she wants, as long as the last two figures printed on the ticket add up to nine: "**pourvu que** les deux derniers chiffres **fassent** neuf." In addition to expressing necessity or preference, the subjunctive can be used to impose conditions on an action, as chart 41.19 illustrates.

• In exercises 41.20 and 41.21, you agree to do various things if certain circumstances are present. Make each circumstance a condition, using *pourvu que* (41.20) or *à condition que* (41.21) and the subjunctive.

Audio cues (for reference):
41.20 Activation orale: Condition et subjonctif

1. J'irai si vous venez.
2. J'irai si Robert vient.
3. J'irai s'il fait beau.
4. J'irai si ça vaut la peine.
5. J'irai si je ne suis pas trop fatiguée.
6. J'irai si j'ai le temps.

41.21 Activation orale: Condition et subjonctif

1. Je le ferai si vous m'aidez.
2. Je le ferai si elle veut m'aider.
3. J'accepterai si c'est bien payé.
4. Je viendrai si tu peux venir avec moi.
5. Je t'accompagnerai si tu me tiens par la main.
6. J'achèterai un billet si tu le choisis.

41.22 Activation: Verb forms (review)

• In each numbered section, use the appropriate forms of the verb in *italics* in the first sentence to complete the following sentences. Read each section through **before** you begin it, and decide from the context which form to use in each incomplete sentence. For instance, expressions like *hier* or *l'an dernier* would suggest that a past tense is needed; *à partir de maintenant* would suggest the future, and so forth.

√ Check your answers in key 41.22 at the back of the workbook.

41.23 Activation: Dialogue between Robert and Mireille

Listen to the conversation between Robert and Mireille and memorize Mireille's lines, imitating and repeating as usual.

TOWARD FREE EXPRESSION

41.24 Words at large

Proceed as usual. (If necessary, refer to lesson 27 for directions.)

41.25, 41.26 Role-playing and reinvention of the story

In 41.25, Mireille and Robert are standing in front of a ticket booth for the national lottery. Imagine their conversation.

In part A of 41.26, Mireille is only 17, and lives at 17 rue de Vaugirard. What lottery ticket would Robert tell her to pick?

In part B, Mireille and Hubert are arguing about the national lottery, which Hubert is against. Imagine their discussion.

• **Suggested written assignment.** Write a version of the debate about the lottery in 41.26, part B. Write ten sentences. Send this assignment to your instructor (see the course syllabus for details).

OPTIONAL EXERCISES FOR WRITING PRACTICE

• Listen again to exercises 41.10 and 41.21 on the audio recording and write out the audio cues you hear.

√ Check what you have written against the printed text in the study guide.

SELF-TESTING EXERCISES

• Complete and check exercises 41.27, 41.28, and 41.29 as usual.

SUMMARY QUIZ

Consult the course syllabus or check with your instructor for information about completing and handing in summary quiz 41.

LESSON 42
A matter of chance II

The story

Early Thursday morning Robert informs a sleepy Mireille that they have won 400,000 francs! She brings him part of the way down to earth by explaining that he only bought a partial ticket and so they'll actually get a tenth of 400,000. Still, that's not too shabby. How will he spend his winnings? Mireille makes a few comically exaggerated suggestions, including exploration on the Amazon river, but Robert would rather they explore France together. Mireille had been considering some more exotic projects for the summer, but she's willing to meet him to discuss the matter. No, not right away! Let's say at ten o'clock, in the Luxembourg Garden.

Mireille hurries Marie-Laure through breakfast and phones Hubert to arrange a luncheon date. Then at 10:10 she meets Robert, who has been waiting for twenty minutes and whose insistance begins to sway her. Anyway, she couldn't leave in less than two weeks because of an exam and because of some children she works with. Besides, she needs camping equipment. No problem! Let's grab a cab and see what's available. She agrees. Just looking around in a store doesn't commit you to buying anything.

She starts to get into a cab, but suddenly recoils. There was a man in there, a strange man in black. As if to pull her in, he reached out a hairy hand with black fingernails. This gets curiouser and curiouser!

Notes on culture and communication

• **Entretenir une danseuse.** Mireille jokingly suggests that Robert follow the French tradition, popular in the nineteenth and early twentieth centuries among rich bourgeois and noblemen, of keeping a fashionable mistress, for instance a dancer from the Paris Opera Ballet.

• **Are Americans just overgrown kids?** In this episode we see Robert full of childish enthusiasm for winning in the lottery, ready to take off at once with Mireille on a camping trip *à deux* all over France. Probably the most common cliché the French have about Americans is that they are just *de grands enfants*. By that they mean that Americans seem to be spontaneous, uninhibited in their activities, unburdened by social rules and historical tradition, continually seeking the formation of personality but never quite

124

achieving it because they are always tempted by new opportunities and occasions. This may be why Robert and Marie-Laure are such natural friends and allies, although we can already see in Marie-Laure an independent personality that is fully formed. Americans want children to show their independence through their sense of adventure, through their willingness to move outside the family. For the French, independence means independence of personality and judgment within the circle of the family.

Content and learning objectives of lesson 42

This lesson will familiarize you with ways in which French speakers evaluate situations from good to bad and express the degree to which a given description applies.

The following points are highlighted in lesson 42 (you should concentrate on sections marked with a √):

√ • Fractions (42.11, 42.12)
  • *Pas encore, déjà, dès*
√ • Position of *déjà* and *encore* (42.16, 42.17)
√ • *Plus rien, jamais rien* (42.18–42.21)
√ • Subjunctive with *pourvu que, à moins que, bien que* (42.22–42.27)

ASSIMILATION OF THE TEXT

42.1–42.4 Text work-up, aural comprehension, and oral production

Proceed as usual in these sections. (Refer to lesson 28.1–28.4 for directions, if necessary.) Work with the text of lesson 42 in the textbook, as in previous lessons.

TOWARD COMMUNICATION

42.5, 42.6 Activation: Pronunciation; quality of the vowels /e/, /ɛ/, and /i/ (review)

• Repeat the words and expressions you hear, remembering (1) to pronounce /e/, /ɛ/, and /i/ as distinctly separate sounds, and (2) to keep each vowel constant, not allowing its quality to change as you move to the following consonant.

42.7, 42.8 Observation and activation: Evaluations

After pointing out to Robert that he hasn't won 400,000F after all, Mireille looks at the positive side of the situation. There is nothing wrong with 40,000F: "Ce n'est pas si mal que ça!" Indeed, she finds she can go a little higher than that. In fact, 40,000F is not bad at all: "C'est déjà pas mal!" Chart 42.7 shows how these and related expressions can be used to evaluate a situation in graded terms, from not bad (degree 1) to very good (degree 4).

• In exercise 42.8, you will hear comments about various amounts won in the lottery. Decide whether each applies to a smaller or a larger winning, and mark the appropriate box on the grid in your workbook.

√ Check your answers in key 42.8 at the back of the workbook.

42.9, 42.10 Observation and activation: Degrees

A minute before Robert's call at 7:15 in the morning, Mireille was sound asleep: **complètement** *endormie*. By the time she picks up the phone, she is **à moitié** *endormie*. Chart 42.9 illustrates how *un peu*, *à moitié*, and *complètement* can be used to indicate to what degree a particular description applies to someone or something.

• In exercise 42.10, people don't seem to be hearing, understanding, staying awake, or working very well. Say it's because they're partly incapable of each activity, using *à moitié* and the appropriate adjective from the list in your workbook.

Audio cues (for reference):
42.10 Activation Orale: Degrés

1. Tu crois qu'elle nous entend? Qu'est-ce qu'elle a? Elle n'entend pas?
2. Il ne comprend jamais rien! Mais qu'est-ce qu'il a?
3. Tu dors debout? Tu es mal réveillée ou quoi?
4. Mais qu'est-ce que tu as? Ça ne va pas? Tu travailles trop! Tu es fatigué, hein?

42.11, 42.12 Observation and activation: Fractions

In buying a lottery ticket, Robert has bet that a certain number will win, but he has not taken as big a risk on that number as he might have. He has not bought *un billet* **entier**, which would entitle him to much larger winnings (and would have been more expensive to purchase), but *un* **dixième** *de billet*, which entitles him to only a tenth of the value of the number if it wins, since nine other people have bought its remaining value. Chart 42.11 contains this and other expressions for common fractions.

• In exercise 42.12, decide which of the expressions containing a fraction best answers each of the questions you hear and mark the corresponding box on the grid in your workbook.

√ Check your answers in key 43.12 at the back of the workbook.

42.13-42.15 Observation and activation: As time goes by

Mireille and Robert arranged to meet at the Fontaine Médicis in the Luxembourg Garden at ten. Robert arrived ten minutes early, at 9:50. Mireille showed up ten minutes late, at 10:10. At 10:05, Robert was beginning to get impatient and Mireille had not yet appeared.

Chart 42.13 contains four expressions that are used to refer to these relationships in time:

Pas encore indicates that something anticipated has not yet taken place.

Ne . . . que is used here to stress how late Mireille is: she didn't arrive until 10:10.

Déjà refers to an event that has already taken place or that took place before it was anticipated.

Dès is used here to underline the fact that Robert is early: at 9:50 he was already there, pacing up and down in front of the fountain.

• To complete exercise 42.14, first familiarize yourself with the sentences in the grid in your workbook. Then mark the one that represents the most appropriate response to each of the phrases you hear.

√ Check your answers in key 43.14 at the back of the workbook.

• In exercise 42.15, you will be asked whether various things have or haven't happened yet. Give negative answers, saying that they won't happen until noon. Use *ne . . . que.*

Audio cues (for reference):
42.15 Activation orale: Le temps qui passe; qu'à 10h

1. Ils n'ont pas encore fini?
2. Hubert n'est pas encore arrivé?
3. Mireille n'est pas encore rentrée?

4. Le plombier n'est pas encore venu?
5. Les ouvriers ne sont pas encore passés?

42.16, 42.17   Observation and activation: As time goes by; position of *déjà* and *encore*

You saw in lesson 38 that the expressions of time *jamais*, *toujours*, and *souvent* are placed **after** the verb: after the single verb form in simple tenses ("Je ne vais **jamais** au cinéma"), and after the **auxiliary**—the **conjugated** part of the verb—in compound tenses ("Robert n'est **jamais** venu en France").

The same patterns apply to *déjà* and *encore*, as chart 42.16 demonstrates.

• In exercise 42.17, you will be asked whether you are ready, whether you are dressed, and whether you have done various things. Say no, not yet, using *pas encore*. Be sure to position *pas encore* after the verb (after the auxiliary in the *passé composé*).

Audio cues (for reference):
42.17 Activation orale: Le temps qui passe; place de déjà et encore

1. Alors, ce billet, tu l'as acheté?
2. Tu as payé l'addition?
3. Tu es prête?

4. Vous avez déjeuné?
5. Tu es habillé?
6. Tu as lu le journal?

42.18–42.21   Observation and activation: Negation; *plus rien, jamais rien*

Charts 42.18 and 42.20 show that when *plus* or *jamais* is used with *rien*, *rien* is placed second. Like *plus*, *jamais*, and *rien* separately, *plus rien* and *jamais rien* come after the verb in a simple tense, after the auxiliary in a compound tense.

• In exercise 42.19, familiarize yourself first with the five verbs given in the workbook. Then listen to the statements on the audio recording. Each statement is about a person who has given up a certain activity. Decide which verb from the list corresponds to that activity and respond, using the appropriate verb and *plus rien*.

Audio cues (for reference):
42.19 Activation orale: Négation; plus rien

1. Il est au régime.
2. Elle fait des économies.
3. Je me tais.

4. Elle a absolument tout oublié.
5. Il est devenue stupide, le pauvre.
6. Elle est retraitée.

● In 42.21, you will be asked if you have ever ordered, bought, found, or won anything in various situations. Say you never have, using *jamais rien*. When a place is mentioned, replace it with *y*.

Audio cues (for reference):
42.21 Activation orale: Négation; jamais rien

1. Est-ce que vous avez déjà pris quelque chose chez Angélina?
2. Vous avez déjà acheté quelque chose à Prisunic?
3. Tu as déjà trouvé quelque chose dans la rue?
4. Vous avez déjà gagné quelque chose?

42.22–42.25 Observation and activation: Subjunctive after *pourvu que* and *à moins que*

Robert tells Mireille to choose any lottery ticket she likes—as long as the last two numbers add up to nine: "**pourvu que** les deux derniers chiffres **fassent** neuf." After they win, he tells her he's not interested in a trip to South America—unless she comes along: "**à moins que** tu **viennes**." The expressions *pourvu que* and *à moins que* are used with the **subjunctive** to indicate a condition that is presented as necessary (Mireille may not choose any ticket she likes if the last two digits don't add up to nine) but at the same time speculative (Robert has no guarantee that such a lottery ticket exists).

Pourvu que expresses a positive condition: other things will or will not happen if the condition **is** present.

A moins que expresses a negative condition: something else will or won't happen if the condition **is not** present.

● In exercise 42.24, various things will come to pass if certain circumstances are present. Restate each circumstance as a positive condition, using *pourvu que* and the subjunctive.

Audio cues (for reference):
42.24 Activation orale: Condition négative; pourvu que

1. J'irai explorer l'Amazone si tu viens.   4. J'irai si vous m'accompagnez.
2. J'irai si vous venez.   5. Elle ira si ça vaut la peine.
3. Il ira si elle y va aussi.   6. Je viendrai s'il fait beau.

● In 42.25, you are not interested unless certain circumstances are present. Restate each circumstance as a negative condition, using *à moins que* and the subjunctive.

Audio cues (for reference):
42.25 Activation orale: Condition négative; à moins que

1. Ça ne m'intéresse pas si tu ne viens pas.
2. Ça ne m'intéresse pas s'il ne vient pas.
3. Ça ne m'intéresse pas si vous ne venez pas.
4. Ça ne m'intéresse pas si on ne peut pas se baigner.
5. Ça ne m'interesse pas si on ne fait pas de camping.

42.26, 42.27 Observation and activation: Restriction; *bien que*

Mireille suggests a number of outlandish ways for Robert to spend his lottery windfall. Now that he has a little cash to spare, she takes advantage of the opportunity to poke fun at his refusal to identify with his banker father. She proposes that he spend his money on an expensive mistress, following the example of the aristocrats and *nouveau riche* bourgeois bankers of the nineteenth century . . . although, she adds, that isn't done much any more: ". . . **bien que** ça ne se **fasse** plus beaucoup." Mireille uses the expression *bien que* to express a restriction. Notice that with *bien que*, as with *pourvu que* and *à moins que*, a verb in the **subjunctive** is used.

● In exercise 42.27, a number of things are possible, but there are certain obstacles to each one. Restate the obstacles as restrictions, using *bien que* and the subjunctive.

Audio cues (for reference):
42.27 Activation orale: Restriction; bien que

1. Tu pourrais entretenir une danseuse, mais ça ne se fait plus beaucoup.
2. On pourrait aller explorer l'Amazone, mais on ne peut pas s'y baigner.
3. On pourrait remonter l'Amazone, mais c'est un peu dangereux.
4. On pourrait faire un voyage en France. Mais je connais déjà un peu!
5. On pourrait faire du camping, mais je n'ai pas de tente.

42.28 Activation: Dialogue between Robert and Mireille

Listen to the conversation between Robert and Mireille and memorize Mireille's lines, imitating and repeating as usual.

● **Suggested oral assignment.** Record the dialogue in 42.28, identifying each character before you say his or her lines. Send this assignment to your instructor (see the course syllabus for details).

TOWARD FREE EXPRESSION

42.29 Words at large

Proceed as usual. (If necessary, refer to lesson 27 for directions.)

42.30-42.32 Role-playing and reinvention of the story

In 42.30, Robert suggests that he and Mireille spend their lottery winnings on travel. Mireille is not as enthusiastic as Robert and raises a number of objections. Imagine the dialogue.

In 42.31, say what you would do if you won the lottery.

In 42.32, make up a series of maxims using Marie-Laure's example as a model.

● **Suggested written assignment.** Write out the description of what you would do if you won the lottery (exercise 42.31). Write fifty to seventy-five words. Send this assignment to your instructor (see the course syllabus for details).

OPTIONAL EXERCISES FOR WRITING PRACTICE

● Listen again to exercises 42.15, 42.19, and 42.24 on the audio recording and write out the audio cues you hear.

√ Check what you have written against the printed text in the study guide.

SELF-TESTING EXERCISES

● Complete and check exercises 42.33, 42.34, and 42.35 as usual.

SUMMARY QUIZ

Consult the course syllabus or check with your instructor for information about completing and handing in summary quiz 42.

LESSON 43
Think vacation I

The story

In a department store. The goldfish salesman can't help, except to direct them to the right department. The camping man shows them a tent, backpacks, and, since Robert has foolishly left his at home, some sleeping bags. The salesman obviously knows the stock well and gives lots of details. Mireille says they'll think it over and come back. Robert needs all kinds of clothing. Mireille tells him to buy his briefs himself and leaves to meet Hubert. She and Robert will talk on the phone. When? Anytime.

On the street, she is accosted by Jean-Pierre who, apparently up to his old tricks, asks her for a light. Not recognizing him at first, she gives him ten francs (much too much) and tells him to buy some matches. He claims not to be surprised that she won the lottery. He isn't superstitious (not much!), but broken glass always brings luck. In answer to Mireille's questions he reveals that he would never walk under a ladder, that he throws salt over his left shoulder after a spill, and that he squishes spiders in the morning, when they are supposed to be most unlucky.

Ironically, Jean-Pierre really does hurt his leg outside the building at number thirteen. We can be pretty sure of that because he says his no-no again. Mireille gives him no sympathy. She departs, saying that tricks like that don't work on her. Serves the creep right.

Notes on culture and communication

• **Body language and social background.** Verbal and nonverbal communication cannot be separated. The voice is produced by the body, and one cannot talk without the whole body participating. However, the amount of body activity and the degree of participation of each part of the body vary according to personality, social background, geographic region, and nationality. "Well-bred" French people are taught not to gesture excessively. Note the difference in body movement when Hubert speaks and when Jean-Pierre speaks. Even without hearing a word he says, one can tell by Hubert's body control that he comes from an upper-class family. On the other hand, Jean-Pierre, *le dragueur*, uses his facial muscles and arms in a most exaggerated manner. For Americans learning French, this exaggeration offers a useful model. As Mireille and Jean-Pierre walk along the rue Saint-Honoré, study Jean-Pierre's behavior carefully and in slow motion if possible. In this short conversation you can observe a caricature of French communication. Do not imitate the manner of Jean-Pierre literally, but if you can get a feeling for it, you may be able to use it in a more genteel, Hubert-like manner. You will learn the basic tension and rhythm of French and be able to avoid the slackness of body and speech that the French observe in Americans.

Content and learning objectives of lesson 43

This lesson presents ways of talking about trips of various kinds. It also shows ways in which French speakers refer to the relationship between the price of an item and its quality.

The following points are highlighted in lesson 43 (you should concentrate on sections marked with a √):

√• Comparatives and superlatives (43.15-43.18)
√• Superlative and subjunctive (43.19, 43.20)

ASSIMILATION OF THE TEXT

43.1-43.4 Text work-up, aural comprehension, and oral production

Proceed as usual in these sections. (Refer to lesson 28.1-28.4 for directions, if necessary.) Work with the text of lesson 43 in the textbook, as in previous lessons.

TOWARD COMMUNICATION

43.5 Activation: Pronunciation; tonic stress (review)

Recall the basic pattern of tonic stress in French: there is a slight stress on the last syllable of a rhythmic group. (This stress is produced by lengthening slightly the vowel sound of the final syllable of the group.) There is no stress inside a word or a rhythmic group.

• Repeat the words and expressions you hear, placing a very light stress on the final syllable of each rhythmic group, **and nowhere else.**

43.6, 43.7 Observation and activation: Trips long and short

Chart 43.6 presents vocabulary used to refer to various kinds of outings, from brief swings around the Luxembourg Garden to lengthy journeys to faraway places.

The expression used is determined by the relative length of the trip: a one-hour trip through Paris on a *bateau-mouche* would be *une promenade*, a day's sail along the coast of Brittany would be *une excursion*, and a slow freighter to Patagonia would be *un voyage*.

The chart also shows the means of transportation most often associated with each expression. Note that *une randonnée* refers to a trip involving physical exercise in the open air.

• In exercise 43.7, determine from the context what kinds of trips are referred to in each sentence, then complete the sentence with the most appropriate expression.

√ Check your answers in key 43.7 at the back of the workbook.

43.8, 43.9 Observation and activation: Divisions

Upon arriving at the fifth floor (*quatrième étage*) of the Samaritaine, Robert and Mireille ask a salesperson for help in selecting camping equipment. He sends them to another part of the store, explaining that he is in the goldfish department: "Je suis au **rayon** des poissons rouges." Chart 43.8 gives the units into which various geographical entities and buildings are divided in France, from the country itself, which is divided into nearly a hundred administrative regions, or *départements* (roughly comparable to American states), and Paris, which is divided into twenty *arrondissements*, to apartment buildings and department stores.

• In exercise 43.9, decide what kind of subdivision is referred to in each sentence, then complete the sentence with the appropriate expression.

√ Check your answers in key 43.9 at the back of the workbook.

43.10-43.12 Observation and activation: Competence and incompetence

The goldfish salesperson says he can't help Mireille and Robert because camping isn't his department: "Ce n'est pas mon rayon." He uses the expression *mon rayon* literally, but it can be used figuratively as well to indicate that you are knowledgeable about something (*c'est mon rayon*) or, on the contrary, that you know nothing about it (*ce n'est pas mon rayon*).

The verb *s'y connaître* can also be used to indicate degrees of knowledgeability, as chart 43.10 demonstrates.

Note that the expression *je n'y connais rien*, without the reflexive pronoun, stresses one's complete ignorance of a subject.

● In exercise 43.11, various people are asked for help of various kinds. Respond by saying that that's really not their department, using the stressed pronoun (*moi, toi, lui, elle,* and so forth) and the corresponding form of *mon rayon*.

Audio cues (for reference):
43.11 Activation orale: Compétence et incompétence

1. Vous pourriez m'aider à programmer cette saloperie d'ordinateur qui ne veut pas marcher?
2. Ma voiture refuse de démarrer. Vous pourriez m'aider?
3. Avec un rôti de porc, qu'est-ce que je devrais servir comme vin, un Bourgogne ou un Bordeaux?
4. Je voudrais acheter du matériel de camping. Vous pourriez me conseiller?
5. Qu'est-ce que c'est, cette nouvelle cuisine dont on parle partout? Vous pouvez me dire?
6. Je voudrais choisir des chaussures pour faire une randonnée. Vous pourriez m'aider?
7. Nous cherchons une station de ski sympathique mais pas trop chère. Vous pourriez nous renseigner?

● In 43.12, you have been asked for help in various areas and you direct the questioner to the people who have the necessary expertise. Add that they know a lot about the subject, using *s'y connaître*.

Audio cues (for reference):
43.12 Activation orale: Compétence et incompétence

1. Vous voulez acheter un poisson rouge pour votre fille? Demandez à Jean-Luc....
2. Votre voiture ne veut pas démarrer? Demandez à Ousmane!
3. Vous cherchez un livre d'art pour l'anniversaire de votre cousine? Vous n'avez qu'à demander à Mireille.
4. Vous voulez refaire le toit de votre maison? Il faut demander aux Belleau....
5. Vous voulez choisir un bon Bordeaux? Il faut me demander, à moi!

43.13, 43.14 Observation and activation: Price/quality ratios

Chart 43.13 shows how speakers of French refer to the relationship between the quality of an article and its price.

The first part of the chart contains expressions that refer to items on sale at a reduced price: *c'est* **en solde**, *c'est* **soldé**. Depending on their cost, some sale items are good deals (*c'est* **une bonne occasion**), others are real bargains (*c'est* **une excellente affaire!**).

● In exercise 43.14, complete the sentences by writing in the words you hear.

√ Check your answers in key 43.14 at the back of the workbook.

43.15-43.16 Observation and activation: Comparison; comparatives and superlatives

Chart 43.15 shows how the comparative and superlative of adjectives are formed, and how they are used in comparisons.

When two objects are compared in terms of a single quality (for example, sleeping bags in terms of price), three kinds of **comparatives** are possible. One sleeping bag can be more expensive than the other, it can be less expensive, or, if they are the same price, it can be as expensive. In French, these relationships are expressed by *plus*, *moins*, or *aussi* placed **before** the adjective. Notice that the adjective describing the term being compared is followed by *que* and the term **to which** it is being compared: "Il est moins cher **que l'autre.**"

In the **superlative**, only two kinds of degrees are possible. A sleeping bag can be either the most or the least expensive of a given group of sleeping bags. In the superlative, *plus* and *moins* are preceded by the **definite article** that stands for the term being compared, and the adjective is followed by *de* or *des* and the term to which it is being compared: "C"est **le** moins cher **de tous.**"

• In exercise 43.16, determine the relationships described in the sentences you see and complete each sentence by writing the appropriate comparative or superlative.

√ Check your answers in key 43.16 at the back of the workbook.

43.17-43.20 Observation and activation: Superlatives; superlative and subjunctive

Charts 43.17 and 43.19 give examples of constructions in which superlatives are used in an absolute sense, with no mention of a specific context in which the term being referred to is best or worst, most expensive or cheapest, and so on. The implication is that there is **nothing** better, worse, more expensive, etc., to be found anywhere. "**C'est ce qu'**il y a de mieux" and "**c'est ce qu'**on fait de mieux" indicate that it is simply the best there is or the best that's made, period.

Note, in chart 43.19, how the **subjunctive** may be used to modify or limit the applicability of a superlative expression. "Ce sont les derniers **que nous ayons**" does not suggest that they are the last ones anywhere; it merely says that within the frame of reference of the ones we have, they are the last.

• In 43.18, you will hear that nobody makes anything worse or better, or
that that there is none worse, better, more beautiful, or more expensive. Say
it's the worst or best that's made, or it's the most beautiful, or most
expensive there is, using *c'est ce qu'on fait* or *c'est ce qu'il y a* and the
superlative.

Audio cues (for reference):
43.18 Activation orale: Superlatifs

1. On ne fait pas pire!
2. On ne fait pas mieux!
3. Il n'y a pas mieux!
4. Il n'y a pas pire!

5. Il n'y a pas plus beau!
6. Il n'y a pas plus cher!
7. Il n'y a pas moins cher!

• In 43.20, you will hear that no better, more luxurious, cheaper, or
more attractive accomodations are to be found, in the speaker's opinion. Say
they are the best, most luxurious, etc., within this limited frame of reference,
using the superlative and the subjunctive.

Audio cues (for reference):
43.20 Activation orale: Superlatif et subjonctif

1. Je ne connais pas de meilleur hôtel.
2. Il ne connaît pas d'hôtel plus luxueux.
3. Nous ne connaissons pas de meilleur restaurant.
4. Vous ne pouvez pas trouver de chambre moins chère.
5. Nous n'avons pas de plus belle chambre.

43.21, 43.22 Observation and activation: Insufficiency

Robert has come to France unprepared to go camping; as he points out,
he has nothing more than a bathing suit: "**Tout ce que** j'ai, c'est un maillot
de bain." Chart 43.21 shows how the expression *tout ce que* is used to
express insufficiency.

• In exercise 43.22, you question various people about what they have,
what's left, and what they know, and they tell you the situation is more
limited than you expected. Ask if that's all they have, all that's left, or all
they know, using *tout ce que.*

Audio cues (for reference):
43.22 Activation orale: Insuffisance

1. --Qu'est-ce que vous avez comme vin?
   --Du Beaujolais.
2. --Qu'est-ce que vous avez comme viande?

--Du rôti de porc.

3. --Qu'est-ce que vous avez comme légumes?

--Des haricots verts.

4. --Il vous reste du fromage?

--Un peu de camembert.

5. --Qu'est-ce que tu connais comme jeu de cartes?

--Euh...la belote.

6. --Tu as de l'argent?

--10 francs.

43.23 Activation: Dialogue between Mireille and Jean-Pierre

Listen to the conversation between Mireille and Jean-Pierre and memo-rize Jean-Pierre's lines, imitating and repeating as usual.

TOWARD FREE EXPRESSION

43.24 Words at large

Proceed as usual. (If necessary, refer to lesson 27 for directions.)

43.25-43.27 Role-playing and reinvention of the story

In 43.25, reconstruct the dialogue between Robert and the salesperson in the sporting goods department.

In 43.26, Jean-Pierre runs into Mireille, who has just won at the lottery. Reconstruct the dialogue.

In 43.27, Mireille has decided to leave with Robert and is telling her mother. Imagine the dialogue.

• **Suggested written assignment.** Write out the dialogue between Mireille and her mother in 43.27. Write ten sentences. Send this assignment to your instructor (see the course syllabus for details).

OPTIONAL EXERCISES FOR WRITING PRACTICE

• Listen again to exercises 43.20 and 43.22 on the audio recording and write out the audio cues you hear.

√ Check what you have written against the printed text in the study guide.

SELF-TESTING EXERCISES

• Complete and check exercises 43.28, 43.29, and 43.30 as usual.

SUMMARY QUIZ

Consult the course syllabus or check with your instructor for information about completing and handing in summary quiz 43.

LESSON 44
Think vacation II

The story

At the tea-room, we learn that Hubert is vehemently opposed to the national lottery. He says it discourages industry and thrift and rewards laziness and dependence on luck. He himself bets on the horses, but that's different. He's contributing to the improvement of the equine race.

Meanwhile, Robert, trying to buy shoes, has a misunderstanding with a salesman about sizes.

Aunt Georgette finds, in Mireille's account of the lottery win, an opportunity to gripe about her own situation. Then, waxing nostalgic as they cull lentils, she tells Mireille about a beautiful young man with whom she once planned to open a dog-grooming salon.

It was the hostility of Mireille's parents that killed both the project and the romance. Georgette's suggestion for using the lottery money is a donation to the French SPA (the SPCA for Minouches and Fidos) and some help with her own pet project, a dog cemetery.

Back at the store, Robert tries on a pair of the kind of shoes he needs. The right one fits perfectly, but the left is too tight. They won't sell him just one shoe, so he takes the pair. That does it! We are definitely not going to give him the "Shrewd Shopper of the Week" award.

Notes on culture and communication

• **Le Tiercé** is a form of state-controlled horse betting in which, to win, one picks the first three horses to come in—either at random or in the order in which they actually finish (in which case the winnings are higher).

• **French faces.** This is a perfect episode in which to study French facial expression because the camera stays focused on Hubert, Robert, and Georgette. Besides, the idea of winning the lottery evokes strong emotions and naturally encourages strong facial expression.

Stirred by the very idea that working people could make money by chance instead of by hard work, Hubert loses his usual control over expression. His lips tighten, his shoulders and head move forward aggressively, his

141

eyebrows rise, his eyelids tighten, and his forehead wrinkles. His lips move energetically to extreme positions, especially on the words *honte* and *chance*. Studying Hubert, you can see how actively French speakers use their lips.

Content and learning objectives of lesson 44

This lesson shows ways in which speakers of French announce news, give advice, and indicate similarity or dissimilarity.

The following points are highlighted in lesson 44 (you should concentrate on sections marked with a √):

√ • Subjunctive indicating purpose (44.14, 44.15)
√ • Subjunctive and implicit negation (44.16–44.18)
  • Demonstrative pronouns, review
√ • Relative pronouns *ce qui*, *ce que*, *ce qu'* (44.20–44.24)

ASSIMILATION OF THE TEXT

44.1–44.4 Text work-up, aural comprehension, and oral production

Proceed as usual in these sections. (Refer to lesson 28.1–28.4 for directions, if necessary.) Work with the text of lesson 44 in the textbook, as in previous lessons.

TOWARD COMMUNICATION

44.5, 44.6 Observation and activation: Pronunciation; don't let your consonants explode!

Recall from lesson 26 that in English, the consonant sounds /p/, /k/, and /t/ tend to be followed by a release of air, a little puff of breath that comes between the consonant sound and the following vowel sound, making the consonant slightly percussive: p*ike*, t*ake*, c*ool*. This puff of air is not heard, however, when the /p/, /k/, and /t/ sounds are preceded by *s:* sp*ike*, st*ake*, sc*hool*.

French /p/, /k/, and /t/ are never followed by a puff of breath. In this respect, they are similar to the corresponding sounds in *spike*, *stake*, and *school*.

• Repeat the words and expressions you hear in exercise 44.6 as you look at them in the workbook. Say the vowel sound immediately after the consonant printed in *italics*, with no puff of air in between.

44.7, 44.8 Observation and activation: Announcing news

Chart 44.7 presents a number of expressions used by French speakers to draw the attention of others to some interesting bit of news they have to announce and to react to such announcements. The announcements range from simple queries ("Vous savez?") through more tantalizing questions ("Tu sais la nouvelle?") to intriguing challenges ("Vous n'allez pas me croire!"), depending on how unexpected (or unbelievable) the information to be communicated is.

In responding, one may be inquisitive ("Quoi?"), impatient at being left in the dark ("Comment veux-tu que je le sache?"), or excitedly curious ("Dis-le moi tout de suite!").

• In exercise 44.8, decide whether each expression you hear represents an announcement or a reaction, and mark the corresponding box on the grid in your workbook.

√ Check your answers in key 44.8 at the back of the workbook.

44.9-44.11 Observation and activation: Miscellaneous advice; *suggérer, proposer, conseiller, recommander*

Chart 44.9 presents four verbs and the corresponding nouns that are used to introduce a piece of advice. These four expressions are ranked according to the strength with which the person offering advice believes in it and expects it to be followed.

Suggérer indicates advice to which the giver is not strongly committed and that the recipient is free to accept or reject.

Proposer suggests a course of action that the proposer favors and is submitting for the recipient's approval in the expectation that it will be followed.

Conseiller is used to introduce advice given by people who have some knowledge or experience of the matter at hand; it represents a considered judgment that the giver believes is in the recipient's best interest.

Recommander indicates strong encouragement toward a course of action that the person making the recommendation has already experienced personally and found worthwhile.

Notice that all four verbs may be used with *de* and an infinitive to refer to the course of action being advised. Note, too, the noun that corresponds to each verb. *Suggestion*, *proposition*, and *recommandation* are introduced by *faire*, but *conseil* is used with *donner*.

• In exercise 44.10, decide whether the statements you hear represent suggestions, proposals, advice, or recommendations, and mark the appropriate box on the grid.

√ Check your answers in key 44.10 at the back of the workbook.

• In 44.11, complete the second part of each sentence with the appropriate form of the verb that corresponds to the noun you see in the first part.

√ Check your answers in key 44.11 at the back of the workbook.

44.12, 44.13 Observation and activation: Discrimination

When Hubert denounces the immorality of the lottery, Mireille reminds him that he himself plays the horses. That's different, he says: "Ce n'est pas la même chose!" Chart 44.12 presents this and other expressions that are used to indicate dissimilarity and similarity.

• In exercise 44.13, you will hear a series of statements. Decide whether they refer to dissimilarity (*différence*) or similarity (*pas de différence*), and mark the appropriate box on the grid.

√ Check your answers in key 44.13 at the back of the workbook.

44.14, 44.15 Observation and activation: The subjunctive used to indicate purpose

The shoe salesman at the Samaritaine tells Robert to sit down so he can measure his feet: "Asseyez-vous **que je prenne** vos mesures." Chart 44.14 shows how the subjunctive is used after *pour que* or *que* by itself to indicate intent or purpose.

Asseyez-vous is the main message the salesman wishes to get across, and so it is said to be in the **main clause** of the sentence. The salesman's reason for telling Robert to sit down is subordinate to his main objective, and so the subjunctive *prenne* is said to be in a **subordinate clause**.

The subordinate clause is introduced by *que*. Most of the subjunctives you have encountered occur in subordinate clauses introduced by *que* (see lessons 36, 39, 41, 42, and 43). Like most subjunctives, *prenne* is a projec-

tion. It does not indicate that the taking of Robert's measurements is
actually happening or about to happen; it expresses the salesman's **intention**.

• In exercise 44.15, you will hear people told to do various things,
followed by an explanation of the reason why. Restate each command and
express the reason as an intention, using *que* and the subjunctive.

Audio cues (for reference):
44.15 Activation orale: Subjonctif indiquant le but

1. Venez! Je veux vous dire quelque chose.
2. Téléphonez-moi! Je veux savoir ce qui se passe.
3. Approche-toi! Je veux te dire un secret.
4. Venez! Je veux pouvoir vous parler.
5. Asseyez-vous! Je veux prendre vos mesures.
6. Prévenez-moi! Je veux partir en même temps que vous.

44.16–44.18 Observation and activation: The subjunctive and implicit negation

In lesson 43.19, you saw how the subjunctive can be used to limit the
applicability of superlative expressions. "C'est le dernier **que nous ayons**"
indicates that within the limited category of what we have, the item we're
talking about is the last.

Chart 44.16 shows how expressions such as this are based on **negative**
assumptions: that we have **no** other or more beautiful item, that there is
nothing more immoral than the *loto* and the *tiercé*, and so forth.

• In exercise 44.17, you are asked whether you and others have other
things, know other people and languages, or carry other styles. Answer
negatively, saying those are the only ones you (or they) have, know, or carry.
Use *ce sont les seul(e)s* + noun + *que* and the appropriate form of the
subjunctive.

Audio cues (for reference):
44.17 Activation orale: Subjonctif et négation implicite

1. Vous avez d'autres bottes?
2. Tu as d'autres chaussures?
3. Vous avez d'autres lunettes?
4. Mireille connaît d'autres Américains?
5. Robert sait d'autres langues étrangères que le français?
6. Ils font d'autres modèles?

• In 44.18, you will be asked what or who, apart from certain things and
people, is such and such or does so and so. Reply negatively, saying that

nothing is or no one does. Use *il n'y a que* + noun + *qui* and the appropriate form of the subjunctive.

Audio cues (for reference):
44.18 Activation orale: Subjonctif et négation implicite

1. A part les films muets, qu'est-ce qui est intéressant?
2. A part les pataugas, qu'est-ce qui plaît à Robert?
3. A part les touristes, qui est-ce qui prend les bateaux-mouches?
4. A part Hubert, qui est-ce qui est contre la loterie nationale?
5. A part Mireille, qui est-ce qui fait du karaté dans la famille?
6. A part Robert, qui est-ce qui sait l'anglais dans le groupe?
7. A part Mireille, qui est-ce qui connaît le musée de Chartres?

44.19 Activation: Demonstrative pronouns (review)

• In exercise 44.19, supply the appropriate forms of the demonstrative pronoun (*celui*, *celle*, *ceux*, or *celles*—see lesson 13).

√ Check your answers in key 44.19 at the back of the workbook.

44.20–44.24 Observation and activation: Relative pronouns

You saw in lesson 24 that the relative pronouns *qui* and *que* can refer to either people or things. *Qui* functions as the **subject** of the verb that follows it. *Que* functions as the **direct object** of the verb that follows it.

Recall that the people or things *qui* and *que* refer to are known as their **antecedents**. In "vous pouvez acheter **la voiture que** vous voulez," the antecedent of *que* is *la voiture*.

Chart 44.20 introduces the use of *qui* and *que* with an antecedent that is not specified. With an unlimited bank balance, you can buy not just the boots you want or the car you want but **whatever** you want: "Vous pouvez acheter **ce que** vous voulez."

The pronoun *ce* is used to refer not to a precise thing but to a vague, limitless expanse of possibilities. It can be extended even further by adding *tout*: "Robert croit **tout ce que** Mireille lui dit."

• Exercise 44.21 will help you review the use of *qui* and *que* with specific antecedents. You will hear pairs of sentences that recount events from the story of Mireille and Robert. What is being talked about in the first sentence is mentioned again in the second sentence. Decide whether it is the **subject** or the **object** of the verb in the second sentence, then combine the two sentences into one, using *qui* or *que* (*qu'*).

Audio cues (for reference):
44.21 Activation orale: Pronoms relatifs: qui, que (qu')

1. Mireille a rencontré un jeune homme. Il s'appelle Robert.
2. Robert a vu des manifestants au Quartier Latin. Il les a suivis.
3. Robert a écrit une lettre. Il l'a envoyée à sa mère.
4. Les Belleau ont une maison de campagne. Elle est près de Dreux.
5. Hubert a envoyé des roses à Mme Belleau. Elle les a bien reçues.
6. Robert et Mireille ont acheté un billet de loterie. Ce billet a gagné 40.000 F.
7. Robert a trouvé des chaussures. Elles sont très bien.
8. Mireille a beaucoup d'amis étrangers. Elle les a rencontrés à la Sorbonne.
9. La mère de Robert a une amie à Paris. Cette amie est aussi la marraine de Mireille.
10. Robert et Mireille ont vu un film de Rohmer. Ce film leur a beaucoup plu.

• In 44.22, if something tempts, pleases, doesn't please, or amuses Robert and Mireille, they buy, discard, or do it. Say they buy, discard, or do whatever tempts, pleases, doesn't please, or amuses them, using *ce qui*.

Audio cues (for reference):
44.22 Activation orale: Pronoms relatifs; ce qui

1. Si quelque chose tente Robert, il l'achète.
2. Si quelque chose ne plaît pas à Robert, il le jette.
3. Si quelque chose plaît à Robert, il le fait.
4. Si quelque chose plaît à Robert et Mireille, ils le font.
5. Si quelque chose amuse Mireille, elle l'achète.
6. Si quelque chose plaît à Mireille, Robert l'achète.

• In 44.23, if various people say something, others believe it; if they see something, they buy it; if they hear something, they repeat it, and so forth. Say they believe, buy, repeat, etc., everything that they or others say, see, hear, etc., using *tout ce que* (*tout ce qu'*).

Audio cues (for reference):
44.23 Activation orale: Pronoms relatifs; ce que, (ce qu')

1. Si Mireille dit quelque chose, Robert le croit.
2. Si Robert voit quelque chose, il l'achète.
3. Si Marie-Laure entend quelque chose, elle le répète.
4. Si on donne quelque chose à Robert, il le perd.
5. Si on dit quelque chose à Robert, il l'oublie.

• In 44.24, decide whether the thing referred to is the **subject** or the **object** of the last verb in the sentence, and write *ce qui* or *ce que* (*ce qu'*), as appropriate.

√ Check your answers in key 44.24 at the back of the workbook.

44.25 Activation: Dialogue between Mireille and Hubert

Listen to the conversation between Mireille and Hubert and memorize Hubert's lines, imitating and repeating as usual.

TOWARD FREE EXPRESSION

44.26 Words at large

Proceed as usual. (If necessary, refer to lesson 27 for directions.)

44.27, 44.28 Role-playing and reinvention of the story

In 44.27, reconstruct two dialogues: the discussion Robert has with the shoe salesman (part A) and Mireille's conversation with Tante Georgette (part B).

In 44.28, invent a new version of Tante Georgette's love story.

• **Suggested oral assignment.** Record Georgette's monologue in 44.28. Say ten to twelve sentences. Send this assignment to your instructor (see the course syllabus for details).

OPTIONAL EXERCISE FOR WRITING PRACTICE

• Listen again to exercise 44.21 on the audio recording and write out the audio cues you hear.

√ Check what you have written against the printed text in the study guide.

SELF-TESTING EXERCISES

• Complete and check exercises 44.29, 44.30, and 44.31 as usual.

SUMMARY QUIZ

Consult the course syllabus or check with your instructor for information about completing and handing in summary quiz 44.

LESSON 45
Think vacation III

The story

Uncle Guillaume invites Mireille to tea to celebrate her win. In quick succession, he shoots down Aunt Georgette's doggy plan, Aunt Pauline's wish to sell Mireille her old car, and Cousin Philippe's suggestion that she buy stocks. Guillaume's notion is that she should spend her loot on a series of splendid meals in the great restaurants of Paris. If she's concerned about her liver, he names several mineral waters that will help cleanse her system.

At this point, Mireille admits, for the first time, that she is probably going to take a trip around France with Robert. Meanwhile, that young man is still in the store, still making less-than-judicious purchases. He rationalizes a ridiculously bright jacket by saying he'll be visible from a distance and so will be less likely to get lost. Then he buys a pair of pants without trying them on. After an Abbott and Costello routine on the word *slip* (which refers to briefs in French, not to women's slips), he leaves.

It would be hard to imagine a more bizarre taxi driver than the one who seems to be waiting for Robert. Eyes blinking in time with erratic pressure on the accelerator, he takes off in the wrong direction. Robert jumps out at a slow spot (his first sign of brain activity in a few hours) and the cab speeds off, its turn signals flashing in Morse code.

Notes on culture and communication

• **L'Exode de 40.** Uncle Guillaume is referring to the southward flight of the French civilian population in World War II as German troops advanced on Paris in May and June of 1940.

• **Une cure d'eau de Vichy.** Vichy mineral water is renowned as an aid to digestion and in the treatment of stomach and liver diseases. This is why Uncle Guillaume suggests Vichy water to remedy the side-effects of a gastronomic tour of the three-star restaurants of Paris.

• **Depuis Pétain.** Mireille is being facetious when she tells Uncle Guillaume that her father has banned Vichy mineral water from the Belleaus' dinner table. She is alluding to the period between July 10, 1940, and August 20, 1944, during World War II when the French government, headed by Marshall Pétain, moved from Paris to the famous spa of Vichy in the Massif

150

Central. The Vichy government has remained a very controversial period in French history because of its policy on cooperation and collaboration with the Nazis.

   • **The individual versus the French family.** As our view of Mireille's family life becomes clearer we see how tight and complicated it is. Mireille feels very close to her aunts and uncles and cousins. She has asked the advice of several of them as to how the lottery money should be spent. She enjoys the excitement of sharing her amusing news with them. Traditionally, members of a French family have a significant influence on each other's lives. Remember Aunt Georgette's bewailing the fact that Mireille's father had broken up the only great romance she ever had. (An American would wonder what business he had meddling in her love life.) Sometimes the tyranny of families is more than even the French can bear: witness the French writer André Gide's cry, "Familles, je vous hais!"

Content and learning objectives of lesson 45

   This lesson shows ways in which French speakers express ignorance, talk about finances and handling money, refer to typical behavior and close resemblance, express satisfaction, and talk about suitability.

   The following points are highlighted in lesson 45 (you should concentrate on sections marked with a √):

   √• *Personne* and *rien* in simple tenses, review and extension (45.16–45.19)
   √• Use of the subjunctive in relative clauses (45.20–45.22)

ASSIMILATION OF THE TEXT

45.1–45.4 Text work-up, aural comprehension, and oral production

   Proceed as usual in these sections. (Refer to lesson 28.1–28.4 for directions, if necessary.) Work with the text of lesson 45 in the textbook, as in previous lessons.

TOWARD COMMUNICATION

45.5, 45.6 Observation and activation: Pronunciation; the consonant /r/ (review)

   Although the /r/ sound is made in the back of the mouth, what happens in the front of the mouth as it is being said is equally important. To produce a French /r/, the tip of the tongue lies lightly against the lower

teeth. In a word that contains an /r/ sound after another vowel or consonant sound, it is important that the tongue return to its position against the
lower teeth for /r/. This is especially critical when /r/ follows the consonant sound /t/, as in *travail* or *trois*. For the /t/ sound, the tongue is
pressed against the ridge behind **upper** teeth. Remember to bring it back
against the **lower** teeth for /r/.

• In exercise 45.6, repeat the words and expressions you hear, as usual.

45.7 Observation: Ignorance

Chart 45.7 groups a number of expressions that French speakers use
when they do not know something. (*Ignorer* and *ignorance* refer to lack of
information, not refusal to pay attention or lack of education.) The expressions related to *je ne sais pas* and *je n'ai aucune idée* are arranged from
least emphatic to most emphatic, from simple lack of knowledge to complete
bafflement. The more emphatic the expression, the more it can suggest
uninvolvement or denial of responsibility as well. Robert, telling the salesman
he doesn't know his waist size, says simply, "Je ne sais pas." Marie-Laure,
trying to duck responsibility for getting jam on the tablecloth, would be more
emphatic: "Je n'ai pas la moindre idée!"

Je ne saurais vous le dire is a polite or formal way to say you don't
know something.

Je me le demande and the expressions related to it suggest perplexity or
curiosity in addition to lack of information.

45.8, 45.9 Observation and activation: The subject is money

The examples and the chart in 45.8 bring together basic expressions that
relate to finances and the handling of money.

Gagner, as the examples show, can refer to the process of making money
or earning one's livelihood (**gagner** *de l'argent*, **gagner** *sa vie*) and to winning
at the lottery (**gagner** *à la loterie*).

Once one has cash in hand and the decision is made not to spend it or
give it away but to hang onto it, one can be thrifty (*économiser*, *épargner*)
and put it into a bank account, or one can invest it in various ways (*placer*,
investir), including in the stock market (*acheter des actions à la Bourse*).

The chart shows the nouns that correspond to the verbs of money
management used in the examples.

• In exercise 45.9, decide from the context of each sentence which of the expressions in chart 45.8 is most appropriate, and write the missing word. In practice, all you need to do in the first five sentences is supply the noun that corresponds to a money-management verb used earlier in the sentence. In number six, however, you will need to supply a verb.

√ Check your answers in key 45.9 at the back of the workbook.

45.10, 45.11 Observation and activation: Typical behavior; resemblance

When Mireille tells Uncle Guillaume that his sister has urged her to donate money to a pet cemetery, he says that is just like Georgette: "C'est Georgette tout craché!" Chart 45.10 shows how this expression can be used to refer to typical behavior and in situations where one person bears an uncanny resemblance to another. Notice that either a person's name (*c'est* **Robert** *tout craché*) or a stressed pronoun (*c'est* **lui** *tout craché*) comes after *c'est*.

• In some of the sentences in exercise 45.11, certain people have said or done typical things; say it's just like them. In the remaining sentences, various individuals are described as closely resembling others; say they look just like them. In both cases, use *c'est* + the appropriate stressed pronoun + *tout craché*.

Audio cues (for reference):
45.11 Activation orale: Comportement typique; ressemblance

1. Elle a dit ça? Ça ne m'étonne pas.
2. C'est fou ce qu'elle ressemble à son père.
3. C'est extraordinaire comme Marie-Laure ressemble à Tante Georgette.
4. C'est fou ce qu'elle te ressemble.
5. Elle ressemble beaucoup à son père.
6. Ma fille me ressemble trop.
7. Il n'y a que toi pour dire des choses pareilles.
8. Ah ça, c'est bien lui.
9. Il n'y a que ton père pour faire des choses comme ça.

45.12-45.15 Observation and activation: Satisfaction; suitability

Robert rejects the salesman's offer to show him something a little daintier in the way of underwear by saying he has everything he needs: "J'ai tout ce qu'il me faut." Chart 45.12 presents this and a related expression with *avoir besoin* as ways of indicating that one's needs have been met.

Note that the pronoun *me* in *j'ai tout ce qu'il* **me** *faut* is an **indirect object** pronoun. When the individual whose needs have been satisfied is not the first person singular, the indirect object pronoun will, of course, change accordingly: "**Ils n'ont besoin de rien**" ⇒ "**C'est tout ce qu'il leur faut.**"

Chart 45.14 shows how *c'est ce qu'il faut* is used with the appropriate indirect object pronoun (*c'est ce qu'il* **lui** *faut*, *c'est ce qu'il* **nous** *faut*, and so forth) to indicate that something is suitable or meets your expectations. If the match between what you wanted and what you are offered is especially good, you can signify this by adding an expression like *exactement* or *tout à fait* after *c'est*.

• In exercise 45.13, you and others are asked whether you would like anything more. Say no, you have everything you need, using *tout ce qu'il* + indirect object pronoun + *faut*.

Audio cues (for reference):
45.13 Activation orale: Satisfaction

1. Tu as besoin de quelque chose?
2. Tu veux autre chose?
3. Mesdames, est-ce que je peux vous proposer un dessert....Non? Un café peut-être?
4. Vos parents ont-ils besoin de quelque chose?
5. Messieurs-dames, vous n'avez besoin de rien?
6. Robert a besoin d'autre chose?

• In certain sentences in 45.15, you will be asked whether things suit you and others. Answer yes. In other sentences, you will hear that things fit you and others to a T. Agree. In both situations, say it's exactly what you (and others) need, using *c'est exactement ce qu'il* + indirect object pronoun + *faut*.

Audio cues (for reference):
45.15 Activation orale: Convenance

1. Ça vous plaît?
2. Ça vous va comme un gant!
3. Ça te plaît?
4. Tu crois que je devrais le prendre?
5. Ça te va comme un gant!

6. Ça me va comme un gant!
7. Ça lui va bien!
8. Vous croyez qu'ils en seront contents?
9. Qu'est-ce qu'on fait? On le prend?

45.16–45.19 Observation and activation: *Personne* and *rien* in simple tenses (review and extension)

Recall from lesson 40 that *personne* and *rien* can be either **subjects** or

objects of a verb. In either case, they replace the negative word *pas*, and in either case, of course, they are used with *ne*.

Chart 45.16 reviews the use of *personne* and *rien* in **simple** tenses (that is, tenses where there is only one verb form, like the present or the future, as opposed to **compound** tenses like the *passé composé,* where there are two).

When *personne* or *rien* are used as **subjects** (**rien** *ne lui plaît*), they occupy the normal position of subject words.

When they are used as **objects of a preposition** (*je n'ai besoin* **de rien**), they are placed immediately after the preposition.

When they are used as **direct objects** (*je ne cherche* **rien**), they occupy the normal place of direct object words—immediately after the verb.

• In certain of the sentences in exercise 45.17, you will be asked whether various individuals know or need specific people and whether they have, like, are interested in, or need specific things. In other sentences, you will be asked whether specific people or things please them. In each sentence, determine whether the person or thing is a subject, a direct object, or the object of a preposition, and answer negatively, using *personne* or *rien* as appropriate.

Audio cues (for reference):
45.17 Activation orale: Personne et rien aux temps simples

1. Il ne connaît pas les Pinot-Chambrun?
2. Vous n'avez pas d'immeubles, de terrains, d'actions?
3. Ils n'ont pas de sac à dos, de sac de couchage, de tente?
4. Robert n'aime pas les pieds de porc, les tripes, la tête de veau?
5. Il ne s'intéresse pas à la cuisine française?
6. Mireille ne lui plaît pas?
7. Son hôtel ne lui plaît pas?
8. Les amis de Mireille ne lui plaisent pas?
9. Tu as besoin d'argent?
10. Tu n'as pas besoin de moi?

• In 45.18, you will be asked about your own experience of people and things. As in 45.17, decide whether each person or thing functions as a subject, a direct object, or the object of a preposition, and answer negatively, using *personne* or *rien*, as appropriate.

Audio cues (for reference):
45.18 Activation orale: Personne et rien aux temps simples

1. Tu connais des gens?
2. Qu'est-ce qui t'intéresse?
3. Vous connaissez beaucoup de gens?
4. Qui est-ce que vous connaissez à Paris?
5. Qu'est-ce que tu veux?
6. Qu'est-ce que tu fais?
7. A quoi penses-tu?
8. A qui penses-tu?

9. De quoi as-tu envie?
10. Chez qui habites-tu?
11. Avec qui sors-tu?
12. Qui est-ce qui te plaît?
13. Qu'est-ce qui te plaît?
14. A quoi est-ce que ça engage?
15. Qu'est-ce que tu faisais?

• Exercise 45.19 will give you practice using *personne*, *rien*, and the relative pronouns *qui*, *que*, *ce qui*, and *ce que* studied in lesson 44.20. Read each numbered passage through before you complete it, decide from the context which expressions are missing, and supply them.

As you complete the exercise, bear in mind the following:

1. When the missing word occurs in a **negative** expression, it will be either *personne* or *rien*; you will only need to figure out from the context whether the missing element is a person or a thing.

2. You will use *qui* when a noun in the first part of the sentence is the **subject** of the verb in the second part, and *que* (*qu'*) when it is the **direct object**.

3. When the subject of the following verb is not specified, or is an entire **situation** rather than a person or a thing, use *ce qui*. When the direct object of the following verb is unspecified or a situation, use *ce que* (*ce qu'*).

√ Check your answers in key 45.19 at the back of the workbook.

45.20-45.22 Observation and activation: Specification; use of the subjunctive in relative clauses

In the Samaritaine, Robert is looking for a jacket that won't show the dirt. Although he is sure of what he wants, he is not certain that the Samaritaine (or any other store) has such a jacket, so he identifies it as an ideal: "Je voudrais un blouson qui ne **soit** pas salissant." Chart 45.20 shows how the subjunctive may be used after the relative pronouns *qui* and *que* to specify things that exist in the speaker's mind but that may not actually be available in reality.

Note. Recall from lesson 24 that the function of a relative pronoun is to link or relate two parts of a sentence through a noun they have in common. The part of the sentence introduced by the relative pronouns *qui* and *que* is known as a **relative clause**.

• In exercise 45.21, each of various places and things doesn't please you, isn't on the seashore, doesn't have a view, is too close to the restrooms, and so forth. Say you would like to find one that does please you, is on the shore, does have a view, isn't too close to the restrooms, etc.—presuming it exists. Use *qui* and the subjunctive.

Audio cues (for reference):
45.21 Activation orale: Spécification; emploi du subjonctif dans les propositions relatives

1. Non, cet endroit ne me plaît pas.
2. Non, cet hôtel n'est pas au bord de la mer.
3. Non, cet hôtel n'a pas de vue.
4. Non, cet hôtel n'a pas de restaurant.
5. Non, cette table est trop près des toilettes.
6. Non, ce menu ne me plaît pas.

• In 45.22, you are able to read Mireille's and Robert's thoughts about each other. In each numbered passage, one of our heroes describes a flaw in the other, then expresses a preference for a companion who would not have this flaw. Complete each passage, using the verbs you see in *italics* in the appropriate form of the subjunctive. Remember that the ideal companion is the **opposite** of the real one; accordingly, when the verb in *italics* that describes the flaw occurs in a **negative** expression, you will put it in a **positive** expression, and vice versa.

√ Check your answers in key 45.22 at the back of the workbook.

45.23 Activation: Dialogue between Robert and the salesman

Listen to the conversation between Robert and the salesman and memorize Robert's lines, imitating and repeating as usual.

TOWARD FREE EXPRESSION

45.24 Words at large

Proceed as usual. (If necessary, refer to lesson 27 for directions.)

45.25, 45.26 Role-playing and reinvention of the story

In 45.25, reconstruct Mireille's conversation with Tonton Guillaume.

In 45.26, pretend Tonton Guillaume has a nasty disposition and imagine a new version of the scene where Mireille tells him she has won at the lottery.

• **Suggested written assignment.** Write out a version of the new scene between Mireille and Tonton Guillaume in 45.26. Write about ten sentences. Send this assignment to your instructor (see the course syllabus for details).

OPTIONAL EXERCISES FOR WRITING PRACTICE

• Listen again to exercises 45.17 and 45.18 on the audio recording and write out the audio cues you hear.

√ Check what you have written against the printed text in the study guide.

SELF-TESTING EXERCISES

• Complete and check exercises 45.27, 45.28, and 45.29 as usual.

SUMMARY QUIZ

Consult the course syllabus or check with your instructor for information about completing and handing in summary quiz 45.

LESSON 46
Getting away

The story

Mireille explains the travel plans to Hubert, who kindly offers the use of his new little car. But it turns out that the car is just part of a package deal; the rest of the package is Hubert himself. Less than thrilled by the prospect of being caught between Robert and Hubert, Mireille calls her friend Colette and urges her to make it a foursome. Colette had no other plans and wasn't eager to spend the summer in Provins with her parents. She says okay.

The following Sunday, after a meeting with the group of summer campers they led last year, Mireille also invites Jean-Michel, a young man as far to the left of center as Hubert is to the right. At first, and in **very** strong language, Jean-Michel refuses to go anywhere with a "degenerate aristocrat and an American savage," but he really is tired and in need of a change. Besides, Mireille is quite persuasive. We can count him in.

Now Mireille must reveal, first to Robert (who really wanted to be alone with her), and then to Hubert what the new plans are. Hubert is horrified by the thought of five people, including that "dangerous anarchist" Jean-Michel, in his little Méhari. Hubert may have something there. We seem to be preparing for one of those circus acts in which a little car pulls up and disgorges fifteen clowns.

Notes on culture and communication

 • **Un jeune homme à tendances gauchistes.** Jean-Michel is described as a radical leftist and a political revolutionary. There are various types of *gauchiste* movements in France, influenced by different revolutionary leaders around the world (Karl Marx, Leon Trotsky, Mao Zedong, Che Guevara, and so forth). These leftist groups started blooming in the wake of the political and social upheaval of May, 1968 (see lesson 12). Today they are on the outer fringe of French political life.

 • **Qu'est-ce que j'irais f----- dans cette galère?** Jean-Michel misquotes a famous line from *Les Fourberies de Scapin*, a comedy by the seventeenth-century playwright Molière: "Que diable allait-il faire dans cette galère?" Taken metaphorically, Jean-Michel's question means, "Why on earth should I get myself mixed up in this?"

159

• **L'Hexagone**. One important image the French have of their country is specified in a geography problem given to children in grade school. It is phrased something like this: "Take your ruler and draw a line from Dunkerque to Brest, another from Brest to Bayonne, then Bayonne to Perpignan, from Perpignan to Nice, from Nice to Strasbourg, and from Strasbourg to Dunkerque. Question: What geometric figure have you drawn?" The answer, of course, is a hexagon. It may be a bit difficult for a foreigner to make it out, but if you trim and patch a little, it is there. (The cartesian French are surely the only people in the world who attribute a geometric shape to their country.)

• **The uncouth American, the civilizing French.** A basic French cliché about Americans seems to lurk behind Jean-Michel's reference to Robert as "ce sauvage américain." The French word *sauvage* and the English *savage* come from the same Latin word, *silvaticum*, "man of the woods," but over the centuries the meanings in French and English have evolved differently. The English sense emphasizes the meaning "ferocious barbarian," whereas the French meaning has kept the suggestion of "living in the woods," hence uncouth, unsocial, and uncivilized. (Note that the French meaning is not necessarily insulting: the philosopher Rousseau, among others, thought that society is corrupt and therefore the *sauvages* were pure and unspoiled.) This cliché also affects Hubert's attitude toward Robert. Hubert tells Mireille that if she is left alone with Robert she will be bored to death after two days. The implication is that as a *sauvage Américain* Robert is not civilized and has no ideas that might keep an interesting conversation going.

Though their political philosophies are radically different, Hubert and Jean-Michel are both French, and they share an image of their culture that the French have developed over the centuries: that France is the most civilized nation in the world and has the duty to carry its *mission civilisatrice* to the rest of the globe. (The word *civilized* comes from a Latin word meaning city, so a civilized person is cosmopolitan, a social being, the opposite of a man of the woods.) Like most of the ideas people have about their own and other cultures, this one is largely a fantasy—but a powerful fantasy nonetheless.

Content and learning objectives of lesson 46

This lesson will familiarize you with ways in which French speakers exaggerate, stress the location of something, refer to being tired, and refer to right and left both in terms of political beliefs and of right- and left-handedness.

The following points are highlighted in lesson 46 (you should concentrate on sections marked with a √):

- *Quand* and the future
√• The conditional in intentional expressions (46.25, 46.26)
- *Il faut* and nouns, review
√• Relative pronouns *qui*, *que*, and *dont* (46.34-46.36)

ASSIMILATION OF THE TEXT

46.1-46.4 Text work-up, aural comprehension, and oral production

Proceed as usual in these sections. (Refer to lesson 28.1-28.4 for directions, if necessary.) Work with the text of lesson 46 in the textbook, as in previous lessons.

TOWARD COMMUNICATION

46.5, 46.6 Observation and activation: Pronunciation; the consonant /r/ (review)

- In exercise 46.6, repeat the words and expressions you hear, taking care to pronounce a clear /r/ sound at the end of words where it occurs.

46.7, 46.8 Observation and activation: Fatigue

Chart 46.7 contains expressions used to refer to being tired, from simple fatigue (degree 1) to total exhaustion (degree 3).

- In the dictation exercise in 46.8, listen and write the words you hear.

√ Check your answers in key 46.8 at the back of the workbook.

46.9, 46.10 Observation and activation: Denial; *n'avoir rien de*

When Jean-Michel tells Mireille he has no interest in taking a long trip with a degenerate aristocrat and an American savage, she replies that there is nothing savage about Robert: "Mon Américain **n'a rien d'**un sauvage!" Chart 46.9 shows how *n'avoir rien de* is used with nouns to indicate that a certain characteristic or description does not apply.

- In exercise 46.10, you will hear that various people and things are not savages, degenerates, camels, and so forth. Say there is nothing savage, degenerate, camel-like, etc. about them, using *n'avoir rien de* and the noun you hear.

Audio cues (for reference):
46.10 Activation orale: Dénégation; n'avoir rien de

1. Robert n'est pas un sauvage!
2. Jean-Michel n'est pas un anarchiste!
3. Hubert n'est pas un dégénéré!
4. Jean-Michel n'est pas un aristocrate!

5. Hubert n'est pas un chameau!
6. Robert n'est pas un idiot!
7. La Méhari n'est pas un autobus!

46.11–46.13 Observation and activation: *Quelque chose à* or *rien à* + infinitive

Trying to get Colette to join her, Robert, and Hubert on their trip, Mireille says she has a proposal to make: "J'ai **quelque chose à** te proposer." Chart 46.11 shows how *quelque chose à* or *rien à* can be used with an infinitive to indicate that something (or nothing) is waiting to be done.

• In exercise 46.12, you have to do various things. Say they are waiting to be done, using *j'ai quelque chose à* and the infinitive of the verb you hear.

Audio cues (for reference):
46.12 Activation orale: Quelque chose à + infinitif

1. Il faut que je te dises quelque chose.
2. Il faut que je fasse quelque chose.
3. Il faut que j'achète quelque chose.
4. Il faut que je lise quelque chose.
5. Il faut que je te raconte quelque chose.
6. Il faut que je vous fasse voir quelque chose.
7. Il faut que je vous demande quelque chose.

• In 46.13, you are asked if you and others aren't drinking or eating, doing anything, and so forth. Say you have nothing to eat, drink, do, etc., using *n'avoir rien à* and an infinitive.

Audio cues (for reference):
46.13 Activation orale: Rien à + infinitif

1. Tu ne bois pas?
2. Vous ne mangez pas?
3. Tu ne fais rien?

4. Robert et Mireille ne disent rien?
5. Mireille ne propose rien?
6. Tu n'ajoutes rien?

46.14, 46.15 Observation and activation: *En plein*

Mireille tells a skeptical Hubert that the travelers plan to camp their way across France, sleeping right in the fields: "Nous passerons les nuits **en** plein champ." For Robert, this will be quite a change from the bustle of his hotel, which is right smack in the middle of the Latin Quarter, **en plein Quartier Latin**. Chart 46.14 shows how the expression *en plein* is used to stress the location of some thing or action.

● In exercise 46.15, you will be asked whether people do or did various things in certain locations. Say yes, they do or did them right there, using the appropriate form of *en plein*.

Audio cues (for reference):
46.15 Activation orale: En plein

1. Les grands-parents de Mireille habitent à la campagne?
2. Vous avez dormi dans les champs?
3. Le Home Latin se trouve au Quartier Latin?
4. Les manifestants ont fait un feu dans la rue?
5. Vous étiez perdus dans la montagne?
6. Mireille a rencontré Robert pendant la manifestation?

46.16-46.18 Observation and activation: The future (review and extension)

Chart 46.16 points out that while *quand* may be followed by the future, *si* generally is not (the exception is *si* used in an indirect question: "Je ne sais pas s'il **fera** beau").

● Exercise 46.17 will help you review the forms of the future. Various people have decided to do various things. Say they will do them, using the future.

Audio cues (for reference):
46.17 Activation orale: Futur

1. Nous avons décidé de partir dans huit jours.
2. Nous avons décidé de faire du camping.
3. Robert a décidé de louer une voiture.
4. Hubert a décidé de venir avec nous.
5. Robert et Mireille ont décidé d'emporter des sacs de couchage.
6. Nous avons décidé d'aller en France cet été.
7. Colette a décidé d'accompagner Mireille et ses amis.
8. Mireille a décidé d'être actrice et infirmière.

● In 46.18, you hear that people will do certain things **if** other things happen. Say they will do them **when** these other things happen, using *quand* and the future.

Audio cues (for reference):
46.18 Activation orale: Futur

1. On s'arrêtera dans un hôtel si on a envie de prendre une douche.
2. On reviendra si on en a assez.
3. On s'arrêtera si on est fatigué.
4. On mangera si on a faim.
5. On restera à l'hôtel s'il pleut.
6. On prendra les vélos s'il fait beau.

46.19, 46.20 Observation and activation: Exaggeration; *mourir de*

Mireille isn't exactly dying to go off alone with Hubert and Robert: "Je ne **meurs** pas **d'envie** de me trouver seule entre Hubert et Robert." Chart 46.19 presents a number of expressions in which *mourir* is used figuratively with a noun to exaggerate one's degree of fear, shame, hunger, boredom, and the like.

• In exercise 46.20, people are very hungry, tired, afraid, and so on. Say they are dying of hunger, fatigue, fear, etc., using *mourir de* and a noun.

Audio cues (for reference):
46.20 Activation orale: Exagération; mourir de

1. Ce que j'ai chaud!
2. Il a très faim.
3. Nous sommes terriblement fatigués.
4. On a très peur.
5. Nous nous ennuyons.
6. Ce que j'ai soif!
7. Nous sommes impatients de vous voir.
8. Il avait honte.
9. J'ai tellement froid que je claque des dents!
10. Ce que j'ai envie de partir en vacances!

46.21, 46.22 Observation and activation: Of right and left

Chart 46.21 shows how right and left can indicate ideology: **de** *droite* and **à** *droite* (and their equivalents with *gauche*) refer to political beliefs.

Right and left can also be used to refer to handedness: a right-handed man is *droitier*, a right-handed woman, *droitière;* a left-handed man is *gaucher*, a left-handed woman, *gauchère*.

• In exercise 46.22, determine the missing expressions from the context of each sentence, and write them in the spaces provided.

√ Check your answers in key 46.22 at the back of the workbook.

46.23, 46.24 Observation and activation: Changes

Jean-Michel is exhausted and needs a change of scene: "Il faut que je **change d'**horizon." Chart 46.23 illustrates the use of *changer de* and a noun **without** the definite article.

Note that *changer* can also be used **with** a definite article and an indirect object pronoun in an expression like *ça* **te** *changera* **les** *idées*, where the change affects the person directly.

• In exercise 46.24, you will be asked whether various people are no longer at the same address, whether they have a new car, whether they no longer have the same telephone number, and so forth. Confirm that they've changed addresses, cars, telephone numbers, etc., answering negative questions with *non* and positive questions with *oui*, and using *changer de*.

Audio cues (for reference):
46.24 Activation orale: Changements; changer de

1. Elle n'est plus à la même adresse?
2. Tonton Guillaume a une nouvelle voiture?
3. Les Courtois n'ont plus le même numéro de téléphone?
4. Marie-Laure ne porte plus la même robe que tout à l'heure?
5. Tu n'es plus d'accord maintenant? Tu as une autre idée?
6. Mme Courtois ne va plus chez le même boucher?
7. Robert n'est plus au même hôtel?
8. Robert et Mireille ne sont plus assis à la même place?

46.25, 46.26 Observation and activation: Firm decision versus simple intent; future and conditional (review and extension)

Chart 46.25 illustrates how the conditional can be used to express a proposed course of action, the result of an intent rather than of a firm decision. If we have decided to go next Monday, we will definitely leave; the **future** expresses this certainty: "Nous **partirons** lundi prochain." But if we are merely planning to go or thinking of going, the **conditional** expresses the tentative nature of our plans: "Nous **partirions** lundi prochain." (The missing condition, *si nous décidions de partir* or something similar, is understood from the context.)

● In exercise 46.26, some of your travel plans are final; others are still tentative. Where you have decided to leave, return, go, and so forth, say you will leave, return, go, etc., using the future. Where you were merely thinking about taking the train or going to the South of France, say you might take the train or go south, using the conditional.

Audio cues (for reference):
46.26 Activation orale: Décision arrêtée et simple intention; futur et conditionnel

1. Nous avons décidé de partir demain matin.
2. Nous pensions prendre le train de nuit.
3. Nous avons décidé de revenir demain soir.
4. Nous pensions aller dans le Midi.
5. Nous avons décidé d'aller à Paris.
6. Nous pensions faire le tour de France.
7. Nous avons décidé de louer une voiture.

46.27, 46.28 Observation and activation: Questioning assumptions; the conditional (review and extension)

When Hubert tells Mireille she will die of boredom if she goes off on a trip alone with Robert ("Tu vas t'ennuyer à mourir!"), Mireille questions his assumption: "Je ne vois pas pourquoi je m'ennuierais." Chart 46.27 illustrates this use of the conditional to challenge assumptions one finds doubtful.

● In exercise 46.28, you hear a number of commands and predictions of what you will do that reflect certain assumptions. Say that you don't see why you would do any of these things, using the conditional.

Audio cues (for reference):
46.28 Activation orale: Mise en question; conditionnel

1. Vous allez vous perdre!
2. Viens avec nous!
3. Tu vas être crevé!
4. Ça ira mieux demain.
5. Fais-moi plaisir.
6. Tu vas mourir d'ennui.
7. Prête-moi ta voiture.
8. Arrête de faire ça.
9. Vous allez vous ennuyer.
10. Mireille ne sera pas d'accord.

46.29-46.32 Observation and activation: Necessity; *avoir besoin de, il faut* (review)

In lesson 39, you saw how *il faut* is used with *que* and a verb in the subjunctive to express necessity or obligation. Chart 46.29 reviews *il faut*, contrasting it with another expression that refers to necessity, *avoir besoin de* + infinitive.

Chart 46.31 reintroduces a use of *il faut* that you saw briefly in lesson 33. *Il faut* can be used with a **noun** to indicate that someone needs something, with the attention focused on the thing that is needed: "il vous faut **des vacances.**"   Notice that when *il faut* is used in this way, the party in need is identified by an **indirect object pronoun**: *il* **vous** *faut*, *il* **lui** *faut*, etc.

• In exercise 46.30, people need to do various things. Say it is necessary that they do them, using *il faut que* and the subjunctive.

Audio cues (for reference):
46.30 Activation orale: Nécessité; avoir besoin de + infinitif, il faut + subjonctif

1. J'ai besoin de partir tout de suite.
2. J'ai besoin de te voir.
3. Tu as besoin de prendre des vacances.
4. J'ai besoin d'aller en ville.
5. Nous avons besoin de changer d'air.
6. J'ai besoin d'essayer autre chose.

• In 46.32, people need various things. Say they must have them, using *il faut* + noun. Don't forget the appropriate **indirect object pronoun** between *il* and *faut*.

Audio cues (for reference):
46.32 Activation orale: Nécessité; avoir besoin de + nom; il vous faut + nom

1. Robert a besoin d'un sac à dos.
2. J'ai besoin d'une voiture.
3. Robert a besoin d'argent.
4. Mireille a besoin d'un sac à dos.
5. Robert et Mireille ont besoin d'une tente.
6. Nous avons besoin d'une grande maison.
7. Tu as besoin de patience.
8. J'ai besoin de repos.

46.34–46.36 Observation and activation: Relative pronouns *qui, que, dont* (review and extension)

You saw in lesson 44 (and earlier in lesson 24) that the relative pronoun *qui* functions as the **subject** of the verb that follows it. The relative pronoun *que* functions as the **direct object** of the verb that follows. Chart 46.34 introduces another relative pronoun, *dont*, that functions as the **object of the preposition** *de* in a relative clause.

In previous lessons, you have come across a number of expressions that use *de* (*profiter de, avoir envie de, avoir besoin de, s'occuper de*, to mention the most frequent ones). Recall that when the verb used with *de* expresses the main message of the sentence, the object of *de* can often be replaced by the pronoun *en: elle* **en** *profite*, *il s'***en** *occupe*, and so forth.

You have seen that the function of relative pronouns is to connect the main clause of a sentence to a relative clause through a noun the two have in common. When this noun—the **antecedent** of the pronoun—functions as the

subject of the verb in the relative clause, the relative pronoun *qui* is used to link the two clauses. When the antecedent is the **object** of the verb in the relative clause, *que* is used. And when it is the **object of the preposition** *de*, the relative pronoun used is *dont*.

- In exercise 46.34, you will hear pairs of sentences. The direct object of the first sentence recurs in the second sentence, where it is the object of the preposition *de*. Combine the two sentences into one, using *dont*. Remember that since objects of *de* can be replaced by *en*, the noun in the first sentence will appear most often as *en* in the second sentence. This *en* is replaced in the final combined sentence with *dont*.

Audio cues (for reference):
46.34 Activation orale: Le pronom relatif dont

1. Hubert a acheté une Méhari. Il avait très envie de cette voiture.
2. Mireille s'est acheté une jupe. Elle en avait envie.
3. Elle est allée chercher un livre à la bibliothèque. Elle en avait besoin.
4. Ils ont acheté un vieux chateau. Personne ne s'en occupait.

- In 46.35, you will hear a series of sentences containing objects of *de*. Restate each sentence, beginning the new version with the corresponding phrase printed in the workbook and adding a relative clause introduced by *dont*.

- In 46.36, determine the antecedent of each of the missing relative pronouns, then figure out in each case whether that antecedent noun is the subject or direct object of the verb in the relative clause, or the object of the preposition *de*. Then write *qui*, *que*, or *dont* in the space provided, as appropriate.

Note. Remember that nouns used possessively are also objects of the preposition *de* and can be replaced by *dont:* "Nous connaissons les parents **de** cette jeune fille" ⇒ "C'est une jeune fille **dont** nous connaissons les parents."

√ Check your answers in key 46.36 at the back of the workbook.

46.37 Activation: Dialogue between Mireille and Colette

Listen to the conversation between Mireille and Colette and memorize Colette's lines, imitating and repeating as usual.

- **Suggested oral assignment.** Record the dialogue between Mireille and Colette in 46.37. Send this assignment to your instructor (see the course syllabus for details).

TOWARD FREE EXPRESSION

46.38 Words at large

Proceed as usual. (If necessary, refer to lesson 27 for directions.)

46.39, 46.40 Role-playing and reinvention of the story

• In 46.39, reconstruct the dialogue in which Mireille attempts to persuade Colette to join her, Robert, and Hubert for the summer.

• In 46.40, Mireille has taken Aunt Georgette's maxim "The more the merrier" seriously, and is inviting still more people to come along. Imagine her conversation with a new prospect.

DOCUMENT

In the textbook chapter for lesson 46 you will find a series of quotations from French writers and thinkers on the subject of traveling:

Georgette Belleau (b. 1938), sustaining member of the Société Protectrice des Animaux; expert in maxims, proverbs, and other forms of traditional expression. Favorite saying: "Children should be seen, not heard."

Charles Baudelaire (1821-1867), one of the best-known poets of the nineteenth century and a vital influence on modern poetry; author of *Les Fleurs du mal*; translator of the tales and poems of Edgar Allan Poe into French.

Claude Lévi-Strauss (b. 1908), anthropologist and philosopher, pioneer in the field of structural anthropology.

François Mauriac (1885-1970), novelist strongly influenced by Catholic themes and concerns; author of the novel *Thérèse Desqueyroux*.

André Suarès (1868-1948), writer devoted to the themes of heroism.

Guillaume Apollinaire (1880-1918), influential poet of love, war, and the modern age; champion of the Cubist movement; author of *Alcools*.

Edmond Haraucourt (1856-1941), writer, author of *Rondel de l'adieu*.

Arthur Rimbaud (1854-1891), visionary poet in rebellion against society and tradition; author of *Les Illuminations*.

OPTIONAL EXERCISES FOR WRITING PRACTICE

• Listen again to exercises 46.15 and 46.28 on the audio recording and write out the audio cues you hear.

√ Check what you have written against the printed text in the study guide.

SELF-TESTING EXERCISES

• Complete and check exercises 46.41, 46.42, and 46.43 as usual.

SUMMARY QUIZ

Consult the course syllabus or check with your instructor for information about completing and handing in summary quiz 46.

LESSON 47
What variety!

The story

At Mireille's house, the five adventurers have met to discuss travel plans. First there is a brief, predictable exchange between Hubert and Jean-Michel on the subject of kings and revolutionaries. Then all talk about the hundreds of cathedrals and churches to see and the many châteaux. Colette throws in an occasional comment about wines and cheeses and Marie-Laure serves as geography expert.

There are zillions of things to see. Luckily, France is not very large. Robert suggests bicycles instead of that cramped car. His idea meets with approval, but naturally leads to talk of the mountain ranges in France. We have a few more clashes between right and left. At last, Mireille insists that they get down to cases. Jean-Michel proposes a counterclockwise *tour de France* beginning in the north. That part of the country interests him because of its workers, what he calls "the real France." Colette, for gastronomical reasons, prefers to start in Normandy. Her evocations of the glorious foods to be found there get everyone to agree. Departure Monday morning, at dawn. First stop: Rouen (even if Jean-Michel still has his heart set on the north). Will the M in B finish the windows in time to tail them? Probably.

Notes on culture and communication

• **Les Rois de France et les géants de '93.** The ideological gap between right and left is a staple of French political life, inherited from the French Revolution (1789-1795). Hubert, as a descendant of the aristocracy, is nostalgic for the bygone days of French royalty, while at the opposite end of the spectrum, Jean-Michel pays homage to the great heroes of the revolution, the spokesmen of the people against the fallen monarchy, and to the oppressed working class.

• **Le Tour de France** is the most famous French bicycle race. Begun in 1903, it takes place every summer along a circuit organized across the hexagon of France, including stretches in flat areas and others over high mountain passes.

• **Cocorico!** cries Jean-Michel, making fun of Hubert's chauvinistic pride in the fact that Mont Blanc—situated in France, of course—is Europe's highest

171

mountain. *Cocorico!* is the crowing of a cock, the bird that has been a symbol of French national pride and feistiness since the days of the Gauls. (The Romans who colonized Gaul called the country *Gallia* and its inhabitants *galli*, which is also the Latin word for roosters.)

• **Variety in unity.** This episode brings us two more essential factors in the image the French have of their country, an image that might be called official because it has been taught in elementary geography and history textbooks for over a hundred years. The first of the factors French people have learned by heart at school is that in the territory of France, smaller than the state of Texas, there is incredible **variety,** as illustrated by the many places, monuments, and kinds of food that Mireille and her friends insist Robert must experience. One could lengthen the list by adding the variety in climate, history, ideology, traditional dress, accent, economy, and so forth,

The great miracle is the cultural and linguistic **unity** of this extremely varied area and of French men and women over the centuries. A crucial theme in French history as it is taught in the schools is an analysis of important people and regimes in terms of their effort to further or hamper the process of unification.

However, because of social, family, geographical, and personal factors, the people of France are divided into *familles spirituelles*, ideological groups that differ violently with each other on questions of politics and culture. This is illustrated by the deep and enduring conflict between Hubert and Jean-Michel. Note, incidentally, even in the expression *familles spirituelles* the emphasis on the idea of **family,** which cannot be overemphasized in the study of French life.

Content and learning objectives of lesson 47

This lesson introduces ways in which French speakers discuss appearances, say that they've reached the limits of their patience, and express doubt and necessity.

The following points are highlighted in lesson 47 (you should concentrate on sections marked with a √):

√ • *Tout* (47.10–47.12)
√ • *Tout/rien, personne/tout le monde* (47.13–47.15)
√ • Restrictive negative *ne . . . que* (47.16–47.20)
  • Subjunctive with expressions of doubt, review
  • *Il faut* + subjunctive, review

ASSIMILATION OF THE TEXT

47.1-47.4 Text work-up, aural comprehension, and oral production

Proceed as usual in these sections. (Refer to lesson 28.1-28.4 for directions, if necessary.) Work with the text of lesson 47 in the textbook, as in previous lessons.

TOWARD COMMUNICATION

47.5 Activation: Pronunciation; The sound /y/ (review)

● Repeat the words and expressions you hear, as usual.

47.6, 47.7 Observation and activation: Appearance; *avoir l'air, paraître, sembler*

Three expressions used to refer to appearances are grouped together in chart 47.6.

Note that all three are used with an **adjective** that specifies **how** the thing or person being discussed looks. The adjective may be preceded by *être* (**d'***être*, in the case of *avoir l'air*).

An **indirect object pronoun** precedes *avoir l'air*, *paraître*, and *sembler* when you wish to emphasize the perception of a particular person: "Ça **me** paraît être intéressant."

Notice that in the *passé composé*, the verb *paraître* may be used to express one's general reaction: "Ça lui **a paru** intéressant."

● In exercise 47.7, you will be asked for your reaction and the reaction of others to various proposals. Say you and they find (or found) them interesting, using *paraître* and the appropriate indirect object pronoun. Notice that when the proposal is specified (*mon idée*, *cette idée*, and so forth), the subject of *paraître* will be *elle*. When the proposal is not specified, use *ça* as the subject of *paraître*.

Audio cues (for reference):
47.7 Activation orale: Apparence; avoir l'air, paraître, sembler

1. Qu'est-ce que tu penses de mon idée?
2. Qu'est-ce que vous en avez pensé?
3. Qu'en pensez-vous, vous deux?

4. Qu'est-ce qu'ils en ont pensé?
5. Comment trouvez-vous mon idée?
6. Comment avez-vous trouvé ça?
7. Qu'est-ce que tu penses de cette idée?
8. Comment Robert trouve-t-il l'idée de faire le tour de la France?

47.8, 47.9 Observation and activation: Satiety (review and extension)

Chart 47.10 presents a series of expressions used to say that you have had all you can take, that you've had it up to here. *En avoir assez*, *en avoir marre*, and *en avoir ras le bol* can be used with *de* and a noun or pronoun to specify the person, thing, or situation you are fed up with. The **stressed** pronoun is used after the preposition *de*: "J'en ai marre **de toi**!"

• In exercise 47.9, various people are beginning to get on your nerves. Say you've had it up to here with them, using *en avoir marre de* and the appropriate stressed pronoun.

Audio cues (for reference):
47.9 Activation orale: Satiété

1. Hubert commence à m'agacer!   3. Vous commencez à m'agacer, vous, là!
2. Marie-Laure commmence à m'agacer.   4. Toi, tu commences à m'agacer.

47.10-47.12 Observation and activation: *Tout*

Chart 47.10 presents two different uses of *tout*: to **modify** a noun or pronoun (**tout** *le monde*, *elle les connaît* **toutes**), and to **replace** a noun (*je fais* **tout**).

When *tout* modifies a pronoun, it is usually placed after the verb in a simple tense (*elle les connaît* **toutes**), or after the auxiliary in a compound tense (*elle les a* **toutes** *vues*).

Note that when the masculine plural form *tous* occurs in front of a noun and its article (**tous** *les châteaux*), the final -*s* is not pronounced. But when *tous* occurs at the end of a rhythmic group or before a verb, the -*s* is pronounced /s/: "Je les connais **tous**/s/;" "elle les a **tous**/s/ vus."

• In exercise 47.11, you and others will be asked whether something is wrong, what you need, what you do around the house, and so forth. Answer that everything is fine, that you need everything, that you do everything around the house, etc., using *tout*.

Note. Listen carefully to the question in each of the sentences you hear. It will help you determine whether to make *tout* the **subject** of your answer (when you hear *il y a quelque chose qui?* or *qu'est-ce qui?*), or the **direct object** (when you hear *qu'est-ce que?*), or an **object of the preposition** *de* (when you hear *de quoi?*).

Audio cues (for reference):
47.11 Activation orale: Tout

1. Qu'est-ce qu'il y a? Il y a quelque chose qui ne va pas?
2. De quoi as-tu besoin?
3. Qu'est-ce que tu fais, toi, dans la maison?
4. De quoi tu t'occupes?
5. De quoi as-tu envie?
6. Qu'est-ce que tu veux?
7. Qu'est-ce qui vous intéresse?
8. Qu'est-ce qui te plaît?
9. Qu'est-ce qui lui a plu?
10. Qu'est-ce que vous avez vu?

• In 47.12, you will be asked which of various things you and others have tasted, seen, or tried, which you like, which you know, and so forth. Say you and they have tasted, seen, tried them all, that you like them all, know them all, etc., replacing the noun you hear with a direct object pronoun, and using the appropriate form of *tout*. Remember that *tout* will appear after the verb (after the auxiliary in a compound tense). Remember also that *tous* in this situation is pronounced *tous*/s/.

Audio cues (for reference):
47.12 Activation orale: Tout

1. Quels crus est-ce que Robert a goûtés?
2. Quels châteaux avez-vous vus?
3. Quels fromages avez-vous essayés?
4. Quels vins avez-vous goûtés?

5. Quels vins aimez-vous?
6. Quelles cathédrales connaissez-vous?
7. Quelles cathédrales avez-vous visitées?

47.13-47.15 Observation and activation: *Tout* or *rien, personne* or *tout le monde* (review and extension)

In lesson 20, *rien* and *personne* were presented as the opposites of *quelque chose* and *quelqu'un*. Chart 47.13 shows that *rien* can also be considered the opposite of *tout*, and *personne* the opposite of *tout le monde*.

In lesson 40, you saw *rien* and *personne* used as both subjects and objects. Chart 47.13 reviews the position of these two expressions and of *tout* and *tout le monde* when they are used as subjects and as objects.

Notice that with a verb in the *passé composé*, *tout* and *rien* used as **direct objects** are placed, like other pronouns, **between** the auxiliary and the past participle. *Tout le monde* and *personne* used as objects are placed **after** the past participle, like other nouns.

• In certain of the sentences in exercise 47.14, you will be told that nothing works, nobody knows, and so forth. In others, you will be asked if you're doing nothing, if you know nothing, etc. Contradict the assumptions of each sentence, using *si!* and replacing *rien* with *tout* and *personne* with *tout le monde*. Remember that with a verb in the *passé composé*, *tout* goes between the auxiliary and the past participle.

Audio cues (for reference):
47.14 Activation orale: Tout ou rien, personne ou tout le monde

1. Rien ne marche!
2. Personne ne le sait.
3. Tu ne fais rien?
4. Tu ne sais rien?
5. Tu ne comprends rien!

6. Personne ne le sait!
7. Personne ne fait ça!
8. Tu n'as vu personne?
9. Tu n'as rien vu?
10. Tu n'as rien compris!

• In 47.15, you will be asked a series of questions about things and people. Decide from each question whether the thing or person asked about is the subject or the object of the verb. (Questions about object things will begin with *qu'est-ce que;* questions about subject things with *qu'est-ce qui;* questions about object persons with *qui est-ce que;* questions about subject persons with *qui* or *qui est-ce qui*). Answer negatively, using *rien* or *personne*. Remember that with a verb in the *passé composé*, *rien* used as an object is placed between the auxiliary and the past participle; *personne* used as an object is placed after the past participle.

Audio cues (for reference):
47.15 Activation orale: Tout ou rien, personne ou tout le monde

1. Qu'est-ce que tu fais?
2. Qui était là?
3. Qu'est-ce qui te plaît?
4. Qu'est-ce qui lui a plu?
5. Qu'est-ce que vous avez vu?

6. Qui est-ce que vous avez vu?
7. Qui le savait?
8. Qui est-ce que tu as invité?
9. Qu'est-ce que tu as perdu?

47.16-47.20 Observation and activation: Restriction; restrictive negative *ne . . . que* (review and extension)

In lesson 39, you were reminded how *ne . . . que* introduces an exception to an overall situation of absence or lack. "Dans le Nord, il **n'**y a **que**

des mines" is not as absolute as "Dans le Nord, il **n'y a rien** à voir." There
is something to see, although it isn't much—nothing but mines.

Notice, in the second and third charts in 47.16, that *que* is placed in
front of the element that represents an exception to the overall negative
situation. We can say that Hubert's uncles build only low-cost housing in the
Paris area (" . . . **que** des HLM"), or we can say that they build low-cost
housing only in the Paris area (" . . . **que** dans la région parisienne").
Likewise, we can say that Mont Blanc is only 4807 meters high, or that only
Mont Blanc is 4807 meters high.

Recall from lesson 44 that the **subjunctive** is used after *il n'y a que* in a
relative clause introduced by *qui:* "Il n'y a que le loto et le tiercé **qui soient**
pires;" "il n'y a que le Mont Blanc **qui fasse** 4807 mètres."

• In exercise 47.17, you will be asked whether you and others have seen
everyone, spoken to everyone, been to all the stores, been to the clothing
department, and so forth. In reality, your situation is limited to the items
listed in the workbook. Express this restriction by answering each question
with *ne . . . que* and the word or expression you see.

Audio cues (for reference):
47.17 Activation orale: Restriction; négation restrictive ne...que

1. Vous avez vu tout le monde?
2. Vous avez parlé à tout le monde?
3. Vous êtes allés dans tous les magasins?
4. Vous êtes allés à tous les étages?
5. Vous êtes allées au rayon d'habillement?
6. Vous avez regardé les caravanes?
7. Ils ont gagné 100.000 francs?
8. Ils vont aller en Italie?
9. Ils vont aller y rester tout l'été?
10. Ils ont beaucoup d'argent?
11. Les Belleau ont des garçons?
12. Mireille a des frères?
13. Les Courtois ont des enfants?
14. Ils ont un grand appartement?
15. Tu comptes sur ton intelligence?

• In 47.18, you will be asked whether you and others have several
sisters, two cars, whether you have seen all the museums, and so forth. In
fact, your situation in each area is limited to the numbers given in the
workbook. Express this restriction by using *ne . . . que* and the expression
of quantity you see; replace the noun in each sentence by *en*.

Audio cues (for reference):
47.18 Activation orale: Restriction; négation restrictive ne...que

1. Tu as plusieurs frères?
2. Tu as plusieurs soeurs?
3. Ils ont deux voitures?
4. Vous avez visité tous les musées?
5. Tu as bu plusieurs Dubonnet?
6. Tu as vu tous les films de Godard?
7. Tu as acheté plusieurs chemises?
8. Elle t'a presenté toutes ses amies?
9. Tu as lu tous ces livres?

● In 47.19, you will hear that nobody can help you except Jean-Michel, nobody knows where he is except Mireille, nothing pleases him except the mountains, and so forth. Say that only he can help you, only Mireille knows where he is, only the mountains please him, etc., using *ne . . . que*, a relative clause with *qui*, and the subjunctive.

Audio cues (for reference):
47.19 Activation orale: Ne...que + relative au subjonctif

1. Rien n'est pire...sauf le tiercé.
2. Personne ne peut vous aider...sauf lui.
3. Personne ne sait où il est...sauf Mireille.
4. Personne ne lui plaît...sauf Mireille.
5. Rien ne lui plaît...sauf la montagne.
6. Personne ne réussit...sauf lui.
7. Personne n'est content...sauf lui.
8. Personne ne veut y aller...sauf lui.
9. Personne n'a envie d'y aller...sauf vous.
10. Personne n'a envie d'y aller...sauf Colette.
11. Personne n'a de voiture...sauf Hubert.
12. Personne ne me comprend...sauf toi.
13. Personne ne se plaint de la publicité...sauf Hubert.

● In 47.20, you will see an excerpt from Aunt Georgette's personal journal. No doubt to confuse future students of French, Georgette has taken out all the restrictive expressions. Reconstruct the original text.

√ Check your answers in key 47.20 at the back of the workbook.

47.21-47.23 Observation and activation: Casting doubt; subjunctive (review)

In lesson 39.16, you saw the subjunctive used with expressions of doubt. Chart 47.21 reviews and extends the list of these expressions. Like many other expressions you have seen with the subjunctive, they simply project an attitude onto the action (in this case, they place it frankly in doubt). The action of the verb in the subjunctive is not seen as actually taking place.

● In exercise 47.22, you will hear a number of statements that seem exaggerated. Say that you would be amazed if each were true, using *ça m'étonnerait que* and the subjunctive.

Audio cues (for reference):
47.22 Activation orale: Mise en doute

1. Il y a des centaines d'églises à voir, en France.
2. On va aller partout.

3. Il y a de tout en France.
4. On peut faire la France à cheval.
5. Le Mont Blanc fait 4810 m.
6. Il n'y a plus de Pyrénées.
7. Les coureurs du Tour de France font trois cols dans la même étape.

• In 47.23, you will hear that various people have climbed all the peaks at Chamonix, know all the wines of France, and so on. Say you doubt they've climbed all those peaks, know all those wines, etc., using *je doute que* and the subjunctive, and replacing *tou(te)s les* + noun with the appropriate direct object pronoun and the proper form of the pronoun *tout*.

Audio cues (for reference):
47.23 Activation orale: Mise en doute, subjonctif, tout

1. J'ai fait toutes les aiguilles de Chamonix.
2. Il connaît tous les vins de France.
3. Ils ont fait toutes les aiguilles de Chamonix.
4. Nous avons vu tous les châteaux de la Loire.
5. Robert a goûté tous les vins de Bourgogne.
6. Marie-Laure a mangé toutes les boules de gomme.

47.24, 47.25 Observation and activation: Necessity; *il faut* + subjunctive

Chart 47.24 reviews the use of the subjunctive with *il faut* (see lesson 39.10). Once again, notice that these sentences do not present the action of the verb in the subjunctive as actually taking place.

• In exercise 47.25, you are discovering that others have never climbed Mont Blanc, toured the châteaux of the Loire, gone to the Alps, and so forth. Tell them they absolutely must climb, tour, go, etc., using *il faut que* and the subjunctive.

Audio cues (for reference):
47.25 Activation orale: Nécessité; Il faut + subjonctif (révision)

1. Vous n'êtes jamais monté au Mont Blanc!
2. Vous n'avez jamais fait les châteaux de la Loire?!
3. Vous n'êtes jamais allé dans les Alpes?
4. Vous n'avez jamais goûté le vin de Saumur?
5. Vous n'avez jamais vu le cirque de Gavarnie?
6. Tu n'es jamais allé à Reims?
7. Tu n'as jamais vu le Mont-St-Michel?
8. Tu n'as jamais descendu les gorges de Verdon?
9. Tu n'as jamais fait le col du Tourmalet à vélo?

47.26 Activation: Dialogue between Hubert and Colette

Listen to the conversation between Hubert and Colette and memorize Colette's lines, imitating and repeating as usual.

TOWARD FREE EXPRESSION

47.27 Words at large

Proceed as usual. (If necessary, refer to lesson 27 for directions.)

47.28, 47.29 Role-playing and reinvention of the story

In 47.28, Reconstruct the discussion among the travelers as they plan their itinerary.

In 47.29, Hubert and Jean-Michel are at it again. Imagine their verbal duel.

• **Suggested written assignment.** Write out a version of the discussion between Hubert and Jean-Michel in 47.29. Write twelve to fifteen sentences. Send this assignment to your instructor (see the course syllabus for details).

OPTIONAL EXERCISES FOR WRITING PRACTICE

• Listen again to exercises 47.19 and 47.22 on the audio recording and write out the audio cues you hear.

√ Check what you have written against the printed text in the study guide.

SELF-TESTING EXERCISES

• Complete and check exercises 47.30, 47.31, and 47.32 as usual.

SUMMARY QUIZ

Consult the course syllabus or check with your instructor for information about completing and handing in summary quiz 47.

LESSON 48
What riches!

The story

Same scene. Next day. The gang convenes. Hubert brings a guide to the châteaux. Colette comes bearing restaurant guides and a selection of cookies and candy for Marie-Laure. When Marie-Laure realizes that they won't take her along, she refuses to share her goodies except with her "beloved cowboy," and even threatens to run away. Finally, she does agree to share.

How about a Tour de France by boat? First the western coastal waters with all their beaches, then through rivers and canals all the way to the Mediterranean. Hubert remembers a family sailboat at Villequiers, but enthusiasm for borrowing it is not very high. No one seems eager to die young. Mireille tells Marie-Laure the story of Victor Hugo's daughter who drowned there in a boating accident.

Naturally, Hubert and Jean-Michel agree on nothing. Hubert seems to be scoring big points about French inventions when the doorbell rings. Marie-Laure answers it. She comes back to report that it was a man in black who claimed to be bringing back her gumdrops. She saw they weren't hers, returned them to him, and he departed. What in the world is this all about?

The gang has to leave. Marie-Laure goes out to play in the Luxembourg Garden. If she comes back no later than 6:00 for dinner, Mireille will take her to a movie. Their parents aren't home. The plot is about to thicken!

Notes on culture and communication

• **Le Canal du Midi.** Built by the French engineer Pierre-Paul Riquet (1604-1680), the Canal du Midi starts in Toulouse and links the Garonne River to the Mediterranean. It was inaugurated in 1680, during the reign of Louis XIV.

• **Se noyer à la fleur de l'âge.** In his poem "A Villequier" (*Les Contemplations*, 1856), Victor Hugo mourns the accidental drowning in the Seine River of his daughter Léopoldine and her husband Charles Vacquerie on September 4, 1853.

181

Content and learning objectives of lesson 48

This lesson will familiarize you with ways in which French speakers refer to seriousness and jesting, ask for confirmation, and identify the location of geographical points on the coast, on rivers, and inland.

The following points are highlighted in lesson 48 (you should concentrate on sections marked with a √):

√ • *Ce qui, ce que, ce dont*, review and extension (48.12–48.14)
  • *Laisser*
  • The future, review
  • Use of the subjunctive with demands
√ • Possessive pronouns (48.21–48.22)

ASSIMILATION OF THE TEXT

48.1–48.4 Text work-up, aural comprehension, and oral production

Proceed as usual in these sections. (Refer to lesson 28.1–28.4 for directions, if necessary.) Work with the text of lesson 48 in the textbook, as in previous lessons.

TOWARD COMMUNICATION

48.5 Activation: Pronunciation; the semivowel /j/ (review)

• Repeat the words and expressions you hear, taking care not to linger on the /j/ sound represented by the letters in *italics*.

48.6, 48.7 Observation and activation: Seriousness and joking

Chart 48.6 groups together expressions that can be used to point out that you are serious or, on the other hand, that you are just kidding around.

• In exercise 48.7, decide whether the statements you hear indicate that the speaker is in earnest (*sérieux*) or in jest (*plaisanterie*), and mark the appropriate box on the grid.

√ Check your answers in key 48.7 at the back of the workbook.

48.8, 48.9 Observation and activation: Coastline and rivers

Chart 48.8 shows how French speakers refer to places that are located on the coast, on rivers, or in the interior of the country.

• In exercise 48.9, look at the map and find the ten cities and towns you see listed. You will be asked whether each is located on the coast, on a river, or inland. In each case, the questioner has got it wrong; give the correct location.

48.10, 48.11 Observation and activation: Confirmation; *c'est bien*

Jean-Michel wants to make sure he has brought the guide he was supposed to bring: "**C'est bien** le Guide Vert de la Normandie et de la Bretagne que je devais apporter?" Chart 48.10 shows how *c'est bien* is used in a question to request confirmation of one's expectations, and in an answer to provide that confirmation.

• In exercise 48.11, people will ask you whether various facts and assumptions aren't accurate. Say they are indeed, using *si* and *c'est bien*.

Audio cues (for reference):
48.11 Activation orale: Confirmation; c'est bien

1. Ouessant, ce n'est pas en Bretagne?
2. C'est pas des berlingots que tu voulais?
3. Ce n'est pas ça?
4. Ce n'est pas à Montélimar qu'on fait du nougat?
5. Ce n'est pas à Marseille qu'on fait la bouillabaisse?
6. Ce n'est pas à St. Jean de Luz que vous allez pour les vacances?
7. Ce n'est pas Louis XIV qui a fait faire le Canal du Midi?

48.12-48.14 Observation and activation: *Ce qui, ce que, ce dont* (review and extension)

You saw in lesson 46 how the relative pronouns *qui*, *que*, and *dont* replace subjects, objects, and objects of the preposition *de*. In lesson 44, you saw *ce qui* and *ce que* used to replace subjects and objects that are not specified. Chart 48.12 reviews these relative pronouns and introduces *ce dont*, used in a relative clause to replace non-specific objects of the preposition *de*.

• In exercise 48.13, you will hear a series of questions about things or situations that are unspecified and that are referred to as *ça*. Answer each question with a confirmation, using *c'est exactement* and *ce qui*, *ce que* (*ce qu'*), or *ce dont*, as appropriate. (You will need to determine whether *ça* functions as the subject, object, or object of the preposition *de*.)

Audio cues (for reference):
48.13 Activation orale: Ce qui, ce que, ce dont

1. Ça t'intéresse, ça?
2. C'est ça que vous voulez?
3. C'est de ça qu'il a besoin?
4. Ça te plaît, ça?
5. Tu as envie de ça?
6. Ça vous ennuie, ça?

7. C'est de ça que tu as peur?
8. Il croit ça?
9. Tu as compris ça, toi?
10. C'est ça que tu cherches?
11. Ils ont peur de ça?

• In 48.14, you will hear statements about various things, followed by questions about those things. Answer positively, using *c'est exactement* and the appropriate relative pronoun, as in 18.13. (You will need to decide whether the things referred to in the questions are subjects, objects, or objects of the preposition *de*.)

Note. In several of the questions you will hear *en* used to refer to the thing that is being asked about. Remember that *en* can be used to replace nouns in two different situations:

1. in partitive expressions ("Est-ce que Mireille a **des frères**?" —"Non, elle n'**en** a pas");

2. in expressions with the preposition *de* ("Robert a **besoin de pantoufles**?" —"Non, il n'**en** a pas **besoin**").

When you hear *en*, be sure to determine whether it is standing in for a partitive expression or a noun used in an expression with the preposition *de* (*avoir besoin de*, *avoir envie de*, and so forth). If *en* replaces a partitive, use *ce que* in your answer. If it replaces an object of *de*, use *ce dont*.

Audio cues (for reference):
48.14 Activation orale: Ce qui, ce que, ce dont

1. Il y a des berlingots. Tu en veux?
2. Il y a des nougats. Tu en as envie?
3. J'ai apporté le guide de la Bretagne. Ça t'intéresse?
4. Robert a acheté de chaussures de marche. Il en avait besoin?
5. Robert et Mireille ont gagné 40.000 F à la loterie. Ils avaient besoin d'argent?

48.15-48.17 Observation and activation: *Laisser*

Chart 48.15 demonstrates how the verb *laisser* is used in several kinds of situations.

Laisser can be used to indicate refraining from involvement or interference, for instance leaving people or things alone: "**Laissez** ça;" "**Laisse**-moi tranquille!" Note that *ça* and *-moi* in these situations are **direct objects**.

Laisser can also be used to say what remains or to indicate the process of leaving something behind: "Ça ne **laisse** pas beaucoup de temps pour l'histoire de l'art;" "Jean-Pierre **a laissé** la table libre."

Laisser is also used with an **infinitive** to refer to allowing something to happen or to giving someone permission for something: "Vous **laissez** tomber des papiers devant elle;" "Tu ne peux pas me **laisser** partir tout seul!" Note that when *laisser* + infinitive refers to allowing someone to do something, the person receiving permission is referred to by a **direct object** pronoun: *elle ne peut pas* **le** *laisser partir tout seul*.

• In exercise 48.16, you and others want to do various things. Say you and they should be allowed to do them, using the imperative form *laissez* and the appropriate direct object pronoun, followed by the verb indicating the action. (Recall that the direct object pronoun *me* becomes *moi* after an imperative.)

Audio cues (for reference):
48.16 Activation orale: Laisser

1. Je veux venir avec vous!
2. Marie-Laure veut aller au cinéma.
3. Il veut partir.
4. Nous voulons écouter la radio.
5. Robert et Mireille veulent aller au théâtre.
6. Je veux dire quelque chose.

• In the dictation exercise in 48.17, write the words and expressions you hear in the spaces provided.

√ Check your answers in key 48.17 at the back of the workbook.

48.18 Activation: Revenge; forms of the future (review)

• Exercise 48.18 will help you review the forms of the future. Imagine you are Marie-Laure, and you are feeling a little spiteful. You are telling Mireille that you know she would like it if you didn't come along, if you told her where you are going, if she left without you, and so forth. Using the future, inform her that exactly the opposite of what she wants will take place. (Where Mireille would prefer that something **not** happen, say that it will. Where she would prefer that it happen, say it won't.)

Audio cues (for reference):
48.18 Activation orale: Revanche; formes du futur (révision)

1. Tu voudrais bien que je ne vienne pas avec vous, hein!?
2. Tu voudrais bien que je te dise où je vais, hein?
3. Tu voudrais bien partir sans moi.
4. Tu voudrais bien faire ce petit voyage sans moi!
5. Tu voudrais bien que j'aille à St. Jean de Luz avec papa et maman.
6. Tu voudrais bien que je ne vienne pas avec vous!
7. Tu voudrais bien avoir un berlingot!
8. Tu voudrais bien savoir ce que je vais faire.
9. Tu voudrais bien pouvoir faire ça.

48.19, 48.20 Observation and activation: Demands; subjunctive (review)

Chart 48.19 reviews the use of the subjunctive in situations where the action of one verb places the reality of the action of another into question. *Je veux que, je tiens à ce que, ils insistent pour que* focus on various demands. The demands themselves are actual, and the verbs that express them are in the **indicative**: *je veux, je tiens, ils insistent*. But the actions demanded are not described as taking place and are not presented as actual; they are expressed by verbs in the **subjunctive**: *que tu sois, que vous veniez, que nous allions*.

• In exercise 48.20, people are told to do various things, and then are told why: because you want them to, because others insist, because it would be better. Tell them that you want them to do these things, that others insist that they do them, and so on, using the subjunctive.

Audio cues (for reference):
48.20 Activation orale: Demandes; subjonctif

1. Viens avec nous. Je le veux.
2. Arrange-toi pour être à l'heure. J'y tiens.
3. Prenez des billets de première classe. J'aimerais mieux.
4. Allons-y demain. Ils insistent.
5. Partez à 6h. Ce serait mieux.
6. Venez déjeuner à la maison. J'y tiens.

48.21, 48.22 Observation and activation: Possession; possessive pronouns

The man in black offers Marie-Laure a package of gumdrops, but she refuses them because they aren't hers: "Ce ne sont pas **les miennes**." Chart 48.21 presents the **possessive pronoun** which, like all pronouns, stands in for a noun and reflects the gender and number of the noun it replaces: *le* **tien**, *la* **tienne**, *les* **tiens**, *les* **tiennes**, and so forth.

Note the circumflex accent on the *o* of *le/la* **nôtre** and *le/la* **vôtre** that distinguishes these forms from the possessive **adjectives** *notre* and *votre*. (Recall, too, that the adjectives *notre* and *votre* are always followed by a noun.) Notice that the first and second person plural forms of the possessive **adjective** (**nos** *vélos*, **vos** *vélos*) are quite different from the corresponding forms of the possessive **pronoun** (*les* **nôtres**, *les* **vôtres**).

• In exercise 48.22, you will be asked whether various things belong to you and others. Say yes, they are yours, his, hers, and so forth, using the possessive pronoun.

Audio cues (for reference):
48.22 Activation orale: Possession; pronoms possesifs

1. C'est bien le vélo de Robert?
2. C'est bien ma madeleine?
3. C'est votre voiture, là-bas?
4. C'est l'appartement des Belleau?
5. Ce sont les boules de gomme de Marie-Laure?
6. C'est le bateau des parents d'Hubert?
7. C'est ta bicyclette?
8. Ce sont les bonbons de Marie-Laure?
9. Ce sont les chaussures de Robert?
10. Ce sont bien mes livres?
11. C'est bien la maison des Courtois?
12. Ce sont bien mes lunettes?
13. Ce sont nos boules de gomme?
14. C'est le chien de Tante Georgette?

48.23 Activation: Dialogue between Marie-Laure and Mireille

Listen to the conversation between Marie-Laure and Mireille and memorize Mireille's lines, imitating and repeating as usual.

TOWARD FREE EXPRESSION

48.24 Words at large

Proceed as usual. (If necessary, refer to lesson 27 for directions.)

48.25-48.28 Role-playing and reinvention of the story

In 48.25, Jean-Michel and Hubert are squaring off on the subject of what Robert should see in France. Reconstruct their conversation.

In 48.26, reconstruct the story of what happened to Victor Hugo's daughter.

In 48.27, say what you would do if you took a tour of France.

In 48.28, make up a conversation between Marie-Laure and the man in black.

• **Suggested oral assignment.** Describe your plans for a tour of France as in 48.27. Say about ten sentences. Send this assignment to your instructor (see the course syllabus for details).

OPTIONAL EXERCISES FOR WRITING PRACTICE

• Listen again to exercises 48.13 and 48.20 on the audio recording and write out the audio cues you hear.

√ Check what you have written against the printed text in the study guide.

SELF-TESTING EXERCISES

Complete and check exercises 48.29, 48.30, and 48.31 as usual.

SUMMARY QUIZ

Consult the course syllabus or check with your instructor for information about completing and handing in summary quiz 48.

LESSON 49
What a nightmare!

<u>The story</u>

By 7:00, Mireille panics and phones Robert to ask if he has seen Marie-Laure. He hasn't, but he rushes over to help. They look in the Luxembourg Garden. There is no trace of her. At 8:00, when the little girl has been gone for three hours, they go home planning to call the police, but they find her in the apartment, calmly straightening the rigging of her sailboat. After a brief bout of hysterics, Mireille sends Marie-Laure to bed and says goodbye to Robert. They and the other travelers will meet tomorrow after Mireille's exam.

A little later, promising to believe her, Mireille persuades her sister to tell what happened. The story is a real plot-thickener. She saw the man in black in the park, looking suspicious (it's hard to imagine him looking anything but suspicious). When he left, she tailed him. He, evidently afraid of being followed, tried to lose her, first in the subway and then by following a guide through the catacombs of Paris. He got away when Marie-Laure was, for a moment, locked in the underground gallery. Not having enough money for the subway, Marie-Laure walked home.

True to form, and in spite of her promise, Mireille believes not a word of the story, and she asks Marie-Laure not to say anything to her parents. Agreed. Mystery and gum drops. By the way, pass me one; it'll help me fall asleep.

<u>Notes on culture and communication</u>

• **Les Catacombes, le Lion de Belfort.** The maxim that history lies all around you in France is never more intimately true than in the catacombs of Paris. (See the document for lesson 49 in the textbook.) The spot was originally a tremendous quarry, the stone from which was used to build most of old Paris. By the end of the eighteenth century the deserted quarry had become a hideout for all sorts of people engaged in nefarious activities, but little was done about the situation until the 1780s when the growth of Paris and of ideas of hygiene made the numerous cemeteries of the city, with their open graves and cadavers stacked up in *charniers*, a threat to public health. It was then decided to remove the bodies to the former quarry. Eventually the bones of five or six million people, some of them dating back to the twelfth century, were moved and piled into the underground vaults.

In the twentieth century, a small portion of the catacombs were made into a tourist attraction. Meanwhile, the surface above this grim area had become a heavily used traffic center. It was at this important intersection that a statue was erected to honor the city of Belfort, in northeastern France, which, lead by General Denfert-Rochereau, held out against the Germans through the War of 1870 and thus remained part of France while the rest of eastern France was annexed to Germany. The sculptor who created "Le Lion de Belfort" was Bartholdi, creator of the Statue of Liberty.

Content and learning objectives of lesson 49

This lesson presents ways in which French speakers give emphatically negative answers and express concern, impatience, perplexity, doubt, and intuition.

The following points are highlighted in lesson 49 (you should concentrate on sections marked with a √):

- *Arriver à*
- *Douter* versus *se douter*
- √ The future of the past (49.19-49.20)
- √ The subjunctive, review and extension (49.21-49.23)

ASSIMILATION OF THE TEXT

49.1-49.4 Text work-up, aural comprehension, and oral production

Proceed as usual in these sections. (Refer to lesson 28.1-28.4 for directions, if necessary.) Work with the text of lesson 49 in the textbook, as in previous lessons.

TOWARD COMMUNICATION

49.5 Activation: Pronunciation; the semivowel /ɥ/ (review)

Recall that to pronounce /ɥ/, tongue and lips are in position to pronounce /y/. The tongue rests lightly against the lower teeth. The /y/ sound is then followed **immediately** by the next vowel sound. The tongue **glides** from the /y/ position to the position of the following vowel.

- Repeat the words and expressions you hear.

49.6, 49.7 Observation and activation: Pronunciation; *os, boeuf, oeuf, oeil*

These four words have a common peculiarity: in the singular, they end in a consonant sound (a semivowel in the case of *oeil*) that is not present in the plural.

• In exercise 49.7, repeat the singular and plural forms you hear.

49.8 Observation: Events; *arriver à quelqu'un*

Chart 49.8 presents the verb *arriver*, used, like *se passer*, to refer to what happens. Events happen **to** people, and *arriver* can be used with an **indirect object** to specify the beneficiary or the victim: "Qu'est-ce qui est arrivé **à Marie-Laure?**" ⇒ "Qu'est-ce qui **lui** est arrivé?"

49.9-49.11 Observation and activation: Insistence; *du tout*

Trying to calm Mireille down after they have found Marie-Laure safe and sound, Robert points out that the little girl is unharmed, that nothing has happened to her at all: "Il ne lui est rien arrivé **du tout!**" Chart 49.9 shows how *du tout* is used to emphasize the negative expressions *ne . . . pas* and *ne . . . rien*.

When *du tout* is used with *rien* in a compound tense, il is placed **after** the past participle ("Il ne lui est **rien** arrivé **du tout**").

• In exercise 49.10, give an emphatic negative answer to the questions you hear, using *du tout*. When the question asks about *quelque chose*, use the negative expression *ne . . . rien*. Otherwise, use *ne . . . pas*.

Audio cues (for reference):
49.10 Activation orale: Insistance; du tout

1. Vous trouvez ça drôle, vous?
2. Tu as eu peur?
3. Tu le connais, ce type?
4. Il t'a dit quelque chose?
5. Il a de la barbe?
6. Il a l'air gentil!

• In 49.11, give emphatic negative answers using *rien* and *du tout*.

Audio cues (for reference):
49.11 Activation orale: Insistance; du tout

1. Qu'est-ce que tu as fait?
2. Qu'est-ce que tu lui as dit?
3. Qu'est-ce qui se passe?

4. Combien est-ce que tu as payé pour entrer?
5. Il lui est arrivé quelque chose?

49.12, 49.13 Observation and activation: Insistence; *mais, pouvoir bien*

Growing more and more anxious about Marie-Laure's absence, Mireille wonders what on earth she could be up to: "**Mais** qu'est-ce qu'elle **peut bien** faire?" Chart 49.12 illustrates how *mais* and *pouvoir bien* are used to emphasize one's concern or impatience.

• In exercise 49.13, you will hear questions about what people did, what happened to them, where they went, and so forth. Ask what in the world they could have done, what on earth could have happened, where in heaven's name they could have gone, etc., using *mais* and *pouvoir bien*.

Audio cues (for reference):
49.13 Activation orale: Insistance; mais, pouvoir bien

1. Qu'est-ce qu'elle a fait pendant tout ce temps!?
2. Qu'est-ce qui lui est arrivé?
3. Où est-elle passée?
4. Où est-elle allée?
5. Qu'est-ce qu'il a fait pendant tout ce temps?
6. Qu'est-ce qu'elle a raconté à ses parents?
7. Qu'est-ce qu'ils ont dit pour la contrarier?

49.14, 49.15 Observation and activation: Perplexity

You have seen how *qui*, *que*, and *où* are used with subjects and verbs to ask questions about people, things, and places: **Qui** *est-ce qu'elle invite?*, **que** *cherchez-vous?*, **où** *va-t-elle?*

Chart 49.14 shows how *qui*, *que*, and *où* are used with infinitives to express more general uncertainty or perplexity. Mireille, wringing her hands over Marie-Laure's disappearance, just doesn't know what to do: "Je ne sais pas **que** faire!"

Qui, *que*, and *où* used in this way as **interrogative pronouns** can be found in two kinds of questions:

1. **Direct** questions—questions one asks directly, with a rising intonation at the end of the question (the written version ends in a *?*): "**Que** faire?"

2. **Indirect** questions in which the question word is enclosed in some other statement. In indirect questions there is no rising intonation and the question mark is absent: "Je ne sais pas **que** faire."

• In exercise 49.15, you are told that various actions must be taken: you must do something, go somewhere, turn to someone, and so forth. Say you just don't know what to do, where to go, whom to turn to, etc., using *qui*, *que*, or *où*. If you hear *quelqu'un* or *à quelqu'un* in the question, answer with *qui* or *à qui*; if you hear *quelque chose*, answer with *que*; if you hear *quelque part*, answer with *où*.

Audio cues (for reference):
49.15 Observation: Perplexité

1. Il faut faire quelque chose!
2. Il faut aller quelque part.
3. Il faut dire quelque chose!
4. Il faut vous adresser à quelqu'un!

5. Il faut parler à quelqu'un!
6. Il faut chercher quelque part!
7. Il faut appeler quelqu'un!
8. Il faut se plaindre à quelqu'un!

49.16-49.18 Observation and activation: Doubt and intuition; *douter, se douter*

Mireille doubts that it's worth the trouble for Robert to go to the Folies-Bergère: "Je **doute** que ça vaille la peine." Returning from Provins in the loaner from Tonton Guillaume's garage, she suspected the headlights wouldn't work: "Je **me doutais** que les phares ne marcheraient pas." Chart 49.16 contrasts the use of *douter* to express doubt and *se douter* to express intuition. Notice that the two expressions have nearly opposite meanings.

The objects of one's doubt or sixth sense can be expressed by *que* and a dependent clause. Or they can be replaced by *en*.

• In exercise 49.17, determine which of the sentences you hear refer to doubt and which refer to intuition, and mark the appropriate boxes on the grid.

√ Check your answers in key 49.17 at the back of the workbook.

• In some of the sentences in 49.18, you and others pretty much **knew** that certain people would come, that they would say this or that, and so forth. Say you (and they) suspected as much, using *se douter que*.

In other sentences, you **don't think** that certain things are worth the trouble, that certain people are sick, and so on. Express doubt, using *douter* *que.* Remember that since *douter que* places the action of a verb in limbo, the verb will be in the **subjunctive**.

Audio cues (for reference):
49.18 Activation orale: Doute et intuition

1. Je savais que tu viendrais.
2. Je ne crois pas que ça vaille la peine.
3. Je ne pense pas qu'elle soit malade.
4. Il savait que je dirais ça.

5. Je pensais bien que ça vous amuserait.
6. Ça m'étonnerait qu'il vienne ce matin.
7. Je pensais bien qu'il serait là.
8. Je ne crois pas que tu veuilles faire ça.

49.19, 49.20 Observation and activation: The future of the past; use of the conditional

Marie-Laure, telling Mireille the story of her pursuit of the man in black, knows her sister won't believe her: "Je **sais** que tu ne me **croiras** pas." Notice that the verb of the main clause, *sais*, is in the **present** because Marie-Laure is talking about a belief she has at that moment. The verb of the dependent clause, *croiras*, is in the **future** because she thinks Mireille will not believe her when she has finished telling her story.

Sure enough, ten minutes later Mireille expresses her utter disbelief, and Marie-Laure refers to her earlier prediction: "Je **savais** que tu ne me **croirais** pas." Now the verb of the main clause, *savais*, is in the **past** (the imperfect), because Marie-Laure is referring to something she knew earlier. The verb of the dependent clause, which ten minutes ago represented a future in relation to the present (*croir*as) still represents a future, but in relation now to the past. This tense is sometimes called the future of the past, and is expressed by the **conditional** (*croir*ais).

• In certain sentences of exercise 49.20, various things will or won't happen; you are sure of it. Say you are sure they will happen, using the present tense to express your certainty and the future to express what you know will take place.

In other sentences, various things did or didn't happen; you guessed as much. Say you were sure they wouldn't happen, using the imperfect to express your certainty and the conditional to refer to what you knew would not take place.

Audio cues (for reference):
49.20 Activation orale: Le futur du passé; emploi du conditionnel

1. Ça ne va pas marcher. J'en suis sûr.
2. Ça n'a pas marché. J'en étais sûr.
3. Ils n'ont pas trouvé Marie-Laure. Je le savais.

4. Il n'a pas fini son travail. Je le savais bien.
5. Il fera beau demain. J'en suis sûr.
6. Ils sont arrivés en retard. Je le savais.
7. Robert n'a pas aimé ça. J'en étais sûr!

49.21-49.23 Observation and activation: Subjunctive (review and extension)

You have seen the subjunctive used in situations where the notion of constraint or necessity is projected onto an action, for example:

Il faut que tu **comprennes** ça.
Tu veux qu'on y **aille**?
Prends n'importe quel billet, pourvu que les deux derniers chiffres
    fassent neuf.

You have also seen the subjunctive used where an action is presented subjectively, for instance when it is colored by some attitude:

J'ai peur que tu **sois** déçu.
Ça m'étonnerait que le Mont Blanc **fasse** 4810 m.

In each of these situations the action of the verb in the subjunctive is not described as actually taking place. The speaker's intent is to present as real not the action represented by the verb in the subjunctive, but the obligation or attitude expressed by the verb in the main clause.

Chart 49.21 presents further examples of situations in which one action is subordinated to another in a way that emphasizes the importance of the verb in the main clause.

● In exercise 49.22, you acknowledge that you and others are not anxious to do certain things. You add, however, that various situations make it important to do them, using *mais* and an expression of necessity or preference. In the sentences you hear, these expressions will be incomplete. Repeat the expression after the word *mais* and complete it, using the subjunctive.

Audio cues (for reference):
49.22 Activation orale: Subjonctif

1. Je sais que ça t'ennuie de partir, mais je veux que tu...
2. Je sais que ça t'ennuie de venir, mais il faut que tu...
3. Je sais que ça t'ennuie de me le dire, mais j'ai besoin que tu...
4. Il sait que ça nous ennuie d'y aller, mais il veut que nous y....
5. Ils sait que ça vous ennuie de venir, mais il aimerait beaucoup que vous...

6. Je n'ai pas envie de lire ce livre, mais il vaudrait mieux que je le...
7. Je sais que tu n'as pas envie d'y aller, mais je crois qu'il serait bon que tu y...

• In 49.23, create sentences that begin with each of the expressions you see. Use the subjunctive.

√ Send your answers for exercise 49.23 to your instructor (see the course syllabus for details).

49.24 Activation: Dialogue between Robert and Mireille

Listen to the conversation between Robert and Mireille and memorize Robert's lines, imitating and repeating as usual.

TOWARD FREE EXPRESSION

49.25 Words at large

Proceed as usual. (If necessary, refer to lesson 27 for directions.)

49.26, 49.27 Role-playing and reinvention of the story

In 49.26, Robert and Mireille have returned from their frantic search for Marie-Laure to find her in her room, peacefully playing with her boat. Reconstruct their conversation.

In 49.27, tell the true story of Marie-Laure's adventure.

• **Suggested written assignment.** Write out a version of Marie-Laure's adventure in 49.27. Write twelve to fifteen sentences. Send this assignment to your instructor (see the course syllabus for details).

OPTIONAL EXERCISES FOR WRITING PRACTICE

• Listen again to exercises 49.10, 49.11, and 49.18 on the audio recording and write out the audio cues you hear.

√ Check what you have written against the printed text in the study guide.

SELF-TESTING EXERCISES

Complete and check exercises 49.28 and 49.29 as usual.

SUMMARY QUIZ

Consult the course syllabus or check with your instructor for information about completing and handing in summary quiz 49.

LESSON 50
More variety, more riches

The story

The gang meets as planned. Hubert and Jean-Michel engage in some good-natured ribbing. Mireille doesn't want to talk about the exam she just took; she'd rather discuss their travel plans.

The trip needs a unifying theme. Châteaux? Churches? Colette (how does she stay so thin?) gets them going for a while on foods, but there are other, less tasty but equally tasteful local artifacts and a great variety of natural phenomena; nothing violent, everything civilized. Spas rather than volcanoes.

At about this time, the quest for a unifying theme is forgotten in the rush to prove that France has a little of everything. There are amber waves of grain and rice paddies, wild horses, cowboys, flamingoes, olive trees. The mention of olive trees brings on a discussion of regional traditions in cooking. All Gaul is divided into three parts, Julius Caesar once wrote. Hubert interprets this as a reference to those parts of France where different cooking fats are dominant: butter in the north, olive oil in the south, and animal fat in central and southwestern France. Jean-Michel has his own interpretation of Caesar: the three parts are the wine-, beer-, and cider-producing regions. Speaking of cider, Colette could go for a bottle right now. There are no objections. The meeting is adjourned to the café across the street.

Notes on culture and communication

• **"Gallia est omnis divisa in partes tres."** Hubert is quoting (somewhat inaccurately) the famous opening sentence of Caesar's historical commentary *De Bello Gallico*, a favorite translation piece from high-school Latin. Of course, Caesar was referring to areas occupied by the tribes he had to overcome in order to conquer Gaul for Rome, not to local habits of eating or drinking.

Content and learning objectives of lesson 50

This lesson presents ways in which French speakers refer to being

198

affected or unaffected by what happens and how they talk about countries, states, regions, provinces, and mountains.

The following points are highlighted in lesson 50 (you should concentrate on sections marked with a √):

√• *Penser de* versus *penser à* (50.6, 50.7)
√• Articles and prepositions with geographical names (50.10-50.17)
• Articles and prepositions with names of mountains
√• The subjunctive, review and extension (50.23, 50.24)

ASSIMILATION OF THE TEXT

50.1-50.4 Text work-up, aural comprehension, and oral production

Proceed as usual in these sections. (Refer to lesson 28.1-28.4 for directions, if necessary.) Work with the text of lesson 50 in the textbook, as in previous lessons.

TOWARD COMMUNICATION

50.5 Activation: Pronunciation; tonic stress (review)

• Repeat the expressions you hear, making sure to place no more than a **slight** stress on the last syllable of each expression.

50.6, 50.7 Observation and activation: Opinion and preoccupation; *penser de, penser à*

Chart 50.6 contrasts two expressions that contain the verb *penser*.

As they leave the theatre, Mireille asks Robert for his assessment of the movie: "Qu'est-ce que tu **penses du** film?" *Penser de* refers to **opinions** and **attitudes**. *Penser de* is used to express opinions about people as well as things: "Qu'est-ce que tu **penses de** lui?" It is mostly used in questions; the answer generally begins, "Je pense **que**. . . ."

Mireille criticizes Colette's preoccupation with food, telling her that's all she thinks about: "Tu ne **penses** qu'à ça!" *Penser à* points to the **target** of one's thoughts, whether things or persons ("Robert ne **pense** qu'à Mireille").

• In exercise 50.7, decide from the context whether the missing element in each sentence refers to opinions or preoccupations. Then complete the sentences using appropriate forms of *penser de* or *penser à*.

√ Check your answers in key 50.7 at the back of the workbook.

50.8, 50.9 Observation and activation: Sensitivity and indifference; *ça vous fait quelque chose?*

When Robert saw Mireille's hair illuminated by a beam of light from one of the stained glass windows at Chartres, he was deeply affected: "**Ça lui a fait quelque chose.**"

Mireille, who doesn't want to think about the exam she just took, asks her friends if they don't mind talking about something else: "Parlons d'autre chose, si **ça ne vous fait rien.**"

Chart 50.8 shows how *ça fait quelque chose* is used with an **indirect object** (*ça* **me** *fait quelque chose*, *ça* **lui** *fait quelque chose*, and so forth) to indicate that someone is strongly affected by something, positively or negatively. When you want to say that they are indifferent to something or that it doesn't affect them one way or the other, *ne . . . rien* is used in place of *quelque chose: ça* **ne** *me fait* **rien**.

• In the dictation exercise in 50.9, complete the sentences with the expressions you hear.

√ Check your answers in key 50.9 at the back of the workbook.

50.10-50.17 Observation and activation: Geography; articles and prepositions in front of the names of countries, regions, and provinces

The charts in this section show how French speakers refer to being in, going to, and coming from various geographical locations that have masculine and feminine names, and how they refer to these places as the origin of various products.

In chart 50.10, these relationships are shown for the names of countries and American states. Note that *en* is used to express movement toward or presence in countries and states with **feminine** names; *au* is used in the case of **masculine** names: **en** *Suède*, **au** *Canada*. *De* is used with no article to say that people or things come from countries and states with feminine names; *du* is used in the case of masculine names: **de** *Chine*, **du** *Japon*.

Chart 50.12 shows ways of expressing these relationships using the names of regions. Note that the pattern for regions with feminine names is the same as for feminine countries and states: *en* refers to movement toward and presence in: **en** *Normandie*, **en** Provence; *de* indicates movement from and origin: **de** *Normandie*, **de** *Provence*. In the case of regions with **masculine** names, *dans* is used with the **definite article** to express movement toward or presence in: **dans le** *Cantal*, **dans le** *Sud-Ouest*. *De* is used, again with the definite article, to say that things and people come from these regions: **du** *Cantal*, **du** *Sud-Ouest*.

As chart 50.15 illustrates, *à la* and *de la* are used to express these relationships in the case of islands with feminine names like Guadeloupe and Martinique.

• In exercise 50.11, you will hear interest expressed in various countries. Determine whether each country is feminine or masculine, listening for *la* or *le* before its name. (You will hear one or two countries whose names begin with *l'* and a vowel: *l'Allemagne*, *l'Afrique*. If your instinct tells you they are probably feminine, you will be right.) Then respond by saying let's go to that country, using *en* or *au* as appropriate.

Audio cues (for reference):
50.11 Activation orale: Géographie; articles et prépositions devant les noms de pays

1. La Grèce m'intéresse.
2. La Belgique m'intéresse.
3. La Russie me fascine.
4. L'Allemagne m'intéresse.
5. L'Afrique m'intéresse.
6. La Tunisie m'attire.
7. Le Canada m'attirerait assez.
8. Le Liban m'intéresse.
9. Le Portugal m'attire beaucoup.
10. La Chine me fascine.
11. Le Japon m'attirerait beaucoup.
12. Le Soudan m'intéresserait assez.

• In exercise 50.13, you will be asked if you aren't familiar with various regions. Say yes, you are, you've been there, using *en* with feminine names and *dans le* (*dans l'*) with masculine names.

Audio cues (for reference):
50.13 Activation orale: Géographie; articles et prépositions devant le nom des régions et provinces

1. Vous ne connaissez pas la Normandie?
2. Vous ne connaissez pas le Midi?
3. Vous ne connaissez pas le Nord de la France?
4. Vous ne connaissez pas la Bretagne?
5. Vous ne connaissez pas la Provence?
6. Vous ne connaissez pas le Cantal?
7. Vous ne connaissez pas l'Est de la France?
8. Vous ne connaissez pas le Sud-Ouest?

• In 50.14, you will be asked if certain people know various regions. Say yes, they've just come back from there, using *ils reviennent* followed by *de* for feminine names, *du* for masculine names.

Audio cues (for reference):

50.14 Activation orale: Géographie; articles et prépositions devant le nom des régions et provinces

1. Ils connaissent la Provence?   4. Ils connaissent le Sud-Ouest?
2. Ils connaissent la Camargue?   5. Ils connaissent la Bretagne?
3. Ils connaissent le Cantal?   6. Ils connaissent l'Alsace?

• In 50.16, decide whether each sentence refers to going to or coming from Martinique or Guadeloupe, and write *à la* or *de la* as appropriate.

√ Check your answers in key 50.16 at the back of the workbook.

• In 50.17, you will be asked where various products come from. The workbook gives you the name of the place of origin. Decide whether each place name is masculine or feminine. Then say that each product comes from the appropriate area, using *venir* + *de* with feminine names, *venir* + *du* with masculine names.

50.18-50.22 Observation and activation: Geography; names of mountains

Chart 50.18 shows that French speakers use the **definite article** with the names of mountainous areas, mountain ranges, and individual mountains.

Chart 50.21 shows that when referring to movement toward or presence in a mountain **range**, *dans* is used with the definite article. In the case of individual **peaks**, *à* is used with the article to indicate movement toward; *sur* and the article are used to talk about activities that take place on the mountain, such as camping.

De and the article are used in both cases to refer to movement away from an individual mountain or a mountain range.

• In exercise 50.19, you will be asked where various peaks are located. The workbook gives you the name of the group or range. Say where each mountain is to be found, using *dans* and the appropriate article.

• In 50.20, you will be asked whether you know various mountainous areas and mountain ranges. Reply negatively, saying you have never gone there; use *dans* and the appropriate article.

Audio cues (for reference):
50.20 Activation orale: Géographie; article défini devant les noms de montagnes

1. Vous connaissez le Jura?   4. Tu connais les Vosges?
2. Vous connaissez le Massif Central?   5. Tu connais les Alpes?
3. Vous connaissez l'Himalaya?   6. Tu connais les Pyrénées?

• In 50.22, you will be asked where various people are going, where they climbed, where they are coming from, where it's possible to ski, and so forth. The workbook gives you each location. Say they are going to the Alps, climbed Mont Blanc, have just come back from the Meije, etc., using *dans* or *de* and the definite article.

50.23, 50.24 Observation and activation: The subjunctive (review and extension)

You have seen in preceding lessons (most recently in lesson 49) that the actions of verbs in the subjunctive are presented as potential occurrences, not real ones. They are projected or envisaged only. Actions expressed by the subjunctive are often colored by some necessity or attitude. The verb expressing this necessity or attitude is the main idea of the sentence and occurs in the **main clause**. The verb in the subjunctive is subordinated to the action of this main verb; it is contained in the **subordinate clause**.

Chart 50.23 contains three further examples of sentences in which the action of the verb in the subjunctive is placed in a kind of twilight zone by the action of the main verb. In each sentence, the speaker's principal intent is reflected in the main verb; the verb in the subjunctive has no reality except as a hypothesis depending on the main verb.

Chart 50.23 also contains an expression in the subjunctive **without** a main clause (the main clause is understood but not expressed). *"Qu'à cela ne tienne!"* is a self-contained exclamation that is used to tell someone who is concerned about a problem not to let it stand in the way.

• In exercise 50.24, you will see a number of statements about Mireille and Robert. You are not completely satisfied with our story; you have some reactions and preferences to express about what happens, and in many cases you would do things differently. Rewrite each statement, giving free rein to your imagination and beginning each new sentence with one or another of the expressions listed in the workbook. Note that all these expressions are followed by the subjunctive.

√ Check the verbs you have put into the subjunctive in key 50.24 at the back of the workbook.

50.25 Activation: Composition

• In exercise 50.25, suppose you went to France. Describe where you would go, what you would like to see, how you would organize your trip. Use the conditional. Write 100–150 words.

√ Send this assignment to your instructor (see the course syllabus for details).

50.26 Activation: Dialogue between Robert and Mireille

Listen to the conversation between Robert and Mireille and memorize Mireille's lines, imitating and repeating as usual.

TOWARD FREE EXPRESSION

50.27 Words at large

Proceed as usual. (If necessary, refer to lesson 27 for directions.)

50.28, 50.29 Role-playing and reinvention of the story

In 50.28, reconstruct the conversation between Robert, Mireille, and Jean-Michel about the variety and richness of France.

In 50.29, imagine the country where you would like to live.

• **Suggested oral assignment.** Record a description of your ideal country in 50.29. Say twelve to fifteen sentences. Send this assignment to your instructor (see the course syllabus for details).

OPTIONAL EXERCISES FOR WRITING PRACTICE

• Listen again to exercises 50.11, 50.13, and 50.14 on the audio recording and write out the audio cues you hear.

√ Check what you have written against the printed text in the study guide.

SELF-TESTING EXERCISES

Complete and check exercises 50.30 and 50.31 as usual.

SUMMARY QUIZ

Consult the course syllabus or check with your instructor for information about completing and handing in summary quiz 50.

LESSON 51
Parade and review

The story

On the terrace of the Deux Magots, famous as a meeting place for the intellectual elite, Hubert orders sparkling cider. The waiter says they don't have any, but Hubert commands, imperiously, that he find some. Now begins a series of coincidences that will strain our suspension of disbelief. As Hubert periodically, and with increasing impatience, reminds the waiter about the cider, we see in rapid succession:

1. Jean-Pierre Bourdon, who can't stop because he's on his way to an assignation with a "superb" number in Martinique.

2. Mme Courtois, talkative as ever, who is taking Minouche to be boarded at the vet's. The Courtois are leaving for Bulgaria, and the cat couldn't get a visa, and so on, and so forth.

3. Ghislaine, who is off to Brighton to meet her boyfriend, Bruce. She'll send postcards.

4. Cécile and her husband on new ten-speed bikes. They're off to Portugal tomorrow. Colette asks them to bring her back a bottle of port.

5. Uncle Victor, in his little car, going fishing in Bordeaux.

6. Uncle Guillaume. The bank at Monte Carlo broke him. Now he's bound for cheap living in Katmandou.

7. A handsome Swede. . . . Does Mireille really know him? Did we see him in Chartres? Was he driving an Alpine? No, he really doesn't have a cent, much less a fancy car. He is going to tour Greece on a motorbike.

8. Aunt Georgette has won big in the lottery on a ticket found in the street by Fido. (Man's best friend!) The next day, she found Georges. Now, with him and her other new toys, she's off to the Orient, to get engaged in the Taj Mahal!

The long-awaited bottle of cider finally arrives, and Robert is given the honor of easing out the cork. It comes blasting forth and Robert, well-meaning but maladroit, succeeds in spraying nearly everyone with cider. The cork ricochets wildly, hitting the man in black, who was seated at a nearby table. He flees, leaving behind a notebook containing information about Mireille and a completely illegible (rats!) "plan of attack."

Notes on culture and communication

• **Les Deux Magots.** In the heart of St.-Germain-des-Prés (see lesson 29), right across from the church, the Café des Deux Magots claims to be the meeting place of the Paris intellectual elite. The Deux Magots, along with its neighbor, the Café de Flore, achieved notoriety in the late 1940s and 1950s, when the most prominent figures of the existentialist movement, Jean-Paul Sartre and Simone de Beauvoir, made them their writing headquarters and favorite haunts.

• **Toujours aussi puant!** Colette's face is a symphony of movement when she says that Jean-Pierre is still the stinker he always was. Note the movement of her shoulders, head, eyes, eyelids, forehead, and lips, in complete harmony with the rhythm of what she says.

Content and learning objectives of lesson 51

This lesson will help familiarize you with colloquial and "correct" versions of a number of everyday expressions. It also shows how French speakers express astonishment, indicate that the costs of things are reasonable, and say where they intend to go and how long they intend to stay.

The following points are highlighted in lesson 51 (you should concentrate on sections marked with a √):

√• Levels of speech (51.8, 51.9)
 • Position of pronouns, review
√• Use of pronouns, *y*, and *en* with imperatives, review and extension (51.13-51.17)
 • *Faire de*
√• Negative infinitives (51.19, 51.20)
 • *Pour* + price, place name, duration

ASSIMILATION OF THE TEXT

51.1-51.4 Text work-up, aural comprehension, and oral production

Proceed as usual in these sections. (Refer to lesson 28.1-28.4 for directions, if necessary.) Work with the text of lesson 51 in the textbook, as in previous lessons.

TOWARD COMMUNICATION

51.5, 51.6 Observation and activation: Pronunciation; intonation

You are familiar with the way in which the pitch of the voice rises at the end of a question, especially a question that calls for an answer of *oui* or *non*. Section 51.5 presents another characteristic pattern of rise and fall of pitch in French.

The sentences in 51.5 are composed of two rhythmic groups—a situation common to a great many sentences in French. Notice that the pitch of the voice rises at the end of the first rhythmic group in these sentences, then returns to where it was, falling slightly at the conclusion of the second rhythmic group.

• Repeat the sentences you hear, making your voice rise at the end of the first rhythmic group.

51.7 Observation: Pronunciation; tonic stress and emphatic stress

Section 51.7 recalls the basic pattern of French pronunciation: a slight stress is placed on the final syllable of a rhythmic group (or the final syllable of a word when that word is said by itself). This **tonic stress** is created primarily by **lengthening** the syllable to about twice its normal (nonstressed) length. It is usually not said any louder, unlike tonic stresses in English.

There is a stress that is produced in French by saying the first syllable of a word **louder** than the other syllables, as the examples in 51.7 demonstrate. French speakers use this *accent d'insistance* to emphasize a word within the rhythmic group.

• Listen and repeat the expressions you hear.

51.8, 51.9 Observation and activation: Levels of speech

Jean-Michel and Hubert occupy different ends of the political spectrum. They have different ways of expressing themselves as well. Jean-Michel's speech tends to be informal, colloquial, even slangy. Hubert's speech is more formal and polished. Levels of speech can reflect background and education, but all speakers vary their levels of speech depending on the situation, the age and status of the person they are communicating with, their mood, and so forth.

Chart 51.8 presents a number of colloquial expressions that Jean-Michel or Marie-Laure might use and their equivalents in the more "correct" French of Aunt Amélie or Hubert's mother.

• In exercise 51.9, substitute more correct versions for the expressions you see in *italics*.

√ Check your answers in key 51.9 at the back of the workbook.

51.10, 51.11 Observation and activation: Surprise

Chart 51.10 groups together a number of expressions used to indicate surprise bordering on astonishment.

• In exercise 51.11, decide whether the speaker in each sentence is surprised or calm to the point of indifference. Mark the appropriate box on the grid.

√ Check your answers in key 51.11 at the back of the workbook.

51.12 Activation: Position of pronouns (review)

Exercise 51.12 will help you review the position of direct and indirect object pronouns (see lesson 39). Recall the pattern when both direct and indirect object pronouns are used with a verb: a first or second person **indirect object pronoun** is placed **before** the direct object pronoun (*elle nous a rendu la monnaie* ⇒ *elle* **nous** l'*a rendue*). When the indirect object pronoun is *lui* or *leur*, however, it comes **after** the direct object pronoun (*elle lui a rendu la monnaie* ⇒ *elle* **la lui** *a rendue*).

• You will be asked whether various people have given you and others change and your tickets. Say yes, they have, replacing nouns with pronouns.

Audio cues (for reference):
51.12 Activation orale: Place des pronoms (révision)

1. La caissière t'a rendu la monnaie?
2. L'ouvreuse t'a rendu les billets?
3. L'ouvreuse t'a rendu ton billet?
4. Tu m'as rendu mon billet?
5. Tu m'as donné les billets?
6. L'ouvreuse nous a rendu nos billets?
7. Pardon, Mademoiselle, vous m'avez rendu la monnaie?
8. La caissière a donné les billets à Mireille?
9. Mireille a donné les billets à Robert?

10. L'ouvreuse a rendu les billets à Robert?
11. L'ouvreuse a rendu leurs billets à Mireille et Robert?

51.13-51.17 Observation and activation: Commands; imperatives, pronouns, *y*, and *en* (review and extension)

Chart 51.13 shows how French speakers tell others to do things and not to do things involving various kinds of objects.

The chart shows that the order of direct and indirect object pronouns, *y*, and *en* is the same in the **negative imperative** as it is in the indicative.

You saw in lesson 25 that in the **positive imperative**, object pronouns, *y*, and *en* all follow the verb. Notice that the order of indirect and direct object pronouns is not the same as in the negative imperative. In the negative imperative (as in the indicative), the indirect object pronoun is placed first **except** when it is in the third person (*lui* or *leur*). In the positive imperative, the direct object pronoun always comes first, followed by the indirect object pronoun.

Recall that the direct and indirect object pronouns *me* and *te* become *moi* and *toi* when they are used in the positive imperative: *il faut* **te** *dépêcher* ⇒ *Dépêche-***toi**!; *il faut* **me** *le dire!* ⇒ *Dites-le-***moi**! Note, however, that this change does not occur when they are used with *en* in the positive imperative: *Achète-moi deux places!* ⇒ *Achète-***m'en** *deux!*; *Occupe-toi de ta poupée!* ⇒ *Occupe-***t'en**!

● In exercise 51.14, various individuals do not know about something; others are not supposed to know about it. When you hear that people don't know, direct that they be told, using the positive imperative. When you hear that they are not supposed to know, direct that they not be told, using the negative imperative. Notice that the **subject** of the sentence you hear will be the **indirect object** of your imperative expression; listen for the subject pronoun of the statement (*elle*, *je*, and so forth) and change it into the indirect object pronoun in your command (*dites-le-***lui**, *ne* **me** *le dites pas*, etc.).

Audio cues (for reference):
51.14 Activation orale: Ordres; impératifs, pronoms, y et en

1. Elle ne le sait pas.
2. Elle ne doit pas le savoir.
3. Il ne le sait pas.
4. Je ne le sais pas.
5. Nous ne le savons pas.
6. Ils ne le savent pas.
7. Elles ne le savent pas.
8. Il ne doit pas le savoir.
9. Je ne dois pas le savoir.
10. Nous ne devons pas le savoir.
11. Ils ne doivent pas le savoir.
12. Elles ne doivent pas le savoir.

• In 51.15, you will be told that certain gumdrops do or do not belong
to you and various other people. When they are yours (hers, ours, and so
forth), direct that they be given back to the owner, using the positive
imperative and the appropriate pronouns. When they are not yours (hers,
ours), direct that they not be given back to the person in question, using the
negative imperative and appropriate pronouns.

Audio cues (for reference):
51.15 Activation orale: Ordres; impératifs, pronoms, y et en

1. Ces boules de gomme sont à moi.
2. Ces boules de gomme ne sont pas à elle.
3. Ces boules de gomme sont à elle!
4. Ces boules de gomme sont à nous!
5. Ces boules de gomme sont à eux!
6. Ces boules de gomme ne sont pas à elle!
7. Ces boules de gomme ne sont pas à moi!
8. Ces boules de gomme ne sont pas à nous!

• In 51.16, you are telling certain people that they will like Katmandou,
others that they won't. Tell the people you think will like it to go there,
using the imperative and *y*. Tell those you think won't like it not to go
there, using the negative imperative and *y*.

Audio cues (for reference):
51.16 Activation orale: Ordres; impératifs, pronoms, y et en

1. Je suis sûr que Katmandou vous plaira.   4. Je suis sûr que Katmandou te plaira.
2. Ça ne vous plaira pas.   5. Ça ne te plaira pas.
3. Je suis sûr que Katmandou nous plaira.   6. Ça ne nous plaira pas.

• In 51.17, rewrite the sentences, replacing nouns with the appropriate
pronouns.

√ Check your answers in key 51.17 at the back of the workbook.

51.18 Observation: Use and disposal; *faire de*

As Uncle Guillaume passes by the Deux Magots in a battered Citroën,
Mireille asks him what he did with his Peugeot 604: "Qu'est-ce que tu **as fait
de** ta 604?" Chart 51.18 shows how *faire de* can be used in the present tense
to refer to the use someone makes of something, and in the *passé composé* to
indicate how one has disposed of it.

51.19, 51.20 Observation and activation: Negation and the infinitive

Chart 51.19 recalls the general pattern for negative expressions in French: *ne* is placed in front of the verb (in front of the auxiliary in compound tenses), and the second negative word follows the verb. The chart also shows that when the verb is in the infinitive, **both** negative words are placed **in front of** the verb.

• In exercise 51.20, people are told to refrain from doing certain things. Tell them to be careful not to do them, using *ne pas* and the appropriate infinitive.

Audio cues (for reference):
51.20 Activation orale: Négatif et infinitif

1. Ne tombez pas!
2. Ne roulez pas trop vite.
3. Ne brûlez pas le feu rouge.
4. Ne tombez pas dans le fossé.

5. Ne laissez pas tomber le plateau.
6. Ne faites pas sauter le bouchon.
7. Ne dépensez pas tout votre argent.

51.21–51.23 Observation: Good buys, destination, intention; *pour* + price, place name, duration

The charts in 51.21, 51.22, and 51.23 illustrate three uses of the preposition *pour*.

Colette, alert to any opportunity involving food or wine, asks Cécile and Jean-Denis to bring her back a bottle of port from Portugal. She has the impression that it's so cheap down there they practically give it away: "Il paraît qu'il est **pour rien** là-bas." Chart 51.21 shows how *pour* + an indication of price can be used to suggest that the cost of something is very reasonable.

Chart 51.22 shows how *pour* can be used with a place name to indicate where one is heading or planning to go.

Chart 51.23 illustrates the use of *pour* to indicate the length of time one intends to be gone or to stay somewhere. Note that *pour* refers to an **intention**; it does not specify the amount of time **actually** spent. *Robert est venu en France* **pour un an**: he has come to France **planning** to stay a year. *Robert est en France* **depuis un mois**: he has **actually** been in France for a month (and he still is).

51.24 Activation: Dialogue between the waiter and Hubert

Listen to the conversation between the waiter at the Deux Magots and Hubert and memorize Hubert's lines, imitating and repeating as usual.

TOWARD FREE EXPRESSION

51.25 Words at large

Proceed as usual. (If necessary, refer to lesson 27 for directions.)

51.26, 51.27 Role-playing and reinvention of the story

In 51.26, Aunt Georgette passes in front of the Deux Magots in a fancy convertible. Reconstruct her conversation with Mireille, Hubert, Colette, and Robert.

In 51.27, you are resigned to the fact that the authors are probably not going to solve the riddle of the man in black. You will very likely have to figure it out for yourself. Take a stab at it, using the suggestions in the workbook to get started.

• **Suggested written assignment.** Write out your solution to the enigma of the man in black in 51.27. Write about fifteen sentences. Send this assignment to your instructor (see the course syllabus for details).

OPTIONAL EXERCISES FOR WRITING PRACTICE

• Listen again to exercises 51.14 and 51.20 on the audio recording and write out the audio cues you hear.

√ Check what you have written against the printed text in the study guide.

SELF-TESTING EXERCISES

Complete and check exercises 51.28 and 51.29 as usual.

SUMMARY QUIZ

Consult the course syllabus or check with your instructor for information about completing and handing in summary quiz 51.

LESSON 52
All's well that ends well . . . or badly

The story

Departure at last. Evidently we've decided to go in Hubert's little car. Hubert suggests a cup of coffee before they leave, but Mireille, spotting the man in black at a nearby café, insists on an immediate getaway. She cuts short the discussion of who will sit where. She's worried.

On the road, Mireille reads up on the museums and churches of Rouen while Colette studies its restaurants. Hubert and Jean-Michel argue about politics, naturally. For a little while we are treated to an ideological-gastronomical counterpoint.

In Rouen, at the place where Joan of Arc was burned at the stake, Robert tells of his dream of being a heroic fireman. He'd arrive on a fiery steed, dash through the smoke, and save Joan of Arc, thus thwarting, says Hubert, the formation of France.

When the restaurant they choose proves to be closed on Tuesdays, Mireille suggests a picnic. The others will visit the cathedral while she shops for provisions. Robert goes with her. He isn't having such a great time. The other two guys' arguments and Colette's food fixation are getting to him, but his idea that he and Mireille leave them and take off by themselves goes over like a lead balloon. That is, until Mireille sees the man in black again and they think back to their numerous previous encounters with him. Mireille is frightened because she doesn't know which of them he is trailing, or why. The man in black has been following a Méhari. To lose him, they must leave it. They grab their things, split the lottery loot, scribble a note, and run.

After a brief ride in a truck bound for Turkey, they commandeer a small plane which Robert, no champion pilot, manages to start and get off the ground. Then, in a remarkably short time, Robert and Mireille see just about all of France from the air. A jet goes by; probably the unsinkable man in black. They're out of gas anyway, so they land and hitch a ride to nearby Lyon, to the railroad station. There, fairly confident that they have lost the man in black (hah!), they board the superspeed TGV train to Marseille. Somewhere on the coast, they hope to relax in the sun. (Hah again! The train may be going at 270 km/h, but look who has caught up with them and is sitting in the same car!)

214

The Hôtel Carlton in Cannes. Adjoining rooms. Balcony with superb view of beach and Mediterranean. Robert, lost in contemplation of sea and sky, maladroit as ever, falls. An ambulance takes him away and Mireille, whose cleverness never ceases to amaze us, guesses that they are taking him to the hospital. She goes there and, dressed as a nurse, spends a while at his bedside saying encouraging things.

Then she returns to the Carlton and there, finally, the decisive encounter with the man in black occurs. He, it turns out, is a filmmaker. It seems Mireille is perfect for the lead role in a film to teach French. Will she accept? Will she! What a day! Not one but two childhood dreams (nurse and actress) realized.

Robert hears on the radio about an explosion and fire at the Carlton. Without even stopping in a phone booth to change, he gets there, rushes in, and a few minutes later is dragged out semiconscious by Mireille. Wait: something's wrong. CUT! Robert reappears an instant later carrying Mireille in his arms. That's better.

A beautiful spring evening. The couple holding hands and walking along the beach into the proverbial sunset is not Laurel and Hardy. It must surely be Robert and Mireille, headed for new adventures.

Notes on culture and communication

• **Jeanne d'Arc** (1412-1431), the illiterate peasant girl who at the age of twelve began to hear supernatural voices summoning her to rescue her country from the English. By 1429, the seventeen-year-old Jeanne and her army had succeeded in freeing several occupied towns and getting King Charles VII crowned in Reims. She was captured and turned over to the English in 1430. Tried in Rouen and condemned as a heretic and a witch by an ecclesiastical court, she was sentenced to death and burned alive at the stake in the Old Market Place in Rouen on May 30, 1431. She was canonized as a saint in 1920. The first and most famous of a long line of powerful women in French history, her life has inspired numerous writers, filmmakers, and artists.

• **Beyond vocabulary and grammar.** The comments on communication in this guide have barely scratched the surface of a vast and fascinating subject. Our hope has been to sensitize you to an aspect of communicating with French speakers that transcends vocabulary and grammar. In summary, here is a quotation from a thinker who has written wisely about communication:

"It is a great mistake to suppose that people always say what they seem to be saying. The words they exchange may refer to automobiles, elections, personal tastes or books; but in talking about these matters they confirm or challenge the social relationship that exists between speaker and listener. In face-to-face communication it is quite possible to talk without conveying any real information about the world outside, but it is not possible to talk without saying something about the relationship between the participants in the communicational situation. . . . Much of the time people talk in order to confirm or to challenge the nature of their relationship to one another, and the world to which their messages refer, albeit obliquely, is the world of status and power, love and protection, hostility and politeness."

—Kurt Danziger, *Interpersonal Communication* (New York: Pergamon, 1976, pp. 27-28.)

ASSIMILATION OF THE TEXT

52.1 Text work-up

Proceed as usual in this section. (Refer to lesson 28.1 for directions, if necessary.) Work with the text of lesson 52 in the textbook, as in previous lessons.

TOWARD COMMUNICATION

By now you should be adequately prepared for communicating with speakers of French. Go directly to the reinvention exercise in 52.2.

TOWARD FREE EXPRESSION

52.2 Role-playing and reinvention of the story

Reinvent the story completely in fifteen or twenty sentences. Or, if you prefer, make up a new version of the five friends' trip and its aftermath. In a postscript, describe what has become of our two main characters now that their story has served its essential purpose—*apprendre le français*.

SUMMARY QUIZ 27

I. Which means of transportation is being described in each of the sentences you hear? Check the appropriate box. (5 pts.)

	1	2	3	4	5
l'avion					
le métro					
la voiture					
le train					
la moto					
le cheval					

II. You will hear a series of statements. From the two possibilities listed for each statement, choose the one that is the most likely continuation of what you hear. (4 pts.)

Example: You hear: Ça ne va pas. Je suis malade.
         You choose: √ a. Je vais rentrer chez moi.
         And not: ___ b. Viens déjeuner! J'ai faim.

Check your choice:

1. _____ a. Vous vous êtes trompée de numéro.
    _____ b. Vous n'avez qu'à prendre le métro.

2. _____ a. J'ai peur.
    _____ b. J'ai faim.

3. _____ a. Vous vous êtes trompé de train.
    _____ b. Vous n'avez qu'à prendre le métro.

4. _____ a. J'y tiens.
   _____ b. J'ai peur!

III. You will hear a statement using a verb in the present indicative.
Complete the response using the same verb in the *plus-que-parfait*.
(10 pts.)

1. Je croyais que vous _____ tout à l'heure.

2. Je croyais qu'il _____ chez les Courtois hier.

3. Je croyais que tu _____ téléphoné à Mireille jeudi.

4. Je croyais qu'ils _____ le petit déjeuner à l'hôtel.

5. Je croyais qu'il _____ ce matin.

IV. Complete the following sentences. (6 pts.)

1-3. —Comment va-t-on au Louvre? _____ pied ou _____

   métro?

   —_____ voiture.

4-5. On peut aller à Rome _____ train ou _____ avion.

6. Il fait beau, allons-y _____ vélo.

SUMMARY QUIZ 28

I. The following questions refer to the text of the lesson. You will hear
two answers to each question. Circle the letter that corresponds to the
correct answer. (5 pts.)

    1. A quelle heure est-ce que le train arrive?   A   B

    2. Où est-ce que Robert et Mireille vont déjeuner?   A   B

    3. Comment est le cycliste après l'accident?   A   B

    4. Qui y a-t-il dans la cathédrale quand Robert

       et Mireille y entrent?   A   B

    5. Qui est-ce que Mireille rencontre?   A   B

II. Choose the expression that best completes each statement you hear.
Check the appropriate box. (4 pts.)

Situation: Il est 4 heures. Robert attend Mireille.

	1	2	3	4
en retard				
à l'heure				
en avance				

III. You will hear two requests. Make each one more polite by rewriting it using the conditional. (4 pts.)

1. Je _____ une assiette de crudités, s'il vous plaît.

2. Est-ce que je _____ parler à Mademoiselle Belleau?

IV. Rewrite the following sentences (which show cause and effect) into hypothetical sentences (showing condition and consequence). (12 pts.)

1. Nous ne prenons pas de taxi parce que nous ne sommes pas pressés.

   Mais si nous _____ pressés, nous _____ un taxi.

2. Nous ne nous arrêtons pas au restaurant parce que nous n'avons

   pas faim.

   Mais si nous _____ faim, nous nous y _____.

3. Elle n'a pas peur parce que je ne conduis pas.

   Mais si je _____, elle _____ peur.

4. Nous n'allons pas au musée parce qu'il ne pleut pas.

   Mais s'il _____, nous _____ au musée.

5. Je ne loue pas de voiture parce que tu ne veux pas.

   Mais si tu _____, je _____ volontiers

   une voiture.

6. Robert n'achète pas de cadeau parce qu'il n'ose pas.

   Mais s'il _____, il en _____ un.

V. Oral Production. Record the following exercises on an audiocassette for submission to your instructor. Before you begin, record your name and today's date.

A. Read the following sentences. (5 pts.)

Elle est belle, ma salade.
Allons à Paris.

B. Order a meal from the menu below. Money is no object. Call the waiter, and tell him what you want. Don't just list the names of dishes; use the expressions you have learned. (20 pts.)

Hors d'oeuvre		Plats garnis	
Crudités	15,00	Rôti de boeuf, pommes	
Coeur d'artichaut	22,00	nouvelles rissolées	45,00
Assiette de jambon		Poulet rôti, frites	38,00
de Paris	22,00	Choucroute garnie	40,00
Oeufs à la russe	16,00	Boeuf bourguignon, riz	40,00

Salade		Glaces et desserts	
Salade maison	24,00	Crème caramel	8,00
Salade niçoise	24,00	Poire Belle Hélène	18,00
Salade exotique	24,00	Tarte aux pommes	8,00
		Fruit	5,00

Fromages		Carte des vins	
Camembert	9,50	Côtes-du-Rhône	22,00
Saint-Nectaire	10,00	Rosé du Tarn	14,00
Roquefort beurre	11,00	Pichet vin maison (25cl)	11,00
Yaourt	5,50		

Service compris 15%

SUMMARY QUIZ 29

I. You will hear a number of statements about means of transportation. Indicate whether each statement refers to an advantage or drawback. Check the appropriate box. (5 pts.)

	1	2	3	4	5
avantage					
inconvénient					

II. Complete by writing the appropriate indirect object pronoun. (5 pts.)

1. — Tu es en retard quelquefois?

   —Non, ça ne _____ arrive jamais.

2. — Est-ce que Mireille et ses soeurs prennent l'aéroglisseur pour aller

   en Angleterre?

   —Ça _____ est arrivé.

3. — Mireille va souvent à la bibliothèque?

   —Ça _____ arrive de temps en temps.

4. — Je ne me trompe jamais!

   —Mais si, ça _____ arrive!

5. — Vous vous perdez dans le métro, vous deux?

   —Nous? Ça ne _____ arrive jamais!

III. Rewrite the following declarations into hypothetical sentences.
Distinguish between past and present. (15 pts.)

Example: You hear: Je suis riche, alors je suis heureux.
You write: Si j'étais riche, je serais heureux.

1. Il fait beau, alors je vais à la plage.

_____

_____.

2. On n'avait pas de voiture, alors on a fait de l'autostop.

_____

_____.

3. Vous n'étiez pas libre, alors je n'ai pas pu vous inviter.

_____

_____.

SUMMARY QUIZ 30

I. You are in the Latin Quarter, looking for the nearest photocopy shop. Someone is giving you directions. As you listen, you jot down the landmarks and street names. Here is your list; put it in order by adding the appropriate number in front of each item. (5 pts.)

_____ boulevard Saint-Michel

_____ rue Cujas

_____ place de la Sorbonne

_____ la Fontaine Saint-Michel

_____ rue Victor Cousin

II. Dictation (10 pts.)

Tenez, je _____ vous montrer. Vous _____ ici.

Vous _____ le Boulevard Raspail jusqu'à Denfert-Rochereau.

Vous _____, c'est une place avec un lion. Vous obliquez à

droite pour _____ l'avenue du Général Leclerc. Vous la

_____ jusqu'à la porte d'Orléans, et là, vous _____ le

périphérique sur la gauche. Vous n'_____ qu'à _____ les

indications pour l'autoroute A6. Vous ne _____ pas vous perdre!

III. Put the sentences you hear into the *passé composé*. (10 pts.)

1. Robert _____ louer une voiture.

2. Il _____ au garage Shell.

3-4. Il _____ une voiture qui lui _____.

5. Il _____ en Bourgogne.

IV. Oral Production. Record the following exercises on an audiocassette for submission to your instructor. Before you begin, record your name and today's date.

A. Put yourself in each of the following situations. In two or three sentences, explain the problem and ask for help. (15 pts.)

1. You have gotten lost driving to Provins. Ask for directions.
2. You wish to rent a car for a week.
3. You are in a café. You want to telephone.

B. Compare each of the conveyances in the pairs below, giving the advantages and the disadvantages of each. Say a couple of sentences for each comparison. (10 pts.)

1. *Le train* versus *l'avion*.
2. *La voiture* versus *la bicyclette*.

SUMMARY QUIZ 31

I. You will hear a series of incomplete sentences. Complete each one by
    selecting the appropriate term from the list below and writing it on the
    appropriate line. (5 pts.)

les phares   la roue
la portière   une voiture
le feu rouge

1. _____   4. _____

2. _____   5. _____

3. _____

II. Complete each sentence by writing the correct form of the appropriate
    verb drawn from the list below. (10 pts.)

ralentir   tomber en panne
déraper   démarrer
s'arrêter

1. Quand tu vois un feu rouge, tu _____ .

2. Il n'y a plus d'essence dans le réservoir. On _____ !

3. Je tourne la clé, je mets le contact, et je _____ .

4. Attention, la route est dangereuse, elle est glissante! Vous allez

   _____ !

5. Vous allez trop vite. _____ !!

III. Put the verb in each sentence below into the *passé composé* by supplying the missing past participle. Don't forget agreement of the past participle if it is needed. (10 pts.)

1. Je dors mal. J'ai mal _____.

2. Il ouvre la portière. Il l'a _____.

3. Vous n'écrivez pas? Vous n'avez pas _____?

4. Elle prend la voiture. Elle l'a _____.

5. Qu'est-ce que tu dis? Qu'est-ce que tu as _____?

6. Vous suivez la rue d'Alésia. Vous l'avez _____.

7. On fait le plein. On l'a _____.

SUMMARY QUIZ 32

I. As you hear the story of Robert's meeting with Mireille narrated in the present, put each of the verbs into the imperfect or *passé composé* as indicated. Don't forget to make the past participle agree with a preceding direct object. (14 pts.)

A. Les circonstances (imparfait)

1. Il _____ beau à Paris.

2. Robert _____ le Quartier Latin.

B. L'action (passé composé)

3. Il _____ un groupe de manifestants.

4. Il les _____.

5. Il _____ dans la cour de la Sorbonne.

6. Il l'_____.

II. Listed below are some terms used to name rooms. Use them to complete the sentences that follow. (5 pts.)

salle
pièce
chambre

Notre appartement a quatre _____. Il y a la _____

de séjour, la _____ à manger, la cuisine (naturellement),

et deux _____ à coucher. Il y a aussi une _____

de bain et les toilettes.

III. Complete the following sentences. You will need to supply the auxiliary verb, reflexive pronouns (where necessary), and articles. (6 pts.)

1. Je _____ tombé. Je _____ fait mal à

_____ jambe.

2. Marie-Laure _____ réveillée à 7 heures. Puis elle

_____ brossé _____ dents.

IV. Oral Production. Record the following exercises on an audiocassette for submission to your instructor. Before you begin, record your name and today's date.

A. Read the following sentences. (5 pts.)

Ils sont bons.
Il sent bon.
Nous, les étudiants.
Nous l'étudions.

B. You are in Paris and your companion has become separated from you. Stop a policeman and explain. Tell him who is lost (your child, your mother, your spouse, your friend . . .), what he or she looks like, what he or she was wearing, and where the lost person was when you last saw him or her. Ask for help. (20 pts.)

SUMMARY QUIZ 33

I. Who is speaking in each of the sentences you hear? Check the appropriate box. (6 pts.)

	1	2	3	4	5	6
Madame Belleau						
Colette						
Hubert						

II. Complete the commands below with the imperative of the verb you hear. (5 pts.)

1. _____ de la patience!

2. _____ attendre, Madame.

3. _____ vos leçons pour demain!

4. _____ généreux!

5. _____ à l'heure!

III. As you hear some of the events of our heroes' trip to Chartres, rewrite them in the past tense, choosing between imperfect and *passé composé*. (14 pts.)

1. Il _____ presque midi quand Mireille et Robert

_____ à Chartres.

2. Ils _____ dans un café pour déjeuner parce

qu'ils _____faim.

3. Pendant qu'ils _____, ils _____

la cathédrale.

SUMMARY QUIZ 34

I. What part of the country house is M. Belleau describing in each of the sentences you hear? Check the appropriate box. (5 pts.)

	1	2	3	4	5
le toit					
les fenêtres					
le garage					
les portes					
la salle de bain					

II. You will hear a series of questions on the text of this lesson. Check the answer that best corresponds to each question. (5 pts.)

1. _____Chers.

   _____Parce qu'ils sont en co-propriété.

2. _____Il y a 20 ans.

   _____Une petite maison près de Dreux.

3. _____Parce qu'ils sont en co-propriété.

   _____Les charges.

4. _____Un coup de sonnette.

   _____Une bonne soeur.

5. _____Parce qu'elle avait de la moustache.

   _____Des billets de loterie.

III. Dictation. (5 pts.)

—Vous _____ cette maison?

—Non, je suis _____. Je trouve que la _____

est préférable à la _____. Et vous?

—J'aime mieux _____.

IV. Complete with the correct form of *faire* or *rendre*, as appropriate. Don't forget the agreement of past participles if necessary. (10 pts.)

1. Quand elle a perdu son chat, ça l'a _____ triste. Ça

   l'a _____ pleurer.

2. Ne _____ pas l'idiot! Tu _____ ta

   mère furieuse!

3. Il nous a fallu trois ans pour _____ la maison

   habitable.

V. Oral Production. Record the following exercises on an audiocassette for submission to your instructor. Before you begin, record your name and today's date.

A. Describe the living room in your house or apartment. Give its size, and name the furniture in it. You might compare it to the living room in the Belleau apartment. Two or three sentences. (10 pts.)

B. You want to sell your car. What can you say about it? Remember you want to present it in a favorable light. Four sentences will be enough. (15 pts.)

SUMMARY QUIZ 35

I. You will hear a conversation among Mireille, Hubert, and Robert, who seem unable for some reason to complete their sentences. Help them by selecting the appropriate term from the list below and writing it on the corresponding line. (5 pts.)

> une vieille maison de paysans   en tuile
> lourd   en dur
> en bois

1. _____

2. _____

3. _____

4. _____

5. _____

II. Rewrite the sentences you hear, using *en* and the present participle. (8 pts.)

1. Elle est tombée en panne _____ de Paris.

2. Robert a vu une Alpine _____ l'autoroute.

3. Marie-Laure est rentrée _____ .

4. Elle est tombée malade _____ son dessert.

III. Dictation. (12 pts.)

Quand _____ridicule

ce désir de _____d'avoir

_____à eux. Maintenant

_____.

SUMMARY QUIZ 36

I. What is being referred to in each sentence you hear? Check the appropriate box. (5 pts.)

	1	2	3	4	5
la Rotonde					
la minuterie					
le *Pariscope*					
L'Amour l'après-midi					

II. Complete the answers to the questions you hear, choosing the appropriate indefinite expression (*quelqu'un/personne, quelque chose/rien*). (5 pts.)

1. Il ne fait _____intéressant.

2. C'est _____ bizarre.

3. Nous mangeons _____bon.

4. Non! Je n'ai rencontré _____ sympathique.

III. Dictation. (5 pts.)

1. Nous allons nous _____. Voulez-vous

_____, s'il vous plaît.

2. Quand tu appuies sur le bouton, la lumière s'_____.

   Elle reste _____ deux minutes, puis elle

   s'_____.

IV. Complete each statement below with the appropriate form of the
   subjunctive. (10 pts.)

   1. —Tu ne prends pas de petit déjeuner?

      —Il faut que tu _____ quelque chose.

   2. —Vous ne finissez pas?

      —Il faut que vous _____.

   3. —Elle ne part pas?

      —Il faut qu'elle _____.

   4. —Ils ne disent rien?

      —Il faut qu'ils _____ quelque chose.

   5. —Je descends? Pourquoi faut-il que je

      _____?

V. Oral Production. Record the following exercises on an audiocassette for
   submission to your instructor. Before you begin, record your name and
   today's date.

   A. Read the following sentences. (5 pts.)

      On construit les murs en dur.
      Le toit est en tuile.

   B. Give clear directions to your house so that the people listening to
      this tape can find it from some well-known landmark in your town
      (from the highway exit, the town square, etc.). Include enough
      details to keep them from getting lost. (20 pts.)

SUMMARY QUIZ 37

I. Choose the best answer to each question you hear and put a check in front of it. (5 pts.)

1. _____Assis à la terrasse du café en face.

   _____En retard.

2. _____Un pourboire.

   _____Rien.

3. _____De la publicité.

   _____*L'Amour l'après-midi.*

4. _____Un jeune cadre dynamique.

   _____Un homme tout en noir.

5. _____L'homme quitte sa femme.

   _____L'homme retourne à l'amour de sa femme.

II. Dictation. (7 pts.)

1. —Qu'est-ce que vous _____?

   —J'_____ un cadeau pour ma mère.

2. Mes vieux *Pariscopes?* Ah, je les _____.

3. Nous partons _____ une heure.

4. Donne-moi un _____ de _____demain.

5. J'ai tout fini _____ une heure.

III. Complete the answer to each question with two personal pronouns.
(8 pts.)

1. —Tu me prêtes ta voiture?

—Oui, je _____ prête.

2. —Vous me recommandez le gigot?

—Oui, je _____ recommande.

3. —Tes parents t'ont payé le voyage?

—Oui, ils _____ ont payé.

4. —L'ouvreuse vous a rendu les billets?

—Oui, elle _____ a rendus.

IV. Complete with the correct form of the subjunctive of the verb in **bold**.
(5 pts.)

1. Vous n'**allez** pas voir ce film? Oh, il faut absolument que vous y
_____!

2. —Tu **peux** venir?

—Non, je ne crois pas que je _____ venir.

3. Elle **sait** que nous avons rendez-vous, mais je ne crois pas qu'elle

_____ à quelle heure.

4. Tu n'**as** pas de patience! Il faut que tu _____ plus de

patience.

5. Ils **sont** toujours en retard. Aujourd'hui, il faut qu'ils _____ à

l'heure!

SUMMARY QUIZ 38

I. Listen and determine which of the landmarks of Paris is being described. Check the appropriate box. (5 pts.)

	1	2	3	4	5
la Madeleine					
le musée d'Orsay					
la Tour Montparnasse					
la Place de la Concorde					
l'Assemblée nationale					

II. Expand the brief answers (printed below) to the questions you hear, as in the example. Be alert! Some of the questions concern the present, others the past. You should use the same verb tense in your answer. (10 pts.)

Example: You hear: Mireille a toujours voulu être actrice?
           You see: Oui, toujours.
           You write: Oui, elle <u>a toujours voulu</u> être actrice.

1. Oui, souvent. Oui, il _____.

2. Non, jamais. Non, il _____son

   passeport.

3. Oui, toujours. Oui, elle _____ avec

   ses parents.

4. Oui, toujours. Oui, il _____ de bonnes

   notes.

III. Rewrite each sentence using two pronouns (direct and indirect object). (10 pts.)

1. Mireille montre la statue à Robert.

   Elle _____ montre.

2. L'ouvreuse rend les billets à Robert et Mireille.

   Elle _____ rend.

3. Hubert a offert ces roses à Madame Belleau.

   Il _____ a offertes.

4. Mireille a emprunté sa voiture à Tonton Guillaume.

   Elle _____ a empruntée.

5. Mireille achète le *Pariscope* à Mme Rosa.

   Elle _____ achète.

IV. Oral Production. Record the following exercises on an audiocassette for submission to your instructor. Before you begin, record your name and today's date.

A. You have just seen a movie. What can you say if:

1. You didn't like it.
2. You thought it was excellent.

Give at least two possibilities for each. (10 pts.)

B. Describe your house: its location (town, city, country), size, number of rooms, garden, etc. If you prefer you may describe the house you wish you had, or you may pretend you are Hubert, Colette, or another character and describe his or her house. (15 pts.)

SUMMARY QUIZ 39

I. Below are some questions about theater in Paris. The answers, given on the audio recording, are not in the same order as the questions. Write the number of each answer in front of the corresponding question. (5 pts.)

_____ Combien de théâtres y a-t-il à Paris?

_____ Qu'est-ce que c'est qu'une salle subventionnée?

_____ Qu'est-ce qu'on joue souvent à la Comédie-Française?

_____ Qu'est-ce qu'on joue au théâtre de boulevard?

_____ Où peut-on aller si on ne veut pas beaucoup penser?

II. Complete by writing the answers to each question using two personal pronouns. Also add agreement to each past participle in the space provided. (10 pts.)

1. —Mademoiselle, quand vous étiez petite, est-ce que votre institutrice

   vous a montré cette fresque de Matisse?

   —Oui, elle _____ a montré____.

2. —Est-ce que l'institutrice a montré cette fresque à ses élèves?

   —Oui, elle _____ a montré____.

3. —Pardon, mademoiselle, vous m'avez rendu les billets?

   —Oui, monsieur, je _____ ai rendu____.

4. —Est-ce que l'ouvreuse a rendu les billets à ce monsieur?

   —Oui, elle _____ a rendu____.

III. Complete by writing the appropriate form of the subjunctive. (10 pts.)

1. —Faites attention!

   —Hein? Qu'est-ce que vous dites?

   —Il faut que vous _____ attention!

2. —Tu vas à la bibliothèque?

   —Oui, il faut que j'y _____.

3. —Est-ce que Marie-Laure veut voir l'exposition de manuscrits

   carolingiens au Grand Palais?

   —Vous plaisantez! Ça m'étonnerait qu'elle _____ voir ça!

4. —Vous allez au théâtre ce soir?

   —Non, je ne pense pas que nous y _____.

5. —Les Folies-Bergère, ça vaut la peine?

   —Non, je ne crois pas que ça _____ la peine.

SUMMARY QUIZ 40

I. Listen and determine what form of entertainment is being referred to. Check the appropriate box. (5 pts.)

	1	2	3	4	5
le music-hall					
le théâtre					
le cinéma					

II. Listen and complete the answers to each question you hear using a personal pronoun, *y*, or *en*. (5 pts)

1. Oui, je _____ ai téléphoné.

2. Non, je n'_____ vais pas.

3. Oui, j'_____ veux.

4. Oui, allons-_____.

5. Oui, j'_____viens.

III. Rewrite the sentences you hear, putting the verb in the future. (5 pts.)

1. Nous _____ au cinéma.

2. Vous _____ en retard.

3. Tu _____?

4. Il _____ prendre un verre.

5. Je ne _____ pas me marier demain.

IV. Listen, and reassure this anxious person by countering his statements with *personne* or *rien*. (10 pts.)

1. Ah, bon? Moi, je _____!

2. Mais non, _____!

3. Tu es fou! Il _____ sous la table!

V. Oral Production. Record the following exercises on an audiocassette for submission to your instructor. Before you begin, record your name and today's date.

A. Read the following sentences. (5 pts.)

Je suis contre le pourboire aux ouvreuses.
Ça doit être intéressant.
Un homme tout en noir.

B. You decide to go to the movies while you are in Paris. Describe each step as you pick out a film, go to the theater, buy a ticket, go in, find a seat, etc. A simple sentence for each step is enough. (10 pts.)

C. What would you say in each of the following situations? One or perhaps two sentences are enough. (10 pts.)

1. You want to purchase the *Pariscope*.
2. You are in a café. Order coffee.
3. You are at the movies. Buy two tickets, then ask when the show begins.

SUMMARY QUIZ 41

I. You will hear a series of questions on the text of this lesson. Write the answer on the corresponding line, choosing the appropriate term from the list below. (5 pts.)

> bonheur   l'argent
> une pièce   l'addition
> un billet   la monnaie
> un ticket

1. Il lui demande _____.

2. Il lui donne _____ de 200 francs.

3. Pour rendre _____.

4. Il laisse tomber _____.

5. Ça porte _____.

II. Respond to each question you hear, completing the expression of indifference given. (4 pts.)

1. Ça n'a pas d'importance. N'importe _____.

2. N'importe _____.

3. Je ne sais pas. . . . N'importe _____.

4. Oh, n'importe _____.

III. You will hear a verb in the imperative. Use the same verb to complete the statement printed below, using the subjunctive. (8 pts.)

1. J'aimerais qu'on _____ un taxi.

2. Il faut que vous _____ attention!

3. Je préfère que nous y _____ à pied.

4. J'aime mieux que tu _____ avec moi.

IV. Write a reply to each of the following questions, using *rien* or *personne*. (And don't forget *ne*!) (8 pts.)

1. —Qu'est-ce que tu as fait?

   —Je _____.

2. —Quelqu'un t'a vu?

   —Non, _____.

3. —Tu as rencontré quelqu'un?

   —Non, je _____.

4. —Quelque chose s'est cassé?

   —Non, _____.

SUMMARY QUIZ 42

I. You will hear a series of incomplete statements. Complete each one, selecting a verb from the list below and putting it into the appropriate form. (10 pts.)

déjeuner   gagner
venir   explorer
faire déjeuner

1. Nous avons _____ 40.000 francs!

2. Tu pourrais _____ les sources de l'Amazone.

3. A moins que tu _____ avec moi.

4. On pourrait _____ ensemble?

5. Il faut que je _____ Marie-Laure.

II. Answer each question you hear with the negative terms indicated. (Don't forget *ne*.) (8 pts.)

1. (rien)

   Non, je _____.

2. (jamais rien)

   Non, je _____.

3. (pas encore)

   Non, elle _____.

4. (plus rien)

   Non, je _____.

III. How are your fractions? Below you will see various quantities left in a liter bottle of cider and a 500-gram block of butter. Choose the correct term to express the corresponding fraction ($\frac{1}{2}$, $\frac{1}{4}$, etc.). Write the letter of the appropriate term in front of each quantity given. (7 pts.)

a. le dixième   c. la moitié

b. le quart   d. les trois quarts

A. Un litre de cidre (=100 centilitres)

_____ 1. 50 cl

_____ 2. 25 cl

_____ 3. 10 cl

_____ 4. 75 cl

B. 500 grammes de beurre

_____ 1. 50 g

_____ 2. 250 g

_____ 3. 125 g

IV. Oral Production. Record the following exercises on an audiocassette for submission to your instructor. Before you begin, record your name and today's date.

A. Read the following words slowly, saying each syllable distinctly. (5 pts.)

mécanique
électrique
comédie
possibilité
télévision

B. Complete the following dialogue. Read Mireille's questions as they are and invent your own answers. Take your cues from what Mireille says. (20 pts.)

Mireille: Allô?
Moi:

Mireille: Comment? Tu as gagné quelque chose? Qu'est-ce que tu as gagné?
Moi:

Mireille: C'est tout?
Moi:

Mireille: Et qu'est-ce que tu vas faire de cet argent?
Moi:

Mireille: Eh bien, tu pourrais m'inviter à déjeuner!
Moi:

Mireille: Oui, avec plaisir. Où? Et à quelle heure?
Moi:

Mireille: D'accord. A bientôt!

Name _____

Instructor _____ Section _____

SUMMARY QUIZ 43

I. Who or what is being referred to in each passage you hear? (5 pts.)

	1	2	3	4	5
le matériel de camping					
un sac à dos					
un sac de couchage					
le verre blanc cassé					
une araignée					

II. You will hear some trips (long and short) described. Indicate the term that best describes each one by checking the appropriate box. (5 pts.)

	1	2	3	4	5
une excursion					
un voyage					
un tour					
une randonnée					
une promenade					

III. Conjugation. (10 pts.)

A. The sentences printed below use five different verbs in the indicative. You will hear five other sentences using the same verbs in the subjunctive. Match indicative and subjunctive by writing the number of the sentence you hear in front of the sentence you see that uses the same verb.

_____ a. Tu viendras?

_____ b. Elle faisait du vélo.

_____ c. Vous êtes en retard.

_____ d. Tout ira bien.

_____ e. J'ai eu peur!

B. Now write the infinitive of the verb from each of the sentences above:

a. _____

b. _____

c. _____

d. _____

e. _____

IV. Complete. (5 pts.)

1-2. Mireille: "J'ai deux soeurs, Marie-Laure et Cécile. Je suis plus

jeune _____ Cécile. Cécile est la plus âgée _____

nous trois."

3-5. —Est-ce que cette tente est moins chère _____ celle-là?

—Oui. C'est la moins chère _____ toutes, mais elle est aussi

moins solide _____ les autres.

SUMMARY QUIZ 44

I. Check the appropriate response to each question or statement you hear. (5 pts.)

1. _____ Alors! Dis-le-moi tout de suite.

   _____ Vous avez quelque chose de moins cher?

2. _____ Elle fait 174 francs.

   _____ 43.

3. _____ 450 francs.

   _____ Elles sont souples et légères.

4. _____ Ce n'est pas mon rayon.

   _____ Oui, voilà.

5. _____ Asseyez-vous que je prenne vos mesures.

   _____ Vous plaisantez!

II. Complete by writing the appropriate relative pronoun (*qui* or *que*), adding *ce* if necessary. (4 pts.)

1. Choisis _____ tu veux.

2. C'est le billet _____ a gagné.

3. Robert et Mireille ont vu un film _____ ils ont aimé.

III. Complete each sentence by writing the appropriate form of the verb indicated. You will need to use various tenses and moods: imperfect, conditional, subjunctive, imperative, etc. (12 pts.)

A. *faire*

1. Si on _____ un tour?

2. Tu veux qu'on _____ un tour?

3. Bon, _____ un tour!

B. *aller*

1. Si j'étais toi, j'_____ aux Folies-Bergère.

2. Tu devrais _____ à la Comédie-Française.

3. Maman veut que vous _____ à la Comédie-

Française.

C. *prendre*

1. Quand nous allions en vacances, nous _____ toujours

le train.

2. Robert et Mireille _____ le train pour aller à

Chartres la semaine dernière.

D. *venir*

1. Si j'avais été libre hier, je _____ avec vous.

2. Tu n'as rien à faire? _____ avec nous!

E. *avoir*

1. Tu boiras quelque chose quand tu _____ soif.

2. Si j' _____ le temps, je vous accompagnerais.

IV. Complete with *celui*, *celle*, *ceux*, or *celles*, as appropriate. (4 pts.)

1. Ces chaussures sont très jolies, mais j'aime mieux _____-là.

2. La chaussure de droite est très bien, mais _____ de gauche
   me serre un peu.

3. —Voilà un très beau blouson.

   —_____-ci?

   —Non, l'autre, à côté.

4. Les vrais voyageurs sont _____-là seuls qui partent
   pour partir.

V. Oral Production. Record the following exercises on an audiocassette for
submission to your instructor. Before you begin, record your name and
today's date.

A. You are in a large department store and are looking for something to
   wear (your choice). Get the attention of the salesperson, explain
   what you need and for what occasion. (10 pts.)

B. What would you do? Complete the following sentence, giving five
   different possibilities. (15 pts.)

   Si j'avais gagné 40.000 francs, je. . . .

SUMMARY QUIZ 45

I. Everyone suggests a use for the money Mireille has won. Listen and match each suggestion with the person making it by checking the appropriate box. (5 pts.)

	1	2	3	4	5
Robert					
Oncle Guillaume					
Tante Georgette					
Monsieur Belleau					
Cécile					

II. The sentences you will hear contain verbs related to the nouns listed below. Complete each statement with the appropriate noun, as in the example. (5 pts.)

investissement   placements
économies   dépenses
épargne

Example: You hear: Je te conseille de **donner** l'argent à une bonne
                oeuvre. Tu ferais. . . .
          You see: Tu ferais _____.
          You write: <u>une donation</u>.

1. Il faut penser à faire des _____.

2. Mets-le à la Caisse d'_____.

3. Ne fais pas de _____.

4. Je peux te recommander un très bon _____.

5. Je connais des _____ très avantageux.

III. Listen, and answer each question with *personne* or *rien*, as appropriate. (10 pts.)

1. Je _____.

2. Non, je _____.

3. _____.

4. _____.

5. Non, je_____.

IV. Dictation. (5 pts.)

Je _____ quelque chose que je_____ en

ville et _____ aussi pour _____ du camping.

SUMMARY QUIZ 46

I. Dictation. (20 pts.)

—Ecoute, j'ai _____ te _____.

Est-ce que _____?

—Oui, je n'ai _____ cet été. Et _____

_____ horizon.

—Bon. Nous _____ dans 15 jours. Nous _____

en _____ champ.

II. Complete by writing the appropriate relative pronoun (*qui*, *que*, or *dont*). (5 pts.)

1. Voilà une chemise _____ n'est pas chère.

2. Voilà une chemise _____ me plaît.

3. Voilà la chemise _____ j'avais envie.

4. Voilà la chemise _____ je voulais depuis longtemps.

5. Voilà la chemise _____ j'ai achetée.

III. Oral Production. Record the following exercises on an audiocassette for submission to your instructor. Before you begin, record your name and today's date.

A. Read the following sentences. (5 pts.)

Araignée du matin, chagrin.
Araignée du soir, espoir.
C'est du verre blanc, ça porte bonheur!

B. You are planning a camping trip. What will you need? (5 pts.)

C. Convince a friend to come along with you on this camping trip. Say where you are going and for how long. Reassure your friend that he or she would be doing you a great favor by coming. Explain why. (15 pts.)

SUMMARY QUIZ 47

I. What is being referred to in each statement you hear? Check the appropriate box. (5 pts.)

	1	2	3	4	5
le Nord					
la Normandie					
les cathédrales					
le Mont-Saint-Michel					
la montagne					

II. Listen and complete the following sentences with the appropriate form of the verb you hear and the restrictive negation *ne . . . que*. (10 pts.)

1. Non, elle _____ dix ans.

2. Non, ils _____ des filles.

3. Non, nous _____ les tentes.

4. Non, ils _____ 40.000 francs.

5. Non, nous _____ au Printemps.

III. Complete the answers below using *rien*, *personne*, or a form of *tout*. (10 pts.)

1. —Mireille ne connaît personne?

   —Au contraire, elle _____.

2. —Robert a tout vu?

   —Mais non, il _____.

3. —Il y avait quelqu'un à la porte?

   —Non, il _____ à la porte.

4. Personne ne sait ça?

   Si,_____ ça.

5. Hubert: Tout m'intéresse.

   Mireille: Ah, ça, ce n'est pas vrai! _____

   _____!

SUMMARY QUIZ 48

I. Listen and determine who is being talked about. Check the appropriate box. (5 pts.)

	1	2	3	4	5
Marie-Laure					
la fille de Victor Hugo					
l'homme en noir					
Jean-Michel					

II. You are apathetic and indifferent. Listen and complete the answers to a friend's questions with *ce* and a relative pronoun (*qui*, *que*, or *dont*). (10 pts.)

1. Je ne sais pas _____.

2. Je ne sais pas _____.

3. Je ne sais pas _____.

4. Je ne sais pas _____.

III. Complete the answers to the questions you hear with the appropriate form of the possessive pronoun (*le mien*, etc.). (10 pts.)

1. Oui, c'est _____.

2. Oui, ce sont _____.

3. Oui, c'est _____.

4. Oui, c'est _____.

5. Oui, ce sont _____.

IV. Oral Production. Record the following exercises on an audiocassette for submission to your instructor. Before you begin, record your name and today's date.

A. Read the following sentences. (5 pts.)

Quand on en a vu une, on les a toutes vues.
Tu as dû étudier ça.

B. A friend asks you about this French course—who are these characters, how do they meet, what do they do? Satisfy your friend's curiosity with eight to ten well-chosen sentences. (The story is not really very complicated, you should be able to give the essential in that many sentences.) Use the present tense—this all takes place in the eternal present of the imagination, doesn't it? (20 pts.)

SUMMARY QUIZ 49

I. True or false? Which of the statements you hear about Marie–Laure's adventures are true? Check the appropriate box. (5 pts.)

	1	2	3	4	5
c'est vrai					
c'est faux					

II. Complete with the subjunctive of the verb you hear. (10 pts.)

Example: You hear: Je sais que tu ne veux pas **partir**, mais . . .
         You see: . . . il faut que tu _____.
         You write: <u>partes</u>.

1. . . . il faut que tu y _____.

2. . . . il faut que vous les _____.

3. . . . il faut que tu _____ là.

4. . . . il faut que vous _____.

5. . . . il faut que vous _____.

6. . . . il faut que tu la _____.

7. . . . il faut que vous le _____.

8. . . . il faut que tu le _____.

9. . . . il faut que tu _____.

10. . . . il faut que vous y _____.

III. Put the sentences you hear into the past. (4 pts.)

1. Je ne _____ pas s'il _____.

2. J'_____ l'impression que ça _____

des étincelles.

IV. Complete by writing the appropriate word. (6 pts.)

1. Je crois qu'il est _____ quelque chose à

Marie-Laure: un accident, par exemple.

2. Je pensais bien que c'était l'homme en noir. Je _____

doutais!

3. J'aimerais bien partir avec quelqu'un, mais je ne sais pas avec

_____ partir.

4. Je ne trouve pas ça drôle _____ tout.

5. Ça m'étonnerait que tu veuilles voir ça. Je doute _____

que tu veuilles voir ça.

SUMMARY QUIZ 50

I. Dictation. (15 pts.)

—Qu'est-ce que _____ film? Ça t'a plu?

—Oh, oui, c'était très émouvant! Ça _____ vraiment

_____. Ça ne t'ennuie pas si on le voit une

deuxième fois?

—Non, _____ du tout!

II. Complete by writing the appropriate preposition or article. (10 pts.)

1-2.—Vous étiez en Europe cet été?

—Oui, nous revenons _____ France.

_____ France nous a beaucoup plu.

3-5. Nous allons faire une randonnée _____ Alpes. Nous irons

_____ Mont Blanc et _____ Aiguille Verte.

6-8. —Vous allez _____ Canada?

—Non, nous allons _____ France. Nous avons loué un

appartement _____ Paris _____ deux mois.

9. J'aime le café _____ Colombie.

III. Oral Production. Record the following exercises on an audiocassette for submission to your instructor. Before you begin, record your name and today's date.

A. Who is the Man in Black? What is he planning? Whom does he work for? Give your analysis of the situation in four or five sentences. (10 pts.)

B. Now that you have completed this course, you consider going to France. Plan the trip: Where will you go? What you will see? (15 pts.)

SUMMARY QUIZ 51

I. You will hear five examples of informal speech. Match each one with its more formal equivalent below. Check the appropriate box. (5 pts.)

	1	2	3	4	5
Ça m'est égal.					
Cet individu est très désagréable.					
Attendez un peu!					
Qui est cette jeune fille?					
Certainement pas!					

II. Rewrite the sentences you hear as shown in the examples, changing the verb you hear into an infinitive. (10 pts.)

Example: You hear: Nous ne partons pas.
You see: Nous préférons _____.
You write: <u>ne pas partir</u>.

Or you hear: Nous partons.
You see: Nous préférons _____.
You write: <u>partir</u>.

1. Nous tenons à _____ à l'heure.

2. Non. J'aime mieux _____ de café. Ça me rend nerveux.

3. Oui, nous commençons à _____ faim.

4. J'aimerais _____ du thé.

5. Oui. Elle commence à _____ Marie-Laure.

III. Rewrite each of the following commands, replacing all nouns by pronouns. Be alert: some of the commands are affirmative, others negative. (10 pts.)

1. Prête ta voiture à Mireille.

   _____.

2. Ne me racontez pas vos ennuis.

   _____.

3. Ne donnez pas d'argent à ces enfants.

   _____.

4. Achète-moi deux billets.

   _____.

5. Apportez-moi du cidre.

   _____.